Honey, Olives, Octopus

The publisher gratefully acknowledges the generous support of the General Endowment Fund of the University of California Press Foundation.

Honey, Olives, Octopus

Adventures at the Greek Table

CHRISTOPHER BAKKEN

Illustrations by Mollie Katzen

UNIVERSITY OF CALIFORNIA PRESS

Berkeley Los Angeles London

University of California Press, one of the most
distinguished university presses in the United
States, enriches lives around the world by
advancing scholarship in the humanities, social
sciences, and natural sciences. Its activities are
supported by the UC Press Foundation and by
philanthropic contributions from individuals
and institutions. For more information, visit
www.ucpress.edu.

University of California Press
Berkeley and Los Angeles, California

University of California Press, Ltd.
London, England

Library of Congress Cataloging-in-Publication Data

Bakken, Christopher.
    Honey, olives, octopus : adventures at the
Greek table / Christopher Bakken.
        p.   cm.
    Includes bibliographical references and index.
    ISBN 978-0-520-27509-6 (cloth, alk. paper)
    1. Cooking, Greek.   2. Bakken,
Christopher.   3. Subject—Social life and
customs.   I. Title.
TX723.5.G8B28   2013
641.59495—dc23   2012026481

Manufactured in the United States of America

22   21   20   19   18   17   16   15   14   13
10   9   8   7   6   5   4   3   2   1

In keeping with its commitment to support
environmentally responsible and sustainable
printing practices, UC Press has printed this
book on Natures Book, which contains 30%
post-consumer waste and meets the minimum
requirements of ANSI/NISO Z 39.48-1992 (R
1997) (*Permanence of Paper*).

For my mother,
Karen Seibel

In the afternoon heat I pick olives,

The leaves the loveliest of greens:

I'm light from head to toe.

Nazim Hikmet

CONTENTS

ACKNOWLEDGMENTS

I owe sincere thanks to those cooks, artisans, restaurateurs, wine folk, agriculturalists, and friends who entertained my questions and invited me to their kitchens and farms: Eva and Stamatis Kouzis, Karolin Giritlioglu, Kyria Konstandina of Dalabelos Estate, Vasilis Petrodaskalakis, Eleftheria Pelekanaki, Pelayia Konsolaki, Nikos Bernikos, Yorgos Babounis, George Atsalinos, Aris and Maria Monovasios, Rita and Yorgos Paraskevopoulou, Dimitris Yerondalis, Markus Stoltz, Yannis and Chris Fekos, Maria Mavrianou, Michalis Makellos, Dimitris Triantafilopoulos, Michalis and Katarina Protopsaltis, Yannis, Maria, and Athanasia Protopsaltis, and Eleni Petrocheilou. Special thanks to Dimitris, Christina, Spyros, and Nikolas Panteleimonitis.

I am grateful to those who offered advice, enthusiasm, and research assistance: Titos and Renna Patrikios, John Psaropoulos and A. E. Stallings, Michael and Kay Bash, David Mason, Leon Saltiel, Jeremiah Chamberlin, David Yoder, Aliki Barnstone, Adrianne Kalfopoulou, Christian Nicolaides, Elaina Mercatoris, Allison Wilkins, Herbert Leibowitz, Willard Spiegelman, Tamar Adler, Scott Cairns and Marcia Vanderlip, Carolyn Forché, Pam Houston, Greg Glazner, and the team at Regal Literary, especially Michael Strong and Markus Hoffman.

The book couldn't have been written without support for research and travel provided by Allegheny College.

Parts of this book have appeared, in somewhat different form, in the following publications: *Parnassus: Poetry in Review, The Southwest Review*, and *Odyssey: The World of Greece*.

Roula Konsolaki, Natalie Bakopoulos, and Joanna Eleftheriou offered helpful comments on the manuscript. For her drawings, I thank Mollie Katzen. For his editorial brilliance and generosity, I am indebted to Ben Downing, *il miglior fabbro*. Thank you, Corey Marks and Darrin Pochan, for your appetites (and thank you for not drowning). Oscar, Karen, and Heidi Seibel: thank you for cheering my wanderlust. Thanks to my brother, Aaron Bakken, for picking olives alongside me. Thanks to my Greek brothers, George Kaltsas and Tasos Kouzis.

And, finally, thanks to my wife, Kerry, and my children, Sophia and Alexander, who sent me off to Greece with their blessings and welcomed me back home with love.

I had just arrived in Thessaloniki and was hungry. The college promised me a nifty apartment on campus, but it was still being painted. In the meantime, I'd be sleeping in a storage room in the basement of the gymnasium, where a rudimentary cot and a reading table had been installed. There was nothing in the refrigerator. Everyone else had gone to the beach for the weekend, so it was up to George Kassiopides, director of physical education, to orient me. Like Jack LaLanne, the exercise guru who had kangarooed through the television commercials of my childhood, Kassiopides was a wasp-waisted calisthenic addict with an inflated chest. He had a big, round, craggy face, atop which a merry mess of blonde curls was splattered, and he sped around campus on a coughing moped, elbows and knees akimbo, tornadoes of pine needles spinning in his wake. Kassiopides knew everything when it came to action and adventure, and it was he who taught me to hunt for octopus later that first year in Greece. I still find ingenious his trick of diving with an old pair of panty hose (nothing else seems to contain a just-harpooned octopus quite as well). But he didn't have much to say about where I should eat on a sleepy Sunday afternoon.

"Take the bus into town and maybe you'll find something," he told me.

So I wound up in a sorry little *taverna* across from the bus stop in the suburb of Harilaou. Seated at a corner table, where I thought I'd be less conspicuous, I tried to decipher the menu with my pocket dictionary. The Greek language grates "like the anchor chain," V. S. Naipaul says, and until I learned six or eight phrases on the soccer field (most of them obscene), Greek was indeed a clattering gibberish to me. I couldn't tell where individual words started and ended. Where did one even place the accents in "Thessaloniki," this city of a million inhabitants where I'd be teaching literature for the next two years?

When the waiter came around, I pointed at three arbitrary items on the menu. It was not a spectacular meal, in hindsight, but it offered a foretaste of the hundreds of exquisite meals I'd have in Greece over the next two decades. First came *chtipiti*, a fiery mash of feta and hot peppers; then *pikantiki*, a salad of raw cabbage, carrot, parsley, and green onions; and last, a tin platter bearing a leg of octopus, still hissing from the grill. What remained on my plate when I finished eating—an acrid puddle of vinegar and oil, a curlicue of charred tentacle, a nubbin of bread, and a morsel of cheese—was evidence that I had made contact with the flavor of Greece. And I wanted more. I still do, twenty years later.

Since that day, almost everything I have learned about Greece I have learned at the table. The country's history is written in the elements of its cuisine: olives, bread, fish, and cheese. Meat, beans, wine, and honey. But the future is closing in. McDonalds and Kentucky Fried Chicken have arrived. The Greek economy is collapsing. Both "slow food" and "local food" have existed in Greece for thousands of years, but the traditional ways are under threat as air-conditioned malls and "big box" stores replace outdoor markets in Greece's cities. Before it was too late, and before those who remembered were gone, I wanted to explore the foundations of the Greek table. To do that properly, I needed to honor what brings everything else together: conversation, friendship, and the leisurely ceremony of dining around which Hellenic culture has evolved for the past several thousand years.

In her classic *Honey from a Weed*, Patience Gray remarks that "a book about food can be as fatiguing as sitting through a six course dinner." Thus, she proposes a "digression" now and then, "offered like a glass of *marc* or *eau de vie* to brace the protagonists." Following her lead, I confess to a meandering method of investigation. Things move slowly in Greece and rarely in a straight line. You see and learn a lot more, I've discovered, while tracing the circuitous route of the goat path.

Plus, I don't live in Greece anymore. After teaching for two years in Thessaloniki, I returned to the United States, married, found employment as a college professor, set up a house, and had a family. I go back to Greece as often as I can, but that's never often enough, since my love affair with the country hasn't dulled one bit. Luckily for me, my wife and children have fallen in love with my Promised Land too. When my nine-year-old daughter learned last week that I'd be heading back to Greece without her, she broke down. "But Dad, I just want to go swimming all day and eat octopus and spanakopita in the afternoon. It's not fair!" I understand her reaction and am myself prone to fits of melodramatic pining for the place and its food.

So the adventures described here correspond to a series of joyous but haphazard returns, spanning roughly four growing seasons. Many of them are set on the island of Thasos—on an obscure little peninsula on a remote bit of Thasian coastline, actually—where I've been retreating, whenever I can, for over two decades. While I'm not Greek by birth, I feel more at home there than almost anywhere else on the planet. It's there, too, on the patio of Pension Archontissa, overlooking three beaches and the ruins of several ancient shrines, that I've eaten some of the best meals of my life.

Greek cuisine, I declare, is the most underappreciated cuisine in Europe. This book is a record of the meals, artisans, cooks, and friends who have

inspired me to make that declaration. "Other countries offer you discoveries in manners, lore, or landscape," said Lawrence Durrell, but "Greece offers you something harder—the discovery of yourself." He's right, but Greece first demands that you discover others. It's not like you'll have a choice.

"Sit," a Greek will command you the moment you arrive, "and eat something with me."

CHAPTER ONE

Olives

The Throumbes *of Thasos*

Tasos of Thasos, whose olives we shall pick, has been drinking *tsipouro* at a wedding all night—until just hours ago, in other words—so when he greets us at the port we can see he's a cheerful disaster. The list of things Tasos Kouzis can do is daunting: with equal proficiency he manages to be a restaurateur, farmer, shepherd, octopus fisherman, rabbit hunter, traditional dancer, and wedding singer. The fact that he served in the Greek Special Forces means he has other skills he cannot disclose. He's also indisputably handsome— black hair, close-cropped beard, irrepressible smile—which helps him play his various roles with perfect *sprezzatura*.

"It hurts me to drive slowly," he tells us, "so put on your seatbelts." In spite of his hangover, he attacks each switchback. We zoom past the massive marble quarries, so huge that the cranes and bulldozers at the bottom look like toys; through the village of Panagia, where the competing, identical *kafenia* in the main square are opening simultaneously; past three deserted beach towns; and around two herds of errant sheep and one lost cow. Abruptly, as we round the southern shoulder of the island, the dense shag of pine and oak gives way to a barren forest of boulders that drops jaggedly down to the sea. Tasos pulls up next to the guardrail on the wrong side of the road so we can orient ourselves. The wind is blowing from the southeast, making visible what is usually obscured: Samothraki, the most haunted and pagan of all the Greek islands, which agitates the horizon like a purple gash. Beyond that we can see the faintly pulsating outline of Asia Minor and the low molars of Limnos, and after two more bends in the road we spy Mount Athos, sacred home of a thousand monks and hermits and not a single woman. (Legend has it no woman has set foot on the peninsula since the Virgin Mary herself).

It was just a few degrees above freezing on the mainland at Keramoti, where I waited for the ferry with my brother Aaron and my friend George Kaltsas two hours earlier. Even the seagulls seemed unwilling to budge from the sea wall. We huddled in a closet-sized *kafenion* on the fishing dock, its proprietor trying to light a little woodstove in the middle of the room. He boiled sweet mountain tea and Greek coffee for us.

George Kaltsas manages a hotel in Kavala, the largest port city in eastern Macedonia, just across the water from Thasos. The air of bureaucratic efficiency he gives off at the hotel belies his brooding, philosophical nature. "A Greek has no walls around him," Henry Miller has remarked, and while I'm sure that's not true about all Greeks, it's certainly true about George. Some years before, he welcomed me to the Hotel Oceanis with old-fashioned hospitality. After settling into my room, George invited me to join him for a bottle of local wine and a table full of *mezedes*, the tapas-like dishes that make up the bulk of Greek dining. Once I'd been fed, George interrogated me for an hour about subjects ranging from the structure of the American electoral system to my thoughts on Greek cheese.

Then I learned his story: on the verge of thirty, having discovered he had cancer, George abandoned chemotherapy, the job that was killing him, and his family. One morning he stripped off most of his clothes and swam from the mainland to Thasos, where he landed dripping saltwater and with nothing but a few drachmas. Inspired by a newly adopted Zorbatic philosophy (Nietzsche filtered through the novels of Nikos Kazantzakis), he lived a life of solitude, vegetarianism, and manual labor, all the while opening his senses to a routine of simple pleasures. For a year, he worked out the kinks in his existence on the island, then returned to his wife and children, his cancer in remission. He's a man of theories, passions, and compulsions and he lives, literally, for ideas and good wine.

Our conversation that first afternoon at the Hotel Oceanis was fascinating, and I found George such a curious and remarkable creature that I also accepted his next invitation: to share a feast of seafood that night on the port, in a seedy *ouzeri* adjacent to the shipbuilding yard. We've been friends ever since.

.   .   .

In order to fetch us at the port, Tasos left his parents behind in the olive grove. So we drop our bags at Pension Archontissa, where we'll be staying, and join them right away. "Don't worry, we came here to work," I remind Tasos. His parents, undistracted by the noisy fowl that surround them—peacocks, geese, ducks, and dozens of chickens—are just pouring the first coffee of the day and unloading a crate full of breakfast: bread, boiled eggs, *tyropites* (cheese pies), and freshly plucked oranges. Tasos's father, Stamatis, rises to greet me with a leathery handshake and two kisses. Though now sporting a harvest costume of flannel and denim, he's a fisherman and looks it: aquiline nose, sunburned skin, a shock of unruly hair. Tasos's mother, Evanthia (or Eva), has something of the Venus of Willendorf about her: she's utterly sturdy, working here all month beside the men, and yet she radiates maternal softness and grace, her voice a joyful lilt, her face always on the precipice of a smile. Both parents seem a little stunned that I've actually come; surely my vow to join their olive harvest, sworn after a long night of drinking the previous summer, was not in earnest. Yet here I am, with brother and George Kaltsas in tow, stocking-capped, combat-booted, and armored in canvas and fleece. Tasos is picking olives in his Armani jeans.

Breakfast in the Olives

Figure 1. Olives ready for harvest at Alyki, Thasos.

He hands us each a *tsougrana*, the only necessary implement: a little plastic rake mounted on a foot-long wooden broom handle. With the *tsougrana*, he demonstrates, you rake—or comb—the olive trees, using choppy downward strokes. We can feel the olives catch in the tines of the *tsougrana*, then fall, but surprisingly most of the leaves and branches remain intact. Beneath us are stretched enormous nylon green nets known as *dychtia* (the same word used for Stamatis's fishing nets), where the olives come to rest. The trees are fifteen feet tall and so dense with silver-green leaves and black olives that you can't see through them.

There is no pattern to our combing, no rule about moving clockwise, say, or keeping some distance from the next person. Where you see olives, you bring them down, shuffling your feet along the nets so as not to trample the booty. I gather three or four branches together at a time, arranging them into a braid before combing out its thousand knots. Just when you think you've

Olives: The Throumbes *of Thasos*

stripped a whole tree side, you part the branches and find another layer in the low canopy, peppering the underside of each scraggly branch.

Meanwhile, above us, Tasos and Stamatis employ a different method entirely. The Italians have invented a mechanical *tsougrana* that runs on compressed air. Mounted at the end of telescoping aluminum wands are pairs of red and black mechanical fingers of varying lengths; when a trigger is pressed these fingers begin furiously clapping. Dragged along the upper branches, the fingers knock olives down about a hundred at a time, raining them upon the heads of those working below. At least once per day I look up to speak only to have an olive drop right into my mouth. Unfortunately, the gasoline-powered air compressor is horribly noisy, always rumbling and revving, its fingers clattering like rusty machine guns. There's no placid conversation, nor the traditional harvest songs I imagined we'd sing. Each of us sinks into an almost catatonic state, sweeping our combs to the racket of Italian technology.

In my first hour, I cover a lot of useless mental territory: reciting every Robert Frost poem I can recall, inventing the lines I don't remember; counting the strokes of my *tsougrana*, then losing count; thinking briefly about the relationship between Czeslaw Milosz and Robinson Jeffers, then, in an inexplicable segue, about the late albums of Bob Marley; wishing for cold beer, then revising that wish to a glass of *tsipouro*, a homemade firewater distilled, like grappa, from the byproducts of winemaking. It's ouzo's evil cousin. Out of such daydreams come beautifully mundane revelations, like this one: olive trees are remarkably clean. In a whole afternoon—and then in the whole week that follows—I don't encounter a single representative of vermin, or even a spiderweb. This strikes me as even more astounding when Tasos confirms that the trees have never been sprayed with anything but rain. At the end of the day, I feel some residue of the trees on my clothes and skin: the leaves wear a faint layer of pollen or dust that smells, not surprisingly, like powdered olive. Nothing is as rugged and stoical as an olive tree; nothing, as it turns out, is as pristine.

The olives themselves vary from black to violet to lime green and all are visibly swollen. Press one between your fingertips and it oozes milky oil. Though I know better, I can't restrain myself from tasting the raw olives I've flown so far to pick. They are bitter and tannic, inducing the worst kind of cotton mouth; after the initial flavor of bright, scratchy oil comes a flood of turpentine, beeswax, and rubber cement, bound together with a mouthful of cornstarch. The unpleasant flavor of the raw olive will not be washed away, and I find myself hawking and spitting for an hour. I'm amazed to see George occasionally stop his furious combing (who knew a hotel manager could work someone else's olives with such gleeful abandon?) and pop a raw olive into his mouth without any visible reaction.

For olives to become palatable, they are usually soaked in brine. Technically, *throumbes* are table olives that have been cured without brine, and they can be found all over Greece. But those produced on this island are of such high quality that one buys *throumbes* hoping that they will be from Thasos. At Titan Foods in the Greek neighborhood of Astoria, New York, for instance, you will find among the olive bins one labeled "Thasos," the island's name being synonymous with its famously wrinkled produce.

Here, a day's work is measured in *telara*, the ubiquitous and sturdy red plastic crates distributed by the local olive oil cooperative. Each *telaro* holds about twenty-five kilos of olives, which typically yield between one and three liters of oil, even more if the olives are particularly plump. To keep Tasos's restaurant supplied with oil for the busy summer, the family needs to gather between three and four thousand kilos of olives, or about one hundred fifty *telara*. When you have brought down all the olives from a tree, which takes nearly an hour with the very largest of the trees, two people gather the green nets together so as to funnel the olives into a single pile, where they can be quickly picked over—to remove the largest twigs and leaves—and then transferred into the *telara*. Today, five of us work an hour to fill two or three of these crates. If we were working for a wage, it would

Figure 2. View from the balcony of Pension Archontissa, Thasos.

certainly be meager. But in fact there is no wage; we work for the oil, which has always been more valuable than money in countries like Greece. With the oil comes nutrition and fuel and light. This is why property is often apportioned according not to acreage but to the number of olive trees growing on it. In Greece one is lucky to inherit trees.

    • • •

I first visited Thasos in the early 1990s, driving from Thessaloniki through the fertile Halkidiki peninsula on my motorcycle, past Kavala to nondescript Keramoti, where ferries churn across to Thasos. The highway runs along the Via Egnatia, the great Roman road from the Adriatic to Constantinople; here in Macedonia, it skirts the edge of the plain where the Battle of Phillipi was fought, in which the young Octavian and Mark Anthony crushed the armies of the assassin Brutus.

An Olive's Worth

"Thasos stands here like the spine of a donkey, wreathed with unkempt forest. . . . It's not a beautiful or lovely place," Archilochus complains in one of his political fragments. I can't think of a more misguided, absurd ancient sentence. When I arrived there in 1992, the island's roads offered a feast of mountain air, pine sap, and wood smoke. A huge portion of the island had recently burned, as it does every decade or so. Even so, I found Thasos beautiful and lovely and green. It reminded me of the more rugged parts of Wisconsin, my home state, but with spring-fed streams and cliff-side beaches instead of pike-stuffed lakes.

My illegal camp on that first visit was at Alyki, a boot-shaped peninsula flanked by calm little swimming coves and bristling with spooky archeology. One can wander among the remains of a very early Christian basilica and the ruins of an ancient sanctuary of the Dioscuri. A dirt road led down to the single fish *taverna*, but the rest of the peninsula was accessible only by foot. I pitched my garish orange pup tent underneath an olive tree next to a black pit into which (according to local legend) temple priestesses would toss male virgins after deflowering them. As I stumbled back to my tent after late dinners at the lonely *taverna*, my flashlight awakened terrifying shadows in that gaping mouth—no wonder I woke every morning there in a cold sweat.

The highlight of the peninsula is the Roman marble quarry, acres of blinding marble excavated for several hundred years with ingenious systems of wooden winches, cranes, and rollers. What remains is a spectacular lunar surface of man-made tide pools, rectangular crevasses, and misshapen rock spines, the kind of place one could reasonably expect to encounter Princess Nausikaa and her maids doing the laundry.

.   .   .

"What do you call that mountain?" I ask during one of our coffee breaks on the second morning of olive picking. We have moved our equipment to the boulder-strewn grove where the Kouzis family grazes its twenty sheep.

Figure 3. Roman-era marble quarry at Alyki, Thasos.

Riddled with caves and jutting ferociously into the low clouds, the crag above us is nearly barren, too steep to support any life but the most determined brambles. From that Cyclopean forehead, the shoulders of the valley drop to the sea, which I can actually hear, since today angry ten-foot waves are detonating below.

"Eineh vouno," Stamatis mutters with a dismissive wave of his hand: "It's a mountain."

"Well, but the old timers, if they want to be specific, call it 'Brachos tou Kleftoyanni,'" Eva interjects. "The Hill of Yannis the Thief."

"Who is Kleftoyannis?" I ask, "and what did he steal?"

But no one responds.

This morning we can see our breath, and a light drizzle has left us damp and cold. No one is in the mood for conversation. We pull our coffee cups

Marble Peninsula

up close to our faces, peel boiled eggs and oranges, and bash open walnuts with stones, staring at the forty or so olive trees we'll need to conquer here. "But as for me," Horace says in one of his odes, "my simple meal consists / of chicory and mallow from the garden / And olives from the little olive tree."

The sheep gather around us and bleat plaintively for handouts. The most persistent ewe has only one good eye (the other was put out by a stalk of bristle grass and is now grey as the yolk of an overboiled egg); she must be shooed away with curses and a stomping of boots. "Oh, my darling, my pretty," my brother says to her each time she approaches, and we are punchy enough to find his flirtations hilarious.

Each year the ewes will escort one or two lambs into this hardscrabble place, where they will drink mother's milk until their throats are cut for the Kouzis family restaurant. One would think that this would make the sheep wary of their human captors. On the contrary, they're tame and cheerful as dogs, though they lack the sympathetic behaviors—whimpering, piteous gazing, and so forth—that dogs use to manipulate us. The moment the sheep hear the idiosyncratic growl of Stamatis's pickup, they begin bleating, trotting off in the direction of the gate where their beloved master will soon arrive, his truck clattering and coughing from the climb. He brings plastic buckets of shell corn for them to gobble.

Now that we've made friends with the beasts, I feel the weight of guilt over the many plates of grilled lamb chops that I've devoured at Pension Archontissa. There they are flash-grilled ten to a plate, flooded with lemon and dusted at the last minute with salt, pepper, and dried oregano. Their flavor has a smoky wildness to it unlike any American lamb I've tasted; seeing now what their mountain grazing consists of—most of it looking about as palatable to me as a tossed salad of thumbtacks and toothpicks— I can understand why. I'm hoping the one-eyed ewe doesn't know how many of her offspring I've eaten, hot blood dripping from my chin. When I offer her the last perfect half of a walnut, she licks my fingers.

Only one ram is currently in service to the flock and he will soon be replaced. "He's dangerous," Tasos warns us. "Don't turn your back on him." Indeed, about an hour later, from inside the mane of an olive tree I'm combing, I see—just a second too late to shout out a warning—the ram slam Stamatis in the back of the knees. Stamatis winces, buckles, but does not fall. He unleashes a string of beautiful curses, bent double in rage and pain. Recovering, he picks up a fallen branch, but Tasos and Eva keep him from braining the beast to death.

"What good will it do? That bastard won't learn a thing from being beaten," Tasos shouts.

"Put him in the stew pot," Eva suggests, "with some baby onions and bay leaves."

Stamatis sits on a boulder, fuming in silence. The ram, having had his fun, joins the ewes by the now empty corn troughs. "That fucker will get the knife soon," Tasos whispers down to me through the branches.

Touchingly, about five glasses of *tsipouro* in to the following evening, Tasos reveals to me that his father—who is about as salty and stoical a creature as I can imagine—is unwilling to butcher the lambs.

"My father feeds them, sings to them, even helps when a ewe has problems giving birth. He has Uncle Nikos do the killing."

"Does your father feel the same way about his fish?"

"No, no, no. Those he clubs across the skull."

.   .   .

We resume our labor. By contrast, yesterday's work was play. The trees were young, virile, and evenly spaced on flat ground. We stretched the nets and attacked. Those branches were heavy with swollen black fruit the size of fat almonds; each robust stroke unleashed a joyful pattering of olives upon nets. Each tree yielded a *telaro*, some considerably more than that. "Some years the larger trees will give ten full *telara* each," Tasos tells me. "This is nothing."

Figure 4. Tasos and Stamatis Kouzis harvesting olives with mechanical *tsougrana*.

Today, beneath Kleftoyannis Brachos, Stamatis surveys his trees with the suspicious, resigned wince farmers everywhere from Attica to Alabama employ when faced with the sight of a lame harvest. Olive trees observe a cycle of fertility—two years on, one year off. Variations in rainfall and temperature also make a difference. This year's drought, which had much of southern Greece on fire, has taken its toll. "But the trees have olives," I say by way of encouragement, scraping my bright red *tsougrana* at the air with exaggerated enthusiasm. "Let's bring them down."

"They have a little . . . no, they don't have shit," Stamatis retorts.

I see what he means. The trees here have drilled into bare rock. Everything green looks pinched, scratchy, and contorted. The outlines of terraces show where some long-dead soul once piled enough rocks for a wall. But the trees have worried themselves into any spot with a few inches of dusty soil, looking like "a time-gnarled / community of elders," as Amy Clampitt describes them in her poem. Today's work will be vertical instead of horizontal; only every third tree has enough to bother harvesting. Where yesterday we disappeared into bejeweled branches, these offer only a wispy sprig or two of produce.

Because olives are (just barely) round enough to roll, and since we'll be making them rain down from the trees onto the ground, we must anticipate how and where they'll fall, arranging nets beneath the trees accordingly. It often takes longer to do that than it does to strip the trees of their fruit. I learn how to situate fallen branches beneath the edges of nets to create hollows into which the olives can tumble and form black pools. Nets are stretched over tall shrubs and evil berry vines that rake our forearms. We perform an absurd, slow-motion dance: balancing on the outer edge of one boot sole while hanging onto a branch with one hand, leaning over jagged stone just to rake down twelve or thirteen olives. Or else we climb into the canopy, nego-tiating a labyrinth of branches, to wipe out one meager colony of black spots.

"What are you doing up there, Aaron?" Tasos calls out when the air compressor suspends its racket. "Leave those for the birds."

"But I'm mad at these ones," Aaron shouts back, his head just visible at the top of the tree. "I've been after them for five minutes."

"Let me," Tasos replies, stripping the little patch of fruit by standing on his toes and stretching out the mechanical fingers so they stutter along the topmost branches.

In the end, most trees yield little more than a single, sorry layer in the bottom of an empty *telaro;* then we must repeat the trigonometry of arrang-ing the nets beneath the next contorted tree. We are cold and discouraged. Thankfully, the drizzle becomes a downpour. Stamatis cuts the power on the compressor for good and shouts, "We're not slaves. Let's behave like free men and quit before we drown."

. . .

A few nights later at the bar, we get a few titillating details about the hill of the elusive Kleftoyannis. We have just eaten a feast of *ortykia*, tiny local quail that Tasos's cousin, also named Tasos, has grilled with astonishing dexterity over the roaring flames of a fireplace in the corner. Every morsel of the quail is as rich and fatty as duck liver, with an added grassiness that must be the result of the birds' nesting in the marshes on the mainland. Even the men at our table know they are being treated to a delicacy, and they nod with reverential gratitude toward the man who shot the birds—a resident of Kavala famous even here, on an island across the water, for his ability to bring down these tiny wildfowl with his gun.

A steady supply of *tsipouro* has us pretty well on the way to inebriation. While drinking *tsipouro*, as with ouzo, one is supposed to eat *mezedes* to keep the demons inside the moonshine at bay. Tonight, only two *mezedes* are served: a bowl of freshly picked *yigantes*—gigantic white beans— oven-roasted with tomatoes, carrots, and parsley, and a slab of the undramatically named *dopio tyri* ("local cheese"), which turns out to be the richest cheese I've ever tasted on Thasos, its equal portions of goat's and sheep's milk held together by a tender membrane of rind. When I begin swooning over the cheese, pestering the men with inquiries, they point to a scarecrow sipping *tsipouro* in the corner. "That's the shepherd there," they tell me. He's busy watching a table of noisy men playing *bilot*, the Thasian card game that dominates the island. When we ask him about the cheese, he tastes a slice from his impossibly weathered fingertips. "It's not mine," he says. "This is some other man's cheese. There's too much goat in this one." With that, he nods and returns to his corner and his drink.

Tasos's uncle, Triandafilos, cuts an imposing figure: his enormous shoulders look even broader because he cradles one arm in a sling at the middle of his chest. A black raincoat has been slung across his shoulders like a cape. His features might betray a hint of foreign ancestry—his loose jaw, flat nose, and cheerful blue eyes are anomalous among the table of Thasian men gathered there, who all look related to one another (and who, it turns out, are). After dislocating his shoulder in a fall some years ago, Triandafilos refused proper treatment and now his right hand has all but seized up; the fingers that protrude from the end of his sling are as swollen as bratwurst, and he moves with the careful deliberation of one in pain. In spite of his injury, it's clear he's still ferociously strong. He's just muttered good night, his good hand raised in farewell, when Tasos implores him to tell us what he knows about Yannis the Thief.

"Who wants to know?" he asks.

"The writer. Mr. Professor Christopher. The American poet."

"During the years when the Turks were here," he explains while refusing a chair with a little lift of the chin, "the people lived off of nothing. They had olives and wild greens, maybe a mountain hare now and then for the stew pot if they had managed to keep a gun."

"No, that story takes place during the years of the Bulgarians," someone from behind us interjects.

"*Po, po, po.* What's the difference? The people were hungry both times," Triandafilos says, with the dramatic backward shrug the Greeks employ to indicate absurdity or exasperation. He continues:

> This man Yannis lived alone, who knows why, and would keep himself alive by pinching a tomato or a watermelon here and there from the gardens of the shepherd's wives. Or he'd make off with a handful of their eggs. Never too much. Everyone understood that the man needed to eat, so out of charity no one reported him. These were human crimes. Anyway, they couldn't have caught him if they wanted to, since he followed paths up into the mountain that only the goats knew, and he kept his loot in a cave there that no one has ever found. The mountain was named for him.

In few landscapes is history as legible as in Greece, where all the place-names bear the weight of classical association: Sparta, Corinth, Thebes. It's difficult to think of them in realistic terms, as the rather destitute and depressing little towns they now are. So I find it refreshing, and somewhat touching, to learn that far more recent history—or mythology—has been inscribed here, on an obscure bluff in an obscure corner of a once famous little island. When Triandafilos leaves, I ask Tasos if all the hills have names, if all the old people have such history in their veins.

"No, people like my uncle are hard to find now. These details are being forgotten," Tasos says.

The famous bird killer of Kavala, depositing one last bit of quail carcass in the ashtray before him, concurs, then raises his glass while proclaiming a village proverb everyone else around the table seems to know: "If you don't have an old man in your family, then you should buy one."

. . .

To get to the olives each morning, we must park about halfway up the thief's mountain (above this point the ruts in the road become veritable trenches), then walk up the steep switchbacks, past a mountain stream that's cut its way into the island shale, and beyond a complex of brightly painted bee boxes arranged between some pine trees. Around the next turn, we come to an enormous purple field of flowering heather that today is a seizure of bees. At first their collective song is almost inaudible, but as soon as we stop walking for a moment and slow our noisy heartbeats, we realize that it is in fact deafening. "What note is that?" I ask my brother, who hums his way up the scale. "They are singing in B flat," he concludes. Then, after another moment's pause, he adds, "But once in a while some of them step up an interval to a harmonic note . . . D sharp, I think."

. . .

Over dinner, our hosts insist that we put aside our hard labor for at least one morning. "Show the island to your brother," Eva implores me as she pours the last of the wine and simultaneously pushes another morsel of calamari onto my empty plate. "Don't worry, there will be plenty of olives to pick when you come back."

The winds of the previous day have gone as quickly as they came, and today the sun is blazing. Aaron and I have shed our insulated vests for T-shirts. Our little car purrs around the coastal road, which in the summer will be abuzz with mopeds and Fiats carrying those sightseers brave enough to venture beyond the port town and their hideous beach hotels for a glimpse of "the other Thasos," the fishing villages and mountain hamlets praised for their "authenticity" in every brochure. But today the road vibrates with the noise of pickup trucks, most of them heavy with crates of gleaming olives on the way to the local oil press, or else precariously loaded with harvest paraphernalia: heaped green nets and robotic forearms, whose compressor-driven clacking I now hear in my nightmares.

Everywhere, we see groups of islanders spreading nets and combing trees, sometimes barely visible underneath the endless olive groves that define those horizons not defined by the sea. In short, there's an urgency in the air that leaves me feeling neglectful, irresponsible—a thousand empty *telara* wait somewhere to be filled, and here we are setting off for a day of lazy exploration.

While we navigate the steep switchbacks along the coast, the shadow of Mount Athos is visible now and then in the distance to the west. Far below—causing instant vertigo when I, the driver, glance down at them—are silent, massive waves, working fruitlessly to erode the white marble of Thasos. Then suddenly the road turns inland and flattens out on a fertile plateau dominated entirely by olives. The air above the trees is alchemized by the silver light their leaves cast when they lift in the slight breeze. Here the work would be easy, we understand by now: with no trees growing at impossible angles, we'd be spared the constant adjustment of our drop nets, the awkward boulder ballet.

Behind the Thasos Oil filling station (the island boasts one productive rig off the southern coast), next to the rusting hulks of five dead semitrailers, two ancient Thasians are gathering olives from their little patch of trees.

They must be over eighty, he sporting a felt fisherman's cap and denim vest, she the usual black dress and black cardigan all the old women here seem to wear. To our surprise, while the man steadies himself on the third rung of his wooden ladder (they have no machinery here), we watch as the old woman climbs up into the branches of the tree, her capped head just visible among the leaves. She begins bashing away with her bamboo cane, just as farmers did for thousands of years before the advent of air compressors and mechanical claws. Later, when the tree has been beaten to death, I know they'll kneel together and pick up by hand what has been brought down with persistence and brute force.

Tracing half the circumference of the island beyond the villages of Limenaria and Potos (where we will return later in the week to deliver a truckful of *telara* to the olive cooperative) takes only about a half hour. Again, on this side of the island, the *kafenia* are devoid of their armies of bead-flipping grandfathers, the minimarts are closed, and even the churches are deserted. Caïques, the traditional fishing boats, are pitifully at rest upon stilts, forlorn in spite of their pastel paint jobs, pulled far up the beach until the olive harvest has ended.

Before long we pull into Thasos Town itself, past the first harbor (modern and ugly, it's dominated by the docks of the competing ferry companies), past about fifty comatose hotels and the papered-over windows of knick-knack shops, down to the sublime ancient harbor, a semicircle of crystalline seawater that's been put to use for at least three thousand years. We smell the bakery but cannot locate it—is there a secret door? We search in vain for a restaurant other than the deservedly deserted Zorba's, which still has a sun-bleached menu with revolting photographs of gelatinous moussaka hanging in the window from the previous summer. After several days of eating in Eva's kitchen, there's not a chance of surrendering to such barbarism.

The only other option is the opulent-looking Taverna Simi, which I'd normally avoid. On Greek islands, ironed white tablecloths and fancy décor usually mean inflated prices, too-attentive service by polyglot waiters, and a pretentious chef. Granted, the place is beautiful, with antique nautical bric-a-brac, black-and-white photographs of the local archeology, and cruciform windows opening out upon the harbor. We are the only customers, and for us to dine they have to turn on the lights.

To our delight, since we are somehow famished yet again, the food is immaculate and fresh: a plate of wilted *horta*, wild greens dressed in the new oil and lemon; a smear of *chtipiti*, mashed feta with hot peppers; a plump tentacle of grilled octopus, drizzled with simple red vinegar and a dash of oregano; and *melitzana tiganiti*, crispy fried eggplant slices, accompanied with *tzatziki*. And at last, I eat an olive—a bona fide *throumba* olive from Thasos. It is as wrinkled as anything ancient should be, a black eye made blind by salt. The flavor of the island is in this fruit. Let all the others give oil; this one has enough meat to stall every other need. Which is not to say we stop with the olives; we eat everything in sight with the focused rapacity of farmhands.

When the waiter comes around to refill our tin carafe of white wine, his curiosity gets the best of him. "So you live in Greece . . . or are you just visiting? You know, we don't see many foreigners on Thasos this time of year."

When I tell him we've paid our own way here, merely to help harvest someone else's olives, he freezes in disbelief, eyeing us beneath a skeptically raised chin.

Later, when the waiter brings our bill, he glances at us devilishly and says, "You know, when you're done paying your friend to harvest *his* olives at Alyki, I'd be willing to let you pay me to harvest *mine*. I've got about two hundred trees down by Limenaria that are waiting to be picked."

.   .   .

When our work is done on the fourth day, Tasos insists that we go mushroom hunting. "We'll gather them along the way. . . . We'll have a bag full in no

An Olive, at Last

time, I promise," he tells us while diving headfirst into a profusion of pine branches thick enough to render him invisible. After another day of working olives in the rain, the idea of mucking around the wet underbrush seems just plain dumb. When we hear Tasos holler a gleeful "Mama mia!" a few minutes later, however, we've got enough curiosity and appetite to bound into the trees ourselves. "Hell, we're already soaked," my brother points out.

We are gathering *piperites*, mushrooms that, like the bees, keep close company with the purple-flowering heather. Though half-covered by fallen pine needles, they're easy to find around the roots of each bush. They're the size and color of small portobellos, but with a delicacy lacking in their mass-produced supermarket counterparts, being slightly fluted at the edges of each cap. Once you locate one, you've located a hundred, since they seem to arrange themselves into little fungic city-states around the roots of the heather. Unfortunately, they're pretty much identical to another kind of mushroom that's entirely poisonous.

"If you see red underneath, throw it away," Tasos tells us. "Brown is OK, but you must crack open the stems to check for worms."

Sure enough, about every other mushroom is riddled with the excavations of disconcerting maggot-like creatures. When I show Tasos a handful of wormless mushrooms, asking him if they're what we want, he replies, "Well, we'll see," which I don't find very comforting.

With our bags full, we resume our descent down the mountain, but Tasos stops abruptly and hushes our conversation with a wave of his flattened palm. I expect he's heard some beast in the brush, am prepared to be charged by a wild boar or rabid billy goat. Instead, from high up on Kleftoyanni Brachos, I hear the echo of someone shouting. At first I can't make out what they're saying, but then Tasos points to a little column of smoke about half a mile away, beneath which, nearly invisible, I see a house, Uncle Nikos's place.

Thus begins one of the oddest conversations I've ever heard: Tasos shouting out greetings, *echo*, his uncle shouting back questions about the olives, *echo*, Tasos asking after his wife, *echo*, his uncle asking after Eva and Stamatis, *echo*, then some discussion of mushrooms, *echo*, where we've found them, *echo*, whether they are big enough to eat, *echo*, and finally, by way of signing off, a cheerful pair of *Ya sous, echo, echo*. When I ask Tasos what on earth that was all about, he smiles and says, "Christopher, that was a Thasian telephone."

. . .

Where I come from, occupation is the key to self-definition; we are what we do "for a living." Americans refer to a work "ethic" for a reason, because in our culture it's unethical to do anything but work—and working hard is the only option. By contrast, Greeks approach all work, from manual labor to bureaucratic paper pushing, with balanced skepticism. A frequently con-quered people, they prize their autonomy, which entails the freedom to act as they see fit, to flout the dictates of the law and even of reason. Above all else, they answer to *philotimo*, a kind of self-pride that defines their individ-ual sense of honor as well as their sense of Greekness. How many times have I waited at the post office or bank while the teller, exercising his or her own autonomy, finishes a cigarette or phone conversation before serving me and the line of people behind me?

Here on Thasos, there's no "workday" per se—Stamatis will work as long as he wants and rest when he wants. We will work and rest along with him, as we see fit. Most days, that means we stop our labor in the early afternoon and retire to the pension for a very civilized lunch: often just leftovers from the previous night, but always accompanied by something fresh from the garden, an arugula salad or a platter of beets and slivered garlic dressed with new oil. And we will have *tsipouro* if we want *tsipouro*, or beer if we want that. And we might take a siesta afterward. Because we can. This isn't to say the Greeks don't work hard. As a college professor no longer accustomed to long days of physical labor, I was astounded to learn just how much stamina is required to maintain a farm, to do the daily chores, not to mention picking the olives, making the wine, distilling the *tsipouro*, catching the fish, and running the restaurant. In spite of all that gets accomplished in a single day at Pension Archontissa, the urgency to live well trumps every other necessity and the pace is always relaxed.

In the evening, our task is to sort the olives that we've collected. We gather inside a little shed lined with straw bales, survey the *telara* brimming with olives, and take our seats before a kind of conveyor belt made of vibrating springs. The olives are dumped in a hopper at one end and make their way down the line, where the gap between the springs slowly widens so that the smallest olives drop first and the largest last, allowing us to sort them by size while we hastily remove twigs, leaves, and other foreign matter. This is as monotonous as any factory work, but it requires just enough speed and dexterity to feel slightly challenging; it helps that there's a little nook next to each spot on the belt where one can nestle a glass of *tsipouro*, to keep things jovial.

When we finish sorting, Tasos agrees to reveal to me the secret I've come here in part to discover: his recipe for *throumbes*. Only the very biggest olives, those that tumble off the end of the belt, those too large to fall between the springs at all, are destined to become *throumbes*. They must be free of blemish and obese with oil. Smooth-skinned Kalamata olives, often pitted and then exported everywhere, offer only two pleasures to the palate: brine and a spongy, uniform texture. Forgive me, Peloponnesians, but I've come to think of Kalamata olives as little more than a delivery system for salt. *Throumbes*, on the other hand, attack the palate with contrasting sensations: though shriveled, their flesh has an almost meaty texture; the flavor, at first nutty, gets swept up in dusky tannins, as with a good red wine, moving on toward notes of bay leaf and bitter thyme. The olive's farewell gesture is its finish: *throumbes* are salty, like most olives, but since they never touch a drop of liquid brine the salt comes at the last moment, with as much grace as salt can muster.

The recipe, which I'm sure must involve bay leaves and perhaps some sort of citrus or other curing agent, turns out to be moronically simple. Tasos leads me to the back of the shed, to a pile of what look like white plastic bricks.

"What's this?" I ask him.

"All you'll need to make your *throumbes*," he replies.

Clearly marked on each brick is "ΑΛΑΤΙ ΓΙΑ ΕΛΙΕΣ" (Salt for Olives). Nothing more, nothing less. No curing agent, no seasoning, no sulfites. Tasos fills a large plastic garbage bag with olives, dumps in a handful of the coarse salt, and then punctures the bottom of the bag with his pocketknife a few times so it can drain. He ties the bag shut with some twine, places a brick on top of it, and walks away.

"That's it?" I ask.

"Yes. They'll be ready in about ten days. You can taste them next summer when you come."

. . .

It isn't easy to work our last day on the island. The weather has turned summery, with the sun glaring down and the wind barely stirring the pomegranate tree outside our balcony. We are supposed to be tackling a little congregation of olives just across the road from the pension, on the edge of a massive cliff that looks over my favorite beach in all of Greece. I'm so distracted by the view that by ten I've already made it known that I'll be going swimming.

That said, the water is absolutely freezing, and we're back on the sun-blasted rocks within a minute, trembling inside our towels.

Late that night, having eaten ourselves into a stupor (octopus roasted in a foil packet over an open fire, potatoes swimming in olive oil, anchovies festooned with dill, roasted chestnuts, and Stamatis's new wine, a fruit-forward *imiglyko*), we make a valiant effort to remain conscious on the balcony of Pension Archontissa. On the table before us, there's a little carafe of *tsipouro* that will never be empty, because Tasos keeps filling it. There's also a plate of last year's *throumbes* and an ashtray for our pits. My brother has mummified himself in a blanket and is nodding off in his chair.

Tasos can't sit still. He's pacing beneath a canopy of decimated grapevines, surrounded by the cats who follow him everywhere he goes, and arguing with his girlfriend, Elpida, on his cell phone; she's on the mainland and he is here—enough to keep the young lovers close to their phones, in a state of agitation, all day long. It's better to avoid the long good-bye, the futile expressions of gratitude, the rehearsal of our friendship, and the many rounds of *tsipouro* that would require, so we leave Tasos to his conversation and drag ourselves to bed.

First thing tomorrow, George Kaltsas (who had to return to Kavala after only one day of olive picking) will meet Aaron and me at Keramoti, and we'll report to him on our labors here before flying back to Athens. Tonight, I'll lie awake in bed another hour and listen to the waves crashing on the rocks below, then drift into dreams through which a billion olives tumble.

.   .   .

Back in Athens, having delivered my brother to the airport, having spent the day talking poetry and politics over numerous coffees with all the expatriate writers and Greek literati I know, I go alone at eleven to my favorite *taverna*, O Karabitis, in Pangrati, a chic neighborhood down the hill from Kolonaki. The place is hideous on the outside, besmeared with filthy stucco and its windows filled with wire mesh, but inside is another matter. One steps down from street level as through a trapdoor into a dungeon, enters a narrow hall walled on one side with enormous wooden wine barrels stacked two or three high, and finds a fire crackling at one end of the room. Beside it, an old man plays a bouzouki and wails poetry put to music by Theodorakis.

I've eaten here five times now, always alone—a bizarre practice in Greece, where food should always be shared. All around me gorgeous couples are leaning close to whisper secrets across their wine; middle-aged men are clumped in satisfied groups, cracking jokes and screaming at one another about the politics of the moment; a quartet of heavily made-up professional women are getting goofy on ouzo; and by the fire, the old man sings Yorgos Seferis:

> On the secret seashore,
> white as a dove
> we thirsted at noon:
> but the water was brackish.

I come for a half-portion of lamb (which the owner's cousin raises outside Nafplio, reputedly), a plate of *horta*, a tin carafe of the *taverna*'s exquisite light red wine from the Peloponnese, and their surprisingly good bread. I add a plate of olives to my order tonight, since it seems appropriate. Alas, they turn out to be the insipid Kalamata olives I can't seem to stomach after becoming so intimate with the *throumbes* of Thasos.

I come also to enjoy my privacy in a public place, my chance to observe the human circus vicariously while reading a good book and eating absent-mindedly, just a forkful now and then—my last chance to do so for some time. Tonight I'm reading a delightful chapter from Patrick Leigh Fermor's *Roumeli*, the one where he attends a wedding feast hosted by Sarakatsan nomads; last time I was here I spilled olive oil on Seferis's poem "Stratis Thalassinos Among the Agapanthi"; the time before that it was Simone Weil (whose work, I found out, is not at all compatible with carnivorous gluttony). Without a dining companion, I must attend to my own thoughts, try to enjoy my own company, and try not to look too conspicuous.

That's going to take a bit of work. I've been living out of a duffel bag for a week and am downright gamey. My lower back is aching and my face is sunburned; my jeans are stained with oil and dirt; there's olive goop beneath my fingernails that won't wash away; and surely there's sheep dung wedged in the tread of my boots. I must look a bit insane.

Am I remembered by the waiters here because I eat alone—the odd foreigner in the corner with his book—or because the first time I was here I left without my brand-new and very expensive coat, which I had to come back to fetch the next day? Not that any of them have really spoken more than a sentence to me. Solitary diners are suspect enough to be left alone. But tonight, perhaps because I'm the last one left (by now even the drunkest of the guests have been graciously ushered out), or because I smell like a shepherd and, after a second carafe of wine, am speaking Greek with the gruff demotic speed of a hired hand, one of the waiters becomes curious enough to ask me where I'm from. Somehow he doesn't seem at all surprised to learn that I'm an American professor who usually comes here to translate Greek poetry written by a famous ex-communist who lives around the corner (this is a very sophisticated neighborhood, after all). But when I tell him I've come this time to pick olives on Thasos, he seems unsettled. He turns away without any response and walks back across the restaurant, to where his cigarette has been patiently smoking itself in an ashtray. I see him relay this information to his boss, who seems equally nonplussed.

When I stand to pay my bill at last, both men rise from their mountain of just-laundered napkins to see me off. "Don't forget your coat this time, Mr. Professor," the older man says, gesturing with an outstretched palm toward the door. "And by the way," he adds with a grin, as if it's just occurred to him, "if you still want to pick some more olives, I've got a beautiful little grove of trees up on Mount Hymmitos that's waiting to be harvested."

Olives: The Throumbes of Thasos

THASIAN OCTOPUS WITH POTATOES AND RED WINE

As a boy, I'd often follow my father into the forests of Wisconsin in the summer, when he'd build blinds and tree stands and do reconnaissance in preparation for deer-hunting season. He'd often test me by pointing across a field at (what appeared to me to be) an unbroken wall of green foliage. "Where's the deer?" he'd ask me. I always failed to see the animals he found by hardly looking, and he'd have to guide my eyes to the exact spot before a tan profile and rack of antlers would come into focus. No wonder I never shot a deer.

My eyes haven't sharpened with age. In fact, I experience a similar blindness when out hunting octopus with Tasos of Thasos. "Where's the octopus?" he'll ask, pointing his speargun in the general direction of some submerged boulders I've just swum past. I know in theory how to find an octopus, sure. I know they'll be tucked into a small crevice or hole and will have made themselves almost invisible by altering the color and pattern of their bodies to match the background. I even know how to spot their gardens (built from the inedible garbage of previous meals). Still, Tasos locates and harpoons three for each one I find. He grew up here and sees into the landscape with a clarity I'll never achieve.

We took six octopuses during an hour of very cold diving one December morning last year, and Tasos taught me this recipe for preparing them. You need:

1 octopus (about 1 kilo)

1 bottle dry red wine

2 tablespoons olive oil

2 large potatoes, peeled and cut into large pieces

1 large onion, sliced

2 green peppers, sliced

2 cloves garlic, sliced

2 bay leaves

2 allspice berries

Black pepper

Having harpooned a large octopus and removed its beak, as well as the organs and innards inside its hood, you must find a good flat stone to whack it against. Be sure there's no sand nearby or you'll likely end up with grit in your finished dish. Smash the octopus against the rock as hard as you can forty times. Then scrub it on the rock in vigorous circles, as if polishing metal; when the muscle begins to break down it will release some white foam. Continue until the foam disappears.

Then, Tasos explains, the octopus must take its "last walk" in the sea. Puncture a small hole in the hood and use a rope to tie it to a stone right where the waves break. The idea here is to let the waves rake the octopus back and forth across smooth stones for an hour, further tenderizing it.

At last, it's ready to cook.

Place the whole octopus, along with the wine, into a deep pot. Simmer while half-covered until the octopus is fork-tender, about 1 hour. Then use tongs to remove the octopus from the pan, reserving the wine in the pot. Cut the octopus into large pieces.

Meanwhile, in a separate pan, heat the olive oil and sauté the potatoes for a few minutes, then add the onion, green peppers, and garlic. Cook them until "they are dead" (Tasos's phrase), or about 5 minutes. Add the pieces of octopus, half of the braising wine, the bay leaves, and the allspice berries. Simmer until the sauce reduces and the potatoes become tender, about 20 minutes. You may add a dash of freshly ground black pepper at the end, but the dish won't want any salt: the octopus will have already delivered that. Serve immediately.

CHAPTER TWO

Bread

The Prozymi *of Kyria Konstandina*

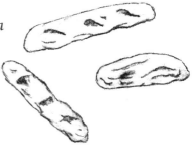

People who have eaten only in tourist restaurants conclude that Greek bread is bad. I hesitate when people tell me this, but they are right. Baskets of nearly crustless, fluffy white slabs with the consistency of marshmallow and the taste of Styrofoam (the qualities of much American bread) litter too many *taverna* tables. Most restaurants in Greece buy in volume from factory bakeries. It's fine for mopping up the mustardy tomato sauce left over in a bowl of mussels *saganaki*, or for smearing with *tzatziki* or *taramosalata*. And even shoe leather would taste good drizzled with Greek olive oil. But bread must be satisfying in its own right. It's the bottom note, the foundation stone, the staff and stuff of life—the rest is beautiful garnish. Chalk up Greece's reputation for bad bread to a half century of booming tourism and globalization, but the story of Greek bread is older than that.

Not long ago, there were two things at the heart of every Greek village: the *fournos* (a wood oven) and the village well (or, sometimes, a bubbling fountain). Bread and water. When times get tough—and in Greece they always do—survival comes down to that. The village baker was more important than the mayor. And every village had its own bread, its uniqueness deriving from the flavor of the local water, the qualities of the grain, the pungency of the oil, and the techniques of the baker. At every *taverna*, your meal was held together by an artisan's bread, and another loaf would be cooling on your own table at home. It is difficult not to romanticize this time, especially now that Greece moves at the speed of any other European nation. Perhaps the loss of good bread is just another cost of the global economy. Village bakeries still exist across Greece, but finding them now takes work. Except on Crete, where it's nearly impossible to find bad bread. Just as Crete was one of the last places in Greece to succumb to the Ottoman juggernaut, it is the very last place resisting barbaric bread.

My friend Roula Konsolaki has been urging me to spend a few days working with master bakers she knows. Within an hour of my arrival on Crete, she leads me down one of the narrow passageways of the old city of Chania. We're visiting a Turkish bath refitted as a charming restaurant called Tamam. Before the waiter makes eye contact, he brings a pitcher of room-temperature *raki* (here on Crete, the liquor of choice still retains its Turkish name and never contains even a hint of anise), a duet of tiny glasses, and a wooden basket of bread. This is the real stuff: brown, with flecks of barley flour, some variegated seeds tattooed upon the crust, and where the loaves have been hacked apart, the visible dips and valleys of a haphazard cell structure—marks of careful kneading and slow fermentation.

Roula understands. My mania for the traditions of village grandmothers might seem pure nostalgia, but she shares in the wonders of the Greek table. Her mother, Pelayia, is one of the best home cooks I've ever met. When Roula began translating my poetry into Greek almost twenty years ago, I visited her in Thebes and enjoyed a series of overwhelming feasts in the Konsolaki family kitchen. I spoke much less Greek then than I do now, but I knew how to smile and eat, and to Pelayia every smile betrayed my helpless desire for more. She'd fill my plate over and over again until I surrendered. Moving to Chania to take a teaching job was, I gather, very difficult for Roula, since it meant leaving her aging parents to fend for themselves and giving up the familiarity of the mainland for Crete. Even for her, the island—floating half-way between Athens and Libya—was exotic, almost another country.

Cretans are notoriously fierce. The men wear knives in their belts and pledge allegiance to Crete first, Greece second. Lawrence Durrell wisely explained it this way: the Cretan "feels about Athens very much what a Sicilian feels about Rome." They are thought, by other Greeks, to be violent individualists, if not murderers. So Crete is to Greece roughly what Texas is to the United States: a vast territory separated by attitude and ideology, pugnaciously defending its homegrown culture. Crete even has an Alamo: Moni Arkadi, a monastery outside Rethymno where 250 men (50 of them monks) held off a massive Turkish assault for several days in 1866 with an absurdly small cache of weapons before blowing themselves up—along with their women and children, 864 people in total—by igniting the gunpowder cache they didn't want to fall into Turkish hands.

Cretan cuisine, however, welcomed outsiders. Many Greek island groups have distinct culinary traditions. As in Italy, regional distinctions follow naturally from what's available and are inflected by invaders. Cycladic islanders might cook their chickpeas in the oven with onions and bay leaves plucked right from the tree (onions and bay laurel being among the few things that grow on the barren Cyclades), while on the Dodecanese Islands chickpeas are often stewed with tomatoes, parsley, and garlic (since Asia Minor is within swimming distance, there's easy access to produce grown just across the water). Beyond such variations, however, Greek cuisine is largely the same from place to place, being founded upon olive oil, legumes, grains, and fish. This is not surprising, as the total land mass of Greece is smaller than that of Wisconsin. It seems infinitely larger, since an archipelago is defined by water, not land. Among seafaring people like the Greeks, there's bound to be fluid boundaries and recipe sharing across its ten thousand miles of coastline. Except on Crete.

At Tamam today we eat *apaki*, a smoked loin of pork sliced succulently thin, and *kalitsunia*, little savory pastries stuffed with wilted mountain greens. Other dishes illustrate Chania's exquisitely mongrelized past. Remnants of the fourteenth-century Venetian presence are visible not only in the harbor architecture but in a dish called *dakos*, which is a swarthy cousin of *bruschetta al pomodoro;* rather than grilled bread, grated tomatoes are heaped upon brown barley rusks called *paximadia*, then bedecked with a rich spoonful of the ricotta-like *myzithra* (made from sheep's milk) or a creamy feta, and drowned in about a pint of scratchy olive oil. And everywhere the Ottomans went, they left behind some version of *börek*, phyllo pies that can be savory or sweet; on Crete, they become *boureki* and hide within their crumbly, buttery embraces a filling of zucchini and potatoes enlightened by the unmistakable (is it African?) presence of mint. It's almost enough to make one forget bread.

"Keep up your appetite, Christopher," Roula remarks when we step from the cool interior of Tamam back into the sweltering alleyway. "My friend Vasilis is coming to Chania to meet you for *mezedes* tonight. You're going to like him. And you're going to like his bread."

. . .

Vasilis owns one of the most progressive agritourism complexes on the island and is one of its best young musicians. With his raspy voice he belts out the rhyming couplets, or *mantinádes*, of Cretan song. He is known for playing the *laouto*, a potbellied lute whose nearest cousin is probably the North African oud. He has rehearsal here later tonight and isn't *really* heading into Chania just to meet me. Roula guides us to a *taverna* tucked in the fortress walls, and Vasilis turns up eventually. Everyone knows him. With a little wave and some words over his shoulder, miniature pitchers of *raki* arrive on our table along with a platter of rusks smeared with fish roe, cheeses, and tapenades. Roula and I left Tamam only about two hours ago, but it's impossible to resist Cretan *mezedes*.

Vasilis embodies a physical paradox: his upper half is burly and hirsute; beneath, he has the legs of a runner. He looks rather like a minotaur. Most of his energy goes to smoking, which he does continuously, and to knocking back shots of *raki*. He moves with the thoughtful weight of a pachyderm. There are sandbags under his bloodshot eyes, and he erupts every few minutes into a fit of coughing. And yet there's an unmistakable quickness about him: except when gripping his *raki* glass, his sausage-like fingers tremble, his eyes dart, and one restless foot—as if accidentally attached to a comatose leg—taps out the speedy percussion of some inaudible music. I initially found his expression sour, brooding, and a little lachrymose for a man just over thirty. But at the most unexpected moments his face suddenly betrays him with a quick, wry smile. I like him.

"So I'll drive to your estate in the morning, if there's bread to bake," I say.

"OK. Can you come early?"

"You mean seven or eight?"

"No, no. Eleven, twelve, one . . . This is Crete. But we're hosting a wedding at the farm this weekend and the lady who runs my kitchen, Kyria Konstandina, needs to teach you about bread in the morning, before they slaughter the lambs. You are lucky, Christopher, since you'll be there to see that too. And then you must go to Kyria Eleftheria in Vatos on Saturday for a different experience."

"And whose bread is better?"

This question elicits a raised eyebrow and a chuckle.

"Listen, both ladies assume their bread is the best on the island, so if you only make bread with one you'll have taken sides in a feud. You must visit Eleftheria after learning what you can from Konstandina. Be careful—here on Crete we take our feuds very seriously."

I remember about the feuds. Twenty years ago, hiking across the mountains of central Crete, a friend of mine was trapped in a quarrel between two villages. He had to hide for a whole day, wedged between boulders in a dry riverbed, while villagers on opposite sides of the valley exchanged volleys. When the gunfire subsided he made a break for it, only to be kidnapped on the

Figure 5. Kyria Konstandina and her Cretan bread.

western edge of the valley. His captors made him endure a night of vehement hospitality: a rowdy feast at a long table with *raki*-drunk cowboys. He got up the courage to ask why they'd been shooting. He never got a satisfactory answer, but it at least became clear that for all but two days per year, a cease-fire was observed. The two villages engaged in ordinary commerce; some recent marriages had even crossed the feud lines. But custom dictated that two days of war would be observed annually: guns loaded, hatred recalled. Bullets would fly.

I don't expect Konstandina or Eleftheria to arrive packing heat, but it seems prudent to follow Vasilis's advice. And since I want to step into the middle of this rivalry armed with as much information as possible about my instructors, I push a little.

"So, whose bread do *you* prefer?" I ask him, clicking his *raki* glass and then downing mine.

"Well, here on Crete, the *real* bread is made with *prozymi*, a wild yeast leaven. *Never* yeast from the supermarket. I think you taste the *prozymi* more in the bread of Eleftheria—maybe because she lives high in the mountains and the yeasts are wilder there. But you'll see and make up your own mind."

"And they both use a wood oven, yes?"

"Sure, but does it matter? Can you tell when the bread is made with wood? For me, it doesn't make much of a difference. The quality of the dough itself is more important."

I agree. But as a *fourno* fanatic, I insist that wood-oven bread has a better crust. When I lived outside Thessaloniki in the early 1990s, I'd visit the neighborhood *fourno*, returning (if I'd been lucky, since they quickly sold out) with a kilo of still-hot *bâtard*, which would cool slowly in my hands on the walk home, just a rumor of wood ash wafting from the crust. I'd never cross the threshold of my apartment with a full loaf, of course, since it was impossible to resist eating at least one of the caramel-colored heels. Occasionally, I would return empty-handed—there was good goat's-milk feta to be bought a few doors down from the *fourno*, and with a handful of *throumbes* that meant an orgiastic half hour on a park bench.

A good crust needs the right moisture, heat, and air. In a vaulted wood oven, air flows in from outside through the door to swirl and convect with the contours of the dome; this is impossible in an ordinary square kitchen oven, even one filled with professional baking stones. For the past three years, I've been trying to make bread in a tiny wood-burning pizza oven in my Pennsylvania backyard. The pizzas are, I admit, pretty sublime—with pizza, one really appreciates wood smoke and some capricious char, not to mention the cracker crust achieved thanks to a super-high-temperature wood oven. But I've not made even one successful loaf of bread, as I can't get a consistent level of heat. The loaves char on the outside and are raw in the middle, or they cook too slowly and the crust never develops. And my dough is lame, its uniform crumb belying my ineptitude at kneading. I fail the physics of gluten and seek Cretan forgiveness. I believe that making (to say nothing of serving) bad bread is among the worst acts of disrespect one can commit. Might as well build your house on sinking sand. I'm relieved to have arrived on an island where people treat bread with the sacramental attention it deserves. And I've attached myself to Vasilis deliberately, since Roula has seen his wood oven in action and tasted the bread of Kyria Konstandina and found it good.

Of course I don't say this to Vasilis, who wouldn't care. It is enough that I've come to sweat in a country kitchen with the hired help.

.   .   .

The Dalabelos Estate stretches atop a verdant crest about five miles from the northern coast of Crete, not far from the city of Rethymno. From its wide patio, in the shadow of a billowing canvas umbrella, I survey its agricultural largesse. Directly underneath are several terraced vegetable and fruit gardens. The pomegranate trees are in flower, as are elephant-eared zucchini plants and huge tomato bushes. A little lower down, sensible lines of grapevines have been inscribed across the hillside, and beyond that is an undulating, silvery spread of olives that goes on forever. Out on the horizon, the low mountains part and all the green dissolves suddenly into blue, beyond which stretches the glaucous expanse of the Mediterranean (the Aegean yields to this parent sea seventy nautical miles north, back at the volcanic cusp of Santorini).

Invisible, but clearly down there somewhere (I hear the tinny gong of bells and a nervous music of bleating) are sheep and goats. And peacocks:

Figure 6. Dalabelos Estate, stretching north toward the coast near Rethymno, Crete.

their otherworldly song echoes off the patio stones. More familiar sounds emanate from within the kitchen—Kyria Konstandina preparing my coffee. Though I came here to work, I am commanded to submit to hospitality first. Vasilis's father, Manolis, joins me. He's also a minotaur, but with a rake's mustache, wisps of white hair, and the potbelly of a privileged gentleman farmer. He glows a little, accepting my lavish praise. The elegant buildings of local stone blend into the vegetative backdrop; in the center is this enormous patio where evening meals are served. There's a restaurant, with two floors of indoor seating for winter and space for twenty tables outdoors. In one corner, a deep clay basin the size of a child's swimming pool has been bricked: here, grapes are stomped in autumn. Gigantic clay amphorae spill over with roses, oleander, and little olive trees, and at every turn one encounters yet another stone staircase leading to another patio; these afford one the pleasant sensation of wandering a sun-blasted Escher print. Only one thing

Dalabelos

sticks out in this gorgeous continuum of soil, leaf, and stone: the gleaming silver cylinders and black chessboards of solar water heaters (each separate building has its own), inorganic but entirely practical. The place was obviously constructed with great care, at great expense. Compared to the billion concrete-block hotels that are the ruination of every landscape from here to Thessaloniki, Dalabelos is a glorious anomaly. It takes real imagination—not to mention talent, patience, and engagement with the land—to build something like this. Today I'm the only guest in the whole place; tomorrow a hundred others will arrive for some lucky couple's wedding.

Konstandina wears an impeccable white apron and T-shirt and has fixed upon her head a conscientious hairnet. I would guess that she is about fifty, but it's hard to tell: Cretans all live forever (they have some of the highest life-expectancy rates in Europe), and she may very well be seventy—for she is perfectly robust. I recognize in her forearms the meaty strength of someone who has spent years battling dough. Her hands on her hips, she grins and motions me, at last, into the kitchen, where a tidy *mise en place* has been set out on a stainless steel table. She takes down a red plastic bowl from atop the highest shelf and shows me the *prozymi*: it's nothing more than flour and springwater that were whisked together once upon a time, "fed" with flour daily (just like a needy pet), then set out in a warm spot to get busy. When I ask her how long she's kept this *prozymi* alive, she explains that it's been in service for seven or eight years. And when she removes the seal of plastic wrap, I recognize the unmistakable sweet-and-sour tang of fermentation—it smells exactly like warm beer. Looking closely, I see the *prozymi* moving.

Of course, anyone can make such a starter using commercial yeast. But why bother when spores of wild yeast are out carousing everywhere? "They're even in Pennsylvania," Konstandina asserts. A simple offering of flour and water is the equivalent of a yeast feast. It's easy to understand why, here on Crete, in this fecund little valley teeming with pollen and grapes and birds and bees, the wild yeast would be especially vigorous. And Cretan bakers are religious about their starters: on one Saturday each spring all the bakers take their profane slurries of water and flour to church to be sprinkled with holy water and blessed by the priest.

Konstandina moves the bowl over to the table, where heaps of flour are waiting for us, and then quickly crosses the *prozymi* several times, having joined her thumb and two forefingers into an Orthodox treble point. Into the *prozymi*, she pours three or four cups of warm water, several gurgles of olive oil from a massive tin, and then the flour: bowl after bowl of yellow, brown, and occasionally some white flour. Her fists work like pistons as she incorporates the dry into the wet. Before long she is sweating and now and then I see her wince; she stops to show me the arthritic swelling in her hands, which are webbed with stringy dough.

Having come here for a recipe, I stand ready with my pen and paper. But there's not a measuring cup in sight. She splashes warm water, then flour, then more water—mashing, kneading, turning, and kneading more. My help is rebuffed with a playful smile—clearly I'm useless, and Konstandina takes some pride in demonstrating her skill. For half an hour this goes on, until the mass of dough is the size of a beach ball and she must transfer it to a larger trough. "When is the kneading done?" I ask, but all she says is "Siga, siga" (Slowly, slowly). Unlike with pastry and cakes, where precision is crucial, bread is forgiving, and one proceeds by instinct, patiently waiting for the right "dough feel," kneading until it achieves the desired tackiness and tensility. Dough will evolve differently on a rainy day, or in winter, so a bread maker has to bend with the atmosphere and improvise. Occasionally, Konstandina gives the now smooth and resilient dough a little punch with her fist and then waits to see the dough's reaction. Finally, it springs back with the right attitude and "Entaxi," she says. It is finished. But wait: in a final act of pragmatic spirituality, she inscribes with her index finger a neat crucifix in the already swelling dough. She then drapes it with towels and ushers us both out of the kitchen quickly, as if our presence might disturb the sacred metamorphosis under way.

Manolis has had his farmhands assemble a heap of olive trash: atrophied branches, dry leaves, and wispy cuttings from the orchard. These he stuffs willy-nilly into the oven, douses with a coffee mug of *raki*, and lights with a wooden match. Flames roil and bellow within the oven's vault but then die down almost as quickly. Manolis repeats the process again and again for the next hour, but the fire won't catch. "The oven hasn't been used since last fall," he mutters, "There's too much water inside." Konstandina and I stand by, hands on our hips, none of our suggestions receiving so much as a nod of the head—here in Crete, the man of the house makes fire and it's best not to kindle his frustration. When Manolis drags out a can of gasoline, Konstandina steps between him and the oven and makes her stand. We'll be baking our bread inside today, "in the other oven," she says. Then, with perfect timing (by now the sun is blasting down upon us), she rushes back out with a tray of cold lemonades. Even though I had my heart set on seeing this wood oven in action, I'm relieved we don't have to watch Manolis blow himself up.

When I ask Konstandina how long the dough will need to rise, she shrugs and looks at me like I've said something inane. "We'll know when it is risen," she remarks inscrutably, leaving me to understand that we'll measure time here according to the mood of the dough, not the numbers on a clock (and that's fine with me, since I misplaced my wristwatch a few days ago). When I return from a stroll around the estate, Konstandina summons me back into the kitchen to shape the loaves and to slash them decoratively with a razor blade. Then into the commercial oven they go—emerging about forty minutes later as gleaming loaves that must be left to cool in the shade. Even though I did only a symbolic amount of work (I shaped one loaf and inscribed my own hash marks on it), I am told again to sit and be served.

While the dough was rising, Konstandina raided the garden and now, suddenly, garden things are arriving before me, having been transformed through her efficient alchemy: *fasolakia* (flat green beans) and *kolokythakia* (baby zucchini), cooked down with grated tomatoes and onions and oil, and a cucumber and tomato salad. Konstandina also brings me lamb cutlets braised in red wine, a decadent mound of *myzithra*, the inevitable pitcher of *raki*, and most enticingly of all, a basket of the bread we've just made. The bread is excellent, I'm not surprised to discover, and I rise to congratulate and thank Konstandina with a kiss on each cheek. That leaves her blushing. We are friends now. Before leaving me to my gluttony, she presents me with a souvenir of our lesson: a little plastic marmalade container holding a precious sample of her *prozymi*, which I'm told to stir now and then before attempting to smuggle it back home in my suitcase the day after tomorrow.

Meanwhile, other business is under way at Dalabelos. Manolis has been pacing for the past fifteen minutes, chattering on his cell phone and noisily loading his pickup truck's bed with buckets and bags. The night chef, Kostas, has arrived and is introduced to me; he's a handsome, stringy fellow with a neat spray of black hair. In one hand he grips a shepherd's crook and in the other an intimidating curved knife, which he drops on the table next to me in order to shake my hand. The lambs. The wedding party bought a small herd, and today is the lambs' unlucky day. "Come and have a look when you're finished," Manolis tells me, but thankfully I'm still involved with my meal when Kostas and Manolis head off in the truck.

I promised myself last night that I would watch. In America, meat arrives precut and hermetically wrapped in cellophane. Disconnecting the idea of "meat" from that of "the animal" is evidently good for business. Since almost all the meat sold in America started in a factory farm and ended on a disgusting factory killing floor, keeping the facts about it under wraps is crucial—if most consumers knew the origins of their meat, the whole sordid industry might come crashing down. The obvious response, of course, is to become a vegetarian, but I find carnivorous longings impossible to put down. As a compromise solution (the ethical nuances of which are probably undercomplicated), I've decided, whenever possible, to face the beast I'm going to eat. Back in Pennsylvania, I've bought several pigs that I'd met personally; I even

Unlucky Lambs

called in the "hit" on them at the local slaughterhouse. So here at Dalabelos, having just devoured a plate of utterly delicious lamb, I feel I should stand up, walk around the last of the outbuildings, climb over the barbed wire fence, and kneel beneath the olive trees to watch the slaughter.

But I'm too cowardly. Hearing it is almost too much for me. First the peacocks begin to panic—as if their necks were on the block—filling the air with insistent, sickly, flügelhorn chortles. Then there are the yips of the dogs, which are no doubt running circles around the lambs, herding them where the men wait beneath the trees with their knives. And finally there's the sound of the lambs themselves: those whinnies and desperate bleats that precede and accompany their murder. My heart is in my throat and my feasting comes to an abrupt halt. Kyria Konstandina has disappeared, I notice, hiding somewhere out of earshot.

Just an hour ago, this valley was filled with air and light: bunches of oleander nodded affirmations in the breeze; Manolis's grandson rode like mad around the patio on his tricycle; cheap silverware turned to gold in the sun; and back in the kitchen, gluten and wild yeast danced the Pentozali through Konstandina's dough. How quickly the earth itself has changed. It's suddenly far too hot—the open palms of grape leaves above me are wilting into fists. Busy ants have retreated into their mounds. And two hawks cruise in ominous circles above the olive grove. I toss back a few shots of *raki* for courage in the face of Thanatos and walk as far down the patio as I can go in the opposite direction, staring out at the impassive sea in the distance.

After a while, Kostas returns on foot, thumping slowly along the stones with his crook and his now warm knife. He looks drained and very, very serious. He rumbles around inside the kitchen—I hear him curse once, and a metallic clatter follows—and then he reemerges into the bright light with a stringer of huge meat hooks, a bucket of knives and cleavers, and some empty plastic tubs. He has a long afternoon ahead of him. I skulk off to my room, hoping no one will notice, and quickly insert the buds of my earphones and turn the music up as loud as it will go. But I can still hear peacocks shrieking over the recorded wail of electric guitar. A few clouds have blown in over the mountains and the sky darkens outside the window. It would seem appropriate to weep, but out of respect (for what, I cannot say) I don't. So I pray for the lily-livered oblivion of a siesta.

Sleeping away several hours of an afternoon feels wasteful at home, where I'm always on the clock: there are papers to grade, lunches to pack, dogs to walk, e-mails to answer, and bills to pay. Given an hour saved from work, I should reenact the sack of Rome with my six-year-old son (the little Visigoth), or teach my nine-year-old daughter how to make a porcini ragu. But from the moment I arrive in Greece, I must do like the dough: rise and recline and rise again at a pace dictated by the heat and my own improvisations. Given so much freedom, it's strange that what takes over isn't sloth, but a kind of animal intensity. In Greece, I risk becoming pure verb: diving, eating, smelling, making, climbing, writing, thinking. No surprise that by the time lunch is over most days, I feel deflated, unable to resist an hour of unconsciousness in the shade. Today, everything having turned sepulchral, it's really the only option.

. . .

> Through the new wound that fate had opened in me
> I felt the setting sun flood my heart
> with a force like that of water when it rushes in
> through a gash in a sinking ship.

So begins "The Sacred Way," the great poem by Angelos Sikelianos. When I dare to step from my room at six o'clock, the air is still and the sky has fallen: long shadows slipped out from beneath the stones while I was sleeping and the tops of trees in the valley are now almost orange. I'm ready to lead a funeral procession into the olive groves.

But I'm drawn by the sound of human voices to the patio, where I find Vasilis seated with a woman at a table beneath a grape arbor. It's Kyria

Eleftheria, I discover, come from Vatos in the south of the island to introduce herself and to shore up our baking plans. When he asks, I assure Vasilis that the afternoon with Konstandina was perfect (indeed it was, though I'm too ashamed to mention my failure with the lambs), and after we spend a moment together gazing at a table full of the bread she made, he goes off to check on some detail of the wedding, leaving me with a beer, a bowl of tiny black olives, and my second Muse of Dough.

Kyria Eleftheria has been learning English for the past year or so—and even though it's more rudimentary than my Greek, she insists that we converse in my mother tongue (not seeming to notice how often she lapses back into her own). As with Konstandina, I can only guess that Eleftheria is around fifty. She keeps her silver hair closely cropped, wears a bright red blouse and a long black skirt, and beams. Vasilis has misled her about my importance in the world, and I think she may be expecting a crew to begin filming us. She's brought a plastic bag full of her bread, which she opens ceremoniously, awaiting my reaction. It's much darker than the bread I made with Konstandina—she's obviously used a much coarser flour. And it's delicious.

Eleftheria is known for more than her bread. She has a kind of studio in the mountains and creates art objects out of the native herbs and flowers: drying, flattening, and framing them attractively and selling them to places like Dalabelos (at one point she gives me a tour of the restaurant walls, where several of her pieces are on display). And though she masquerades—in terms of physical appearance—as an ordinary Cretan woman, I gather from our conversation that she's a kind of unorthodox naturalist. It seems perfectly right that her name means "freedom." Though I waver when she begins suggesting an itinerary for the next day (I am tempted by a restful day at the beach), she insists that I drive to Vatos in the morning, as planned, to make bread with her.

A party has been organized for tonight—my presence having provided a good excuse to throw one—and as the twilight deepens, the headlights of cars come winding up the estate's gravel driveway. Vasilis welcomes the guests, whose names I'm embarrassed to forget almost immediately. Several of them arrive bearing musical instruments in lumpy black cases, and one—the leather-clad Dr. Manolis—has brought an entire case of red wine. A pale moon hoists itself from behind the hillside into the still bluish sky, and we all wander about the patio talking. The party includes some professional women from Rethymno, a trio of bespectacled musicians, and a teacher whose daughter is studying in the United States—intellectuals all. Just before we sit down at our long table, there's one last, late arrival: a kind old hippie from Chania whose Jesus face I recognize from the icons of Christ Pantocrator. Eleftheria, who'd earlier announced her imminent departure, is clearly going nowhere now, and by the time Kostas begins slinging *mezedes* from the kitchen, the *raki* is flowing, conversation has found its rhythm, and cigarettes are rising and falling like fireflies in gesticulating hands. I can't help noticing that sometime during the confusion of arrivals and introductions, Eleftheria stealthily tucked samples of her bread into the baskets already loaded with Konstandina's.

For an hour we drink only *raki:* someone gives a toast to our collective health every few minutes, and many cheers are made for my coming here, and others to the chef. Thank god the cups are miniscule, because such rocket fuel will send one to the stratosphere. Then bottles of red wine are opened; salads, spreads, and cheeses are pushed aside; and our host emerges with platters of steaks, sausages, and of course lamb chops. I'm heaping my plate high once again. The *raki* has rinsed away every trace of this afternoon's unexpected gloom; it's also inspiring in me the delusion that I can comprehend every word of Cretan Greek being spoken. An involved conversation about wine is under way, for which I lack much vocabulary. But I can follow, and people speak enough English for finer points. Dr. Manolis's wine is surely some of the most sophisticated I've had on Crete. He keeps his vineyards in another exquisite microclimate, that of the Amari valley, which is flanked by Mount Psiloritis—Crete's tallest mountain and mythology's

Mount Ida, nursery of baby Zeus. Into this sacred pagan soil, Dr. Manolis has planted old clippings of cabernet and merlot; he combines these in equal portions and ages the wine in French oak barrels. What he pours from this three-year-old bottle is dark as blood and dry as bone, but with a blackberry finish that makes it a perfect complement to lamb. When I plunge my nose as deep as it can go in the glass I swear I can sniff out some of the wild yeast that animated Kyria Konstandina's *prozymi*.

Yet several people are asserting that this is not Cretan wine so much as French wine grown on Cretan soil. The rugged table wines of Crete are pressed from hardy native grapes—such as *romeiko*, *kotsifali*, and *mandilari*—that have been cultivated for many, many generations. "What happens to tradition if you refine it too much?" asks Jesus, who like all of us is well into his third glass.

"You become British," someone shouts from the other end of the table, inspiring some laughter.

As recently as fifteen years ago, I remind the group, it wasn't easy to find anything but cheap *retsina* or watery red plonk at most restaurants.

"That's true," Manolis agrees, "but we've come a long way in the past decade. I've risked making a wine that is very *heavy* by Greek standards. This isn't wine for lunch at the beach."

The subject is pushed and prodded a long time, rhetoric often giving way to lyricism, improvisations moving in the direction of high argument and finally back to mutual assent. Toasts are made to someone's grandfather's wine, and to the wine of Manolis.

Then the party grows diffuse—pairs wandering out into the moonlight to smoke, Kostas clearing the table, Eleftheria insisting she must finally go home. For a while I find myself embroiled in a conversation about Iraq, and another about the impossibility of Obama winning the upcoming election, and then the imminent collapse of the Greek economy. Until, suddenly, Vasilis's fingers are charging up and down the frets of a mandolin, and someone else is playing a percussive accompaniment on the lyre, and everyone is back at the table singing. They all know a thousand songs and I know none. No matter. It would seem wrong for a foreigner to have access to territories so personal and ancient and Cretan. At three in the morning, once all the guests have gone and the wine is killed, I'm treated to a private concert: Vasilis picks up the *laouto* and plays until sunrise—his eyes rolled backward and his lids fluttering in ecstatic concentration—with a pathos that's not lost in translation.

.   .   .

My body, even when demolished by revelry, remembers the road from Rethymno to the southern coast; I spent three weeks in Crete back in my twenties and followed this road numerous times on my motorcycle. It leads to Preveli Monastery, famous for its icons and the beach just beneath its cliff. A cool freshwater stream gurgles out of a mountain gorge there and runs through a forest of palm trees, stopping to rest in a white sand basin before plunging into the Libyan Sea—saltwater yielding to sweet. One weekend back in that distant summer, I ran out of gas miles above the monastery, in the mountains, but momentum and elevation were on my side; I coasted my bike all the way here to the edge of the world. Then I pitched my tent in the shade of some palms and survived on pistachios and *raki* for a few days, wishing never to leave. Eventually hunger made me bum a few splashes of gasoline from the monastery's gardener. I scribbled several pages of heroic couplets about the Battle of Crete down on that beach—thankfully that bit of macho versification hasn't survived. But for years I've wondered about the notebook I lost there, the only record I had of those days, probably fallen from my motorcycle into the dust. Today I resist my nostalgic impulse to return to Preveli; instead, I continue past Spili and Vatos toward the tiny village of Agiou Vasiliou, where Kyria Eleftheria bakes her bread.

I know which is her house without having to ask. There are only ten, and surely Eleftheria's is the one sending wood smoke into the blinding sky. It doesn't matter that I'm several hours late. She's made her dough, which is tucked in beneath impeccably white sheets, and she's feeding branches into the oven when I cross the threshold of her busy little courtyard. Yogurt containers, empty olive oil tins, and buckets mass-produced in China: every empty vessel has been transformed into a planter for herbs and flowers. In a tall yellow cylinder printed with the hideous phrase "JCB Special Gear Oil" grows the largest and most beautiful geranium I've ever seen, in an absolute tizzy of fuchsia blossoms. On one wall, a prickly mountain of dried branches has been piled—fuel for the oven. Opposite that, a rusty wheelbarrow and an aluminum stepladder melt in the sun just out of reach of the shade cast by a bamboo awning. Creeping across the vast expanses of a white plastic table, a little brown snail has set out upon a long journey in the direction of the whitewashed wall. Watching him, it seems perfectly reasonable to believe that time has stopped for good within this bower and that on Crete all things are meted out in units of eternity.

As it turns out, Eleftheria is the source of bread and *paximadia* for Agiou Vasiliou, Vatou, and three other tiny villages. She's not started her oven just to demonstrate her skills for me—indeed, within five minutes of my arrival some local pokes his head through the gate to ask if the bread's ready. Her oven takes up every inch of space inside a cinder-block hut, where it is infernally hot. When I step before the roiling, flame-frenzied vault, I can feel my hair blow back. It might be the ugliest oven I've ever seen: although the brickwork is neat and has been contoured by a skillful mason, the outer dome is covered with a haphazard blanket of silver-backed insulation and even a few layers of entirely flammable cardboard. There's almost no space to work, but once the fire burns down Eleftheria mops out the ashes with a wet rag (secured to the end of a very long pole), and then with great skill she arranges about twenty kilo-sized loaves in a neat spiral to maximize the oven floor's circular space. The moment the dough touches the hot stones I can smell the evaporated sweetness of Cretan yeast.

Bread: The Prozymi of Kyria Konstandina

Oddly, Eleftheria leaves a gap in the center of the oven. When I ask her why, she takes my wrist in her hand and guides me behind the shed where one loaf has been set apart from the others. While the rest are thick and oblong, this one is small and round. She unwraps it carefully and then shows me a small wooden disk with an elaborate woodcut. I study it briefly, trying to figure out what image it would produce in reverse, then notice the conspicuous crosshatch of a crucifix. The solitary loaf is the communion host, Eleftheria explains, and the man who was inquiring about the bread earlier was the village priest. She presses the disk into the dough and the loaf exhales beneath its pressure. Then she loads it on a wooden peel and lands it neatly into its privileged spot, where it gradually swells and turns golden along with the attendant loaves. A free, if not pagan, spirit drives the hill wandering and herb gathering of Eleftheria, and she's no doubt a remarkable source of local knowledge; in another epoch, I imagine she'd be a priestess at the Temple of Demeter. Yet it makes complete sense that some-one with such power over grain would be crucial to the Eucharistic feast in now Christian Crete.

While the bread bakes, Eleftheria shows me into her tidy, slightly lonesome cottage, which is dominated by the kitchen. She directs me to a plate of morsels I've never encountered before: they are *myzithropites*, ravioli-sized pies made from her bread dough and stuffed with *myzithra* and mint, then fried in olive oil. More food is clearly on its way, bubbling atop every burner on her rickety stove. In the back of the house is Eleftheria's studio. Shoe boxes full of dried plants and flowers are stacked from floor to ceiling, each labeled with an illegible scrawl. A drafting table holds her frames and mats and cutting tools, and on one wall there's a gallery of finished work hanging, much of it fascinatingly detailed, with dried blossoms and branches fixed in organized profusion upon colored paper and pressed behind glass. Eleftheria presents me with two small cards, one for each of my children back home. And then she dials up her English teacher, who is enlisted to tell me (in better English than she's able) how proud she is to have me in her home, and how much she wishes she could read the book of poetry I've brought her, and how honored the village of Agiou Vasiliou is to host such a distinguished guest. I nod and smile, in as distinguished a manner as I'm able, and voice my own formal appreciations, which the English teacher translates for Eleftheria.

Once the bread is removed from the oven and put to cool in the shade, we retire to a table covered in oilcloth in the middle of the kitchen. Eleftheria presses a tin pitcher of wine into my hand and then fills the table with food: steaming beets dressed with garlic and vinegar, a bowl of braised greens she gathered on the mountain, and a plate of cracked green olives preserved with lemon. Still sizzling in a cast-iron skillet is an omelet made with fried potatoes and eggs from her neighbor's chickens; when it is finished, she slides it onto a platter and sprinkles it with the florets from a marjoram bush. "If only you stay for dinner, Christopher, we could eat some snails," she implores me, showing me some she has caught and imprisoned in a colander in her sink. I think of the one I saw earlier in the courtyard, which got away.

We eat in relative silence—I've run out of questions about bread, now that the bread has been made, and we exhausted all topics of conversation the night before. But our taciturnity isn't in any way uncomfortable, and I find my new friend to be full of a calm sadness I recognize in myself. A wave of homesick longing for my wife and children has come out of nowhere and it feels as if, after so many days in motion, my dawdling heart has suddenly caught up with my busy body. It takes a few moments to reorient myself. So I hold still in my solitude, while Eleftheria makes peace with her own. Then I think of that great line by Seferis: "Wherever I travel Greece wounds me." I'm leaving for home tomorrow and can already feel the injury of departure.

Eventually, Eleftheria shows me a photograph of her children, both of whom have lives of their own far away. Her husband, I learn, "left" many years ago (speaking in Greek, I gingerly get her to clarify that he abandoned her and didn't actually die) and she's lived alone ever since, surrounded by a village full of old people, most of them suspicious of her interest in art but greedy for her bread. "My children worry about me," Eleftheria confesses, her eyes suddenly brimming, "and I miss them too much." She removes her glasses to wipe her tears away with the back of her hand, then allows herself to sob a little. At last she returns her glasses to her nose, smoothes out the apron on her lap, and smiles up at me. "Alla, ti na kanoume?" she says with a shrug and a deflating sigh, in Greek now, since English cannot do justice to her gorgeous phrase, containing all the pained resignation in the world: "But what can we do?"

By the time I leave, bearing two heavy loaves of Eleftheria's bread wrapped in brown paper, it is late afternoon and all of Crete is asleep. There's not another car on the road, and I must keep myself from nodding off along the switchbacks of the ascent toward Rethymno. I stop my car on the wrong side of the road near the turnoff to Preveli and gaze for a while backward at the Libyan Sea. Nearly indigo and impossibly still, it no doubt scoured the coast of my past long ago.

.　.　.

I sleep restlessly in my hotel in Chania and get up at daybreak to catch a taxi to the airport. There's an American military base here, and a jeep full of drunken soldiers clatters by the taxi stand where I'm waiting with my suitcase, ruining the silence and sending a black cat bounding from a garbage can. The first church bells of Sunday are ringing off in the distance. Ahead of me today are three airplanes and a series of terrible airport meals, but I take comfort knowing that somewhere over the Atlantic, unable to sleep in the hissing confines of a jet, I'll be able to think of my *prozymi* expanding inside that plastic vessel, which Kyria Konstandina sealed with blessings so that—at least for the duration of my flight home—it will contain the yeasty breath of God.

MYZITHROPITES

Unless you have a close friend who owns sheep or goats, finding fresh *myzithra* isn't an easy task outside of places like Greece. But I like to approximate this dish, which I was first served by Kyria Eleftheria of Agiou Vasiliou on Crete, by using a mixture of whole-milk ricotta and chèvre.

English speakers know the word *pita* and associate it with a sort of dry pocket bread that can be stuffed with sandwich ingredients. But *pites* in Greece are actually little pies, and the word can refer to almost anything wrapped in dough, including the famous rotating meat gyro, most commonly ordered to go as a gyro pita in the beloved grease palaces of Athens. Some *pites* are made with phyllo, as with the famous spanakopita, but a simple flour, water, and olive oil dough is just as common. Some, such as *kotopita* (a shredded chicken pie), contain meat, but there are also myriad vegetarian *pites*, including *kolokythopita* (zucchini pie), *prasopita* (leek pie), and finally *tyropita* (a cheese pie most commonly stuffed with feta, but with kasseri you get a *kasopita*, and with *myzithra*, a *myzithropita*). Since Kryia Eleftheria always has bread dough near at hand, she simply uses that, but I've opted here for something closer to a very rustic phyllo.

3½ cups all-purpose flour, plus additional as needed

1 cup water, plus additional as needed

1 tablespoon olive oil

A generous pinch of fine salt

2 cups whole-milk ricotta cheese

8 ounces chèvre

½ cup thinly sliced fresh mint

Olive oil, for frying

Combine the flour, water, olive oil, and salt in a bowl and knead, adding additional flour or water until a soft, elastic mass forms. Add flour just until the dough no longer sticks to your fingers. Seal with plastic wrap and refrigerate for at least 1 hour. Then prepare the filling.

Use a wooden spoon to mix the ricotta, chèvre, and mint.

Once the dough is refrigerated, divide it into 8 pieces and roll each piece out on a lightly floured surface until it is a little thinner than an American pie crust.

Cut the rolled sheets into uniform 4-by-4-inch squares. Place a rounded teaspoon of the filling in the center of each square, then pull one corner across diagonally to form a kind of triangular ravioli. Seal the open edges with the back of a fork, then lightly press down on the filling so it disperses inside the dough. Transfer the assembled pies to a towel.

Heat a quarter inch of olive oil in a skillet until shimmering, then drop the pies into the oil in small batches, being careful not to crowd the pan too much. Fry the pies until lightly golden on both sides, then transfer to drain on paper towels for a moment before serving them hot or at room temperature.

CHAPTER THREE

Fish

Tailing Barbounia

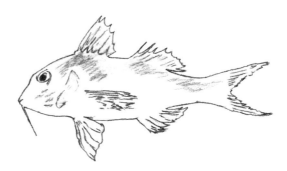

I've been invited to join one of the great food families of Greece for a seaside lunch. My last meal was steamed-mystery-meat-on-plastic-plate, served at thirty-five thousand feet over Greenland, so I'm going in famished.

Dimitris and Christina Panteleimonitis, my hosts, represent different sides of Greek gastronomy. Dimitris sells John Deere and Kubota farm equipment, and for over thirty years he's traveled rural Greece, helping farmers modernize their equipment and their approach to agriculture. He knows how to build sanitary milking parlors for sheep and goats, can install state-of-the-art desalination systems, and is capable of taking a small farm from mere subsistence into profit and export capability. All of which might make him sound like an adversary of artisanal food production. (I think of the American family farms of my mother's generation, many of which went "industrial" and wound up captive to the whims of big seed, pesticide, and farm implement companies, in debt up to their ears, selling out.) But while Dimitris is an entrepreneurial genius with loads of capitalist acumen, his feet are firmly rooted in agrarian tradition. His family comes from a tiny village on Lesbos, and thanks to his childhood there he has an abiding knowledge of the foodways of his grandparents.

As a result, he sees the value of Greece's rural past to its commercial and touristic future.

The agritourism movement is just now beginning to take off in Greece, but Dimitris has been promoting the idea of "farm vacations" for years. "Not everyone who comes to Greece wants to melt on the beach," he told me the first time we met, a decade ago, "and the trick is to create a value-added holiday." A small, fleshy fellow with a few wisps of blowsy hair, a forehead always furrowed by the onset of ideas, and a nautical, mostly Ralph Lauren wardrobe that gives no hint of his rural upbringing, Dimitris has a habit of dropping textbook economics phrases into his otherwise impassioned sentences, constantly theorizing about the way "cost-benefit analysis," say, might apply to someone planning a visit to the Dodecanese Islands. His pet project was the restoration of Ta Mylelia, a two-hundred-year-old water mill on Lesbos. Tinkering with ancient machinery, much of which had to be excavated from a hillside, he created a working farm museum where one can see how island agriculture was practiced in Ottoman times. A spring-fed stream turns the waterwheel, which turns the giant millstone, which grinds hard durum wheat, which makes a short journey from mill to wood oven, where Yannis, a sprightly seventy-something master baker, stands ready to demonstrate bread-making techniques to the hundreds of schoolchildren who come to Ta Mylelia on field trips. For Greeks, the experience is akin to what an American feels wandering colonial Williamsburg.

Christina, meanwhile, is a celebrated chef, the author of several glossy cookbooks, and the mastermind behind Ta Mylelia's line of preserves, teas, sea salts, and unusual pastas (I'm partial to her saffron fettuccine). Hers was the first line of boutique organic food products in Greece, and the business is wildly successful. Christina's an elegant being: tiny, doe-like, and soft-spoken, but with a boisterous mane of reddish hair and gigantic penetrating eyes. She has four sons, all of whom look very much like her, and she is clearly adored by her little army of Panteleimonitis men. Indeed, it's impossible not to adore either Christina or her food, with its island ingredients and perfect balance between sophistication and handmade simplicity.

I'd been buying Ta Mylelia's products for years before I met Spyros, the Panteleimonitis's eldest son, whom they sent to study at the Pennsylvania college where I teach. When Spyros, having come to my office to introduce himself to "the professor who knows Greece," told me he was the son of the Ta Mylelia folks, I nearly kissed his feet. By now, not only Spyros but his three brothers are studying abroad and becoming integrated into the family business. Today's lunch, in fact, celebrates the return of the youngest, Pavlos, from the United Kingdom after his first year of university. He sits next to Christina, clutching her hand and grinning.

We're dining at Mikrolimano, one of those spots that make me forget my troubled relationship with Athens. The city and I have never been on very good terms. My Greek "hometown," Thessaloniki, boasts about a million inhabitants but has the neighborly atmosphere of a large village. There, I bump into people I know on a regular basis. Athens, by contrast, has always felt anonymous, not to mention smoggy and scattered: urban blight from horizon to horizon. But gradually I've made peace with the place, if only because it's hard to love Greece without finding some way to come to terms with Athens.

In truth, there's much to like. There are many quiet little parks and alleyways where one can retreat for espresso or ouzo. The suburbs of Maroussi, Kifisia, and Agios Stephanos are entirely hospitable. The new light-rail system (built for the Olympics) runs from the city center to the beach at Glyfada or Edem, where one can swim and then eat calamari with feet in the sand. There's Mount Lykavitos to climb, with its little whitewashed shrine at the top. Coming down from the mountain, with its spectacular view over the Acropolis all the way to the first Saronic Islands, one strolls through a placid pine forest teeming with Mediterranean nature; during my last descent, I was astonished to glimpse the darting swoops of a gold-crested Hoopoe, the kind of psychedelic bird one would expect to find in Madagascar, not Athens.

Mikrolimano ("Little Port") is another such gem, located just down the coast from suffocating Piraeus. Only fifteen minutes earlier I was dodging traffic near Syntagma Square, and now I'm sitting by the sea, watching minnows harass a fisherman's hooked bait. The Athens Yacht Club—formerly the Royal Yacht Club, before Greek royalty was sent packing—is here, and the place is swanky. (Dimitris is a member, his smart blue sailboat moored a few docks away.) Open-air restaurants line the harbor front, all teeming with well-dressed families out for Sunday afternoon lunch. The scent of salt water and grilled fish is everywhere, and I'm very hungry.

Now, I can cook most kinds of Greek food back home in Pennsylvania, utilizing local organic produce, free-range lamb from a friend's farm in Wisconsin, and the olives, dried chickpeas, and Santorini *fava* (yellow split peas, not the fava beans of Italy) with which I stuff my luggage on every return from Greece. I can crank out sublime moussakas with Pennsylvania eggplants; and in August, with some heirloom tomatoes, local cucumbers, and imported feta (one market in town orders real Greek feta through a warehouse in Pittsburgh), I can assemble a classic *choriatiki* salad. But I crave real seafood all year long.

As a rule, one shouldn't eat fish more than a few miles from salt water. In Greece, that's an easy rule to obey. Back in Pennsylvania, however, that means avoiding fish altogether. There's great fly-fishing where I live, but our streams are so polluted from agricultural runoff that it's unwise to eat more than one trout per month. And I wouldn't touch anything from Lake Erie (which famously once caught fire) with a ten-foot pole. Now and then my piscatory longings become so intense that I raid the grocery store for a plank of frozen salmon, but mostly I save them up for Greece.

Christina offers me a menu out of politeness, but I know from experience to trust her to place our order with the chef—no one has more exacting standards. The waiters know this too, circling her like nervous sparrows.

A salad of arugula and tomatoes arrives, followed by a long wave of things from the sea. First come velvety, flash-fried *langostinos, garides Symi* (little fuchsia shrimp eaten whole, shell and all), and crunchy baby squid (lightly breaded with what I think is semolina flour). And now what's this? A triangular vessel has appeared on the table, filled to the brim with sea urchin roe. The golden eggs are scraped from urchin skeletons during the full moon (when they are most swollen) and then dunked in lemon juice and olive oil. They land on the tongue with a slightly bitter mineral darkness, then depart in a paroxysm of iodine, salt water, and sweet citrus: quintessence of the Aegean. My enthusiasm for them is so obvious that I'm made to drink the remaining roe right from the dish—"like the Japanese do," Christina says. Next comes octopus. Rather than the standard grilled tentacles, however, the chef has braised a small octopus until fork-tender in Mavrodaphne, a cloying dessert wine from Patras. A salty-sweet pool of crimson reduction, voluptuous as demi-glace, serves as the dish's exquisite foundation.

While we chatter on about my family and theirs, and about Pavlos's life in England, all of us relaxing into the Sunday heat, I notice that Dimitris has disengaged from the conversation, evidently at work on one of his big ideas. His jaw's moving a little and his eyes are flashing, and I wonder what he's scheming. He waits impatiently for a break in the conversation, then smacks his lips twice and exclaims, matter-of-factly, "So, Christopher, here's what we must do." He proceeds to tell me that the mayor of the city of Drama, way up in Thrace, has been working for decades to create a seed bank of local grains—many of them very obscure, limited to specific valleys and ecosystems of the southern Balkans. Each seed has a tale to tell, many involving the sad history of war, diaspora, and population exchange that's hardened the people of Thrace. Grain seeds have been carried here and there in the pockets of the displaced. The mayor has set aside a lush valley outside Drama where little plots will be sown with each grain, both as a kind of agricultural and historical exhibition and in order to produce heirloom seeds, which are to be distributed to the locals. Dimitris is so moved by the mayor's altruism that he's ready to make me a deal: he'll provide all the tractors and heavy machinery if I'll go up there and help write the exhibition's catalogue. I'm astonished to find myself the linchpin of the plan, but I listen as he outlines the next two years of my life. What could stop me from pulling up stakes and moving my family to Thrace?

By the time our main courses arrive (two dishes featuring locally farmed mussels) I'm off my head with jet lag and ouzo, imagining life as an anthropologist of grain. I know Dimitris is serious, and I'm taking him seriously, but our attention is diverted again by food: now there's an expertly composed *mydopilafo* to attend to. The chef knows how to handle his arborio, the creaminess of the rice serving to soak up the saline excretions of the mussels. On another plate, a tower of squid-ink linguine has been tossed in slivered garlic and fresh tomatoes and spiked with black mussel shells, each bearing a succulent morsel.

Then suddenly our table is empty, except for a small carafe of the restaurant's own *limoncello* and a bottle of mastic spirits. I raise a glass to whatever the future brings. Finally, we devour a superfluous platter of profiteroles, chocolate cakes, and ice cream.

I must stop to wipe the sweat from my brow, so exhausting is all this pleasure. More satisfaction is impossible to imagine, and yet, thankfully, there's one thing missing from the feast. If not, where would I go from here? From this point on, I announce to my hosts, I'll be following the trail of my favorite Mediterranean fish: *Mullus surmuletus*, which the Greeks call *barbounia*, the French *rouget*, and we Anglophones *red mullet*. Tomorrow I'm headed back to the island of Thasos with a few friends; there, Stamatis the fisherman has promised we shall catch *barbounia* from the comfort of his boat.

. . .

In any good Greek restaurant, guests are invited into the kitchen to inspect fish before buying them. "There, *file mou*, is the Aegean," the proprietor will indicate with his outstretched palm, "and here's the fish" (resting before us on its mattress of crushed ice), "and over there is the grill, ready for your order." The discerning customer will always be on the lookout for the crimson gills and convex, pellucid eyes that indicate freshness. When it comes to selecting mullet, however, there are other things to watch for. There are two kinds of red mullet, and many diners don't know the difference. Both are a species of goatfish, named for the beard-like barbs hanging from their lower lips, which they drag like antennae along the sea bottom. Of the two, the more desirable are my *barbounia* (*Mullus surmuletus*), which are almost bright red after being scaled, with two or three golden stripes running from gills to tail (for this reason, they are sometimes referred to in English as "striped red mullet"). *Barbounia* also boast a single horizontal stripe across their first dorsal fins, though you'd have to handle them to notice it. (Some restaurant proprietors draw a sanitary line here—you fondle the fish, you buy it.) *Mullus barbatus*, which the Greeks call *koutsomoura* ("lame-faced"), are paler and lack the gilded striations of their cousins, though they're also quite beautiful.

Not only tourists but plenty of Greeks wind up paying *barbounia* prices for *koutsomoura*. To be honest, both fish are delicious, but many fishermen insist that *barbounia* are sweeter, and I tend to agree. While both kinds of mullet can grow rather large—some as big as two kilos—it's rare to find them bigger than a quarter kilo. This is not a matter of overfishing (though in some places that is a problem); the smaller mullet are just tastier, perhaps because of their diet of minuscule shrimp. Like most good things, they aren't cheap: *barbounia* average fifty euros per kilo, making it among the most expensive seafood (except for lobster) sold at most *tavernas*. (Trustworthy restaurants sell *koutsomoura* at a more reasonable forty euros per kilo, around the same price as sea bream and John Dory.) That translates to around ten euros per small fish, and my *barbounia* cravings are never satisfied by just one.

Beloved from Tel Aviv to Tarifa, the red mullet has been among the most esteemed Mediterranean fishes since Roman times. Mulletomania afflicted

Fish: Tailing Barbounia

first-century Romans much as the "bacillus of tulipomania" (Zbigniew Herbert's phrase) would infect the Dutch in the 1630s. Predictably, the Romans preferred their mullets massive, since to them bigger was always better, and prices for large ones became so extravagant that Rome's greatest satirical poets—Horace, Martial, and Juvenal—took turns disparaging the idiots who paid more for mullets than they did for quality slaves, or who wasted their time hand feeding those they tried to raise in captivity. In *Natural Questions*, Seneca tartly observes, "The belly of gourmets has reached such daintiness that they cannot taste a fish unless they see it swimming and palpitating in the very dining room." The mullet was prized for its sweet flesh and its delectable liver, but wealthy Romans were even more titillated by the fleeting colors displayed by the fish in its death throes. To those same dainty-bellied gourmets, Seneca continues, "there is nothing more beautiful than a dying [mullet]. In the very struggle of its failing breath of life, first a red, then a pale tint suffuses it, and its scales change hue, and between life and death there is a gradation of color into subtle shades." Leave it to the Romans to combine seafood, avarice, and sadism.

The Greco-Italian connection, as usual, is wonderfully complicated. My friend Titos Patrikios, who spent much of his life in Rome, tells me that the ancient Greeks called the mullet *trigli* (perhaps, James Grout has suggested in his excellent *Encyclopaedia Romana*, because it spawns three times a year) and that modern Italians still refer to the fish as *triglia di scoglio* (for *surmuletus*) or *triglia di fango* (for *barbatus*). But the Venetians brought their love for mullet with them when they colonized parts of Greece in the fourteenth and fifteenth centuries and left behind their dialect name for mullet: *barbone* ("beard-bearing"). So, Titos concluded, now the Italians use the Greek word and the Greeks use the Italian. The Turks, who occupied Greece for seven centuries but who were themselves colonized by Greek seafood-eating habits, still call the fish *barbunya*. I enjoyed the ironies of this linguistic tangle a few summers back while sipping white wine and devouring inexpensive *barbunya* at Gümüşlük, south of Bodrum on the (now) Turkish Aegean coast, where I overlooked the ruins of the ancient Greek city Myndos.

. . .

Stamatis, Eva, and Tasos Kouzis are the closest thing I have to a Greek family; Pension Archontissa, the small hotel they run overlooking the peninsula of Alyki, has become like a second home. Having helped them harvest their olives, and having slung a plate now and then in the restaurant, I feel I've even earned my keep just a little. When I pull in the driveway, I immediately cross paths with Stamatis, who has just gathered up his evening nets and is sorting the catch. I take it as a good omen that at my first Thasian embrace leaves me smelling of fish. Stamatis shows us what he's brought in from the cove: a whole bucket of small *lithrinia* (*Pagellus erythrinus*, known as "pandora" in English), two large squid, a still-throbbing cuttlefish, and a dozen *barbounia*. "We've been waiting for you," Stamatis says when I introduce him to my friends Corey and Darrin—a sentence Eva repeats verbatim a few moments later when we crowd into the busy kitchen. Tasos and his girlfriend, Elpida (who has recently moved here from Thessaloniki and is, I see, now working in the family restaurant), are running like mad from table to table, smiling in welcome. We drop our bags, find a seat near the railing, and take in the view—as familiar to me as my own backyard, but no less gorgeous for that fact. With dusk coming on, the three bays of Alyki are turning violet, and the marbles of the ruined shrine of the Dioscuri, just visible on the far edge of the second bay, are glowing in the last of the sunlight. I should be content to stay here for the next week, eating seafood, sipping *tsipouro*, and watching the vines grow.

But, the truth is, the moment I arrive at Archontissa, a kind of weird oscillation kicks in. I'm thrilled to feel at home here: even the cats look familiar to me, their faces mustached with squid ink. I'm told to help myself to food from the refrigerators in the restaurant kitchen, and am pretty much forbidden to spend anything beyond a symbolic pittance. I have a history here that I slip back into like a second skin. It occurs to me that I've been coming to Alyki for almost twenty years now, and should feel relief upon arrival. But I take one look out across the coves and the gleaming edge of the marble quarry and my mind begins racing, my feet tapping beneath the table. I can't find a way to be still.

All at once I feel the desire to swim (in all three coves), to dive for octopus, to hike up into the nearby olive groves, to chat with Stamatis about the state of the sea, to join Eva in the kitchen (where she's stuffing zucchini flowers with rice, onions, and mint), to read Wallace Stevens out on my patio, to scribble something in my notebook, to throw rocks, and to scream (I don't know what) with all the air in my lungs. Some island calm will wash over me eventually, I trust, but my inquietude never gives up easily.

Dinner will help. With food imminent, Tasos demands I have some *tsipouro*. "You are on Thasos now, Christopher. Plus, this is the best batch I've made in years." I do as he insists, then dive into Eva's *roka-marouli*—a salad of arugula and romaine tossed with capers, dried tomatoes, *throumbes* olives, and feta—and an entire squid grilled over coals. Soon I'm wiping the flavor of the island from my chin, savoring the combination of *tsipouro* anise, squid juice, charcoal, and olive oil that triggers on my tongue the idea of Thasos, its terroir.

Next comes a platter of six *barbounia*. *Barbounia* can be bathed in garlic, bay leaves, allspice, and olive oil, then baked in a wood oven. The fish's delicate flesh also makes it a good candidate for preparations *al cartoccio* (baked in parchment, that is). In the Ionian Islands, *barbounia* are fried and then marinated with vinegar, currants, rosemary, and honey—a centuries-old method of preservation suited to long sea voyages. But I prefer the simplest possible preparation for red mullet: either fried in olive oil until the skin is crisp, or basted with oil and lemon and grilled over wood coals. (Often, very small *barbounia* are not even gutted, since the innards are thought to contribute to the flavor of the fish.) Tonight I've ordered them fried, since I know Tasos has a way with this preparation. The skin has become even redder after its submersion in hot oil and peels back in crisp little wafers to reveal tender white flesh, which I think has a flavor closer to shellfish— oysters in particular—than any other fish. Wash each bite down with some *tsipouro*, I declare, and *barbounia* are indeed the best fish in the sea. "It's a pity you don't eat the heads," Tasos says when he stops by to check on our progress. And so we do, crunchy skull bones and all.

After dinner, when I ask Stamatis when we'll begin fishing in the morning, he delivers two pieces of bad news: tomorrow he's off to see the doctor in Kavala (he had a cardiac shunt installed a few years ago and must go to the mainland for a checkup), and his boat isn't working. He gives me an explanation I don't understand, something about there being too much fresh water in the engine. (*Should there be salt water instead?* I find myself wondering.) The day after tomorrow a mechanic will come from the other side of the island to have a look. Then we shall see about *barbounia*.

Since I've come such a long way to fish, however, Tasos has an idea.

"Tomorrow will be a slow day here at the restaurant, and Elpida can manage," he says. "I haven't been out diving yet this year. Let's go out on my little boat and see what we can catch." Then he looks at my friends. "You can both swim, right?" Corey and Darrin assure him they can.

Later, our host fills us a plastic bottle of *tsipouro* and we head down the goat path to the beach for a nightcap and some stargazing. The universe looks good from here, we all agree, and when Tasos switches off the bright lights of the restaurant, another billion stars swim free from their net of blackness and seem to dart before our eyes. Luckily, the *tsipouro* doesn't hold out for long, and we crawl back up the dark cliff toward bed.

.   .   .

Though I'd anticipated catching fish from the comfort of a bobbing trawler, it would be foolish to miss an opportunity to see how the larger fish make it onto the plate—thanks to the skills of a master skin diver like Tasos. Over the years, I've become fairly adept at spearing octopus in shallow water, which mainly involves locating their dens and finding a way to extricate them. Being among the most intelligent creatures in the sea, octopuses have a talent for finding nooks and crannies where they can squeeze themselves into a knot of marine muscle, adjust their color to match their surroundings, then snag a meal as it swims or creeps by. But housekeeping is their downfall: they like to arrange the inedible portions of their prey in concentric patterns around their dens. This is what Ringo Starr meant when he crooned about an "octopus's garden" back in 1969. It's also what to look for while snorkeling: anomalous patches and patterns in the busy sea floor.

Many divers save themselves this step by installing a simple trap: sinking tires within easy swimming distance from shore. What could be more curious to an octopus than a black tire, incongruous, inorganic, yet entirely habitable?

Such curiosity is the diver's best weapon. Even while wedged safely inside its den, an octopus can't resist the impulse to investigate with one tentacle the sharp textures and metallic sheen of the trident about to impale it. Once shot through with the spear and dragged up to the surface, an additional challenge waits the hunter: treading water and navigating a cloud of black ink and a tangle of sticky, writhing tentacles to incapacitate your dinner. This is either done by reaching three fingers inside the octopus's hood and flipping it inside out, or you can opt for the more dramatic, but probably more humane, coup de grâce Tasos usually employs: biting the octopus—very hard and decisively—right between the eyes.

When it comes to supplying a restaurant with seafood, such inefficient methods of bagging octopus would result in quick bankruptcy, of course. But for many of the Greek men that I know—especially those who grew up on islands—a primary source of weekend entertainment involves donning a full wet suit to hunt fish, eels, and octopus in deep water with a speargun, often at night. This is no more adventurous to them than, say, a weekend of hook-and-bobber fishing would be for my uncles back in Wisconsin, but the Greek sport (I would soon find out) offers many more opportunities for disaster.

Tasos fits us each with fins and checks to see that our snorkel gear is sufficient. Then back down the goat path we go to prepare for fishing. His boat is not a boat at all, but an inflatable orange dinghy patched here and there with duct tape. We take turns manning an air pump, reinflating the thing as best we can. "It's not pretty," Tasos says proudly, "but it will float. I bought it from an Italian friend for only a hundred fifty euros." That's hardly comforting. Into this dubious craft we pile our gear, including a duffel bag covered in old fish scales and a prickly bouquet of spearguns.

"Have I taken you to Bámbouras before, Christopher?" Tasos asks. "It's out on the point—the monsters wait for us there."

Tasos contorts himself into a full wet suit (the rest of us are swimming without), and then off we go, bouncing across the whitecaps, laughing as we're bombarded by spray, the motor screaming, the three of us eager to help Tasos catch dinner. We pass two or three exquisite little coves ("for later," Tasos shouts) and head out across the open water. The sky is cloudless, and heat haze clings to the scrub-covered hillsides, which rise steeply all along the coast. Soon it becomes clear we're headed toward a point where, to spectacular effect, a high horse-shaped cliff has broken off, leaving one megalith of marble at a sharp angle to the water and a half-sunken, smaller one jutting a hundred yards out. Between them lies crystalline water. After Tasos kills the motor and tosses the anchor overboard, I ask him why this is such a good fishing spot.

"Fish come here because of the *revma*. The small fish become confused and so the big ones come to feed. You're all strong swimmers, right? Because there's *revma* here, you know, and sometimes it's strong. If you get tired, just come back to the boat."

Figure 7. The horse-shaped rock at Bámbouras, Thasos.

Corey and Darrin look at me curiously, awaiting translation. "What's *revma?*" Darrin asks finally.

This requires a bit of explanation. *Revma* means "current," and (as in English) can apply to electricity, air, or water. But the word also serves as the root of *révmatismós*, from which we get *rheumatism*, and the link is telling, for Greeks have some curious superstitions about the perils of circulated air. When I first moved to Greece, I wondered why passengers chose to keep the windows shut on stifling buses, why taxi drivers removed the window controls in the backseat, and why electric fans were almost impossible to find. The reason, a Greek friend explained, was *revma:* currents wafting across the back of the neck were thought to cause paralysis. This old wives' tale was so pervasive that even my educated friends bought into it, avoiding the occasional breezes for which I was desperate in summer. But,

I assure Corey and Darrin, a little *revma* in the water off Bámbouras won't do us any harm.

Tasos waits for us to don our fins and then gives us a lecture: "I'll swim with the large speargun, and you must always be careful to stay behind me in the water. I'm fishing for fish, not friends. Christopher, you will hunt with the smaller speargun—but stay close behind, since if I hit a large *rofos* you may need to finish it off with the small gun."

The idea of bagging a big grouper is enough to get us moving, and one at a time we tip backward overboard. The moment my mask is below the surface I see hundreds of fish, so busy avoiding one another that they pay no attention to me. I give an underwater thumbs-up to Corey and Darrin, who paddle along behind me, then point downward, making sure they see that Tasos has made his first dive. I begin the descent with him, but having ruptured my eardrum in the Corinthian Gulf last summer, I don't dare go deeper than about fifteen feet. Thanks to the belt of lead weights Tasos is wearing, in seconds he's gone so deep we can't even see him. He stays down a long time, several minutes on one breath, leaving us to tread water as instructed so we don't get pulled ahead of him. Eventually a chain of bubbles rises from the murk and up comes the black figure of Tasos, with a roughly four-pound *synagrida* (what we call dentex in English) quivering on his spear. I watch him pull a knife from his ankle holster and stab the fish between the eyes to put it out of its misery. Not a bad start.

By the time we've waited for Tasos to tuck the fish into the net he wears around his waist, we've been sucked almost around the point. He dives two or three more times, and we have to swim with all our might back against the current—suddenly very strong—to stay behind him. For my part, I'm swimming with one hand, since I'm trying not to shoot myself through the neck with the speargun in my other. Before long, my heart is thumping way too hard in my chest and I can't seem to get enough oxygen through the narrow tube of my snorkel. When I surface to catch a few breaths, I see Darrin's fins disappearing around the last of the outcroppings. I'm tempted to follow, since I wonder if the current might subside there, but that seems unwise. Plus, I see Corey right behind me, also gasping for breath.

"Want to head back to the boat?" I shout over the crashing water.

"Definitely," he shouts back.

This is easier said than swum. We're on a watery treadmill, as I can tell by marking my progress—or lack thereof—along the rock wall to my right; despite crawling as hard as I can (with one arm), I'm not budging. I know that if I allow myself to succumb to fear, I'll begin to hyperventilate. Though the urge is strong, I resist coming up for air again. It'd only take a few seconds to be pulled out to sea. Just while I'm contemplating how much longer I can manage this pace before my heart explodes, I get a wicked cramp in the arch of my left foot. Now I'm swimming with only one arm and one leg, still trying not to shoot myself with the other hand. I should probably ditch the speargun, but doing so would constitute a fatal blow to my machismo, one I'm not quite desperate enough to resign myself to. At any rate, what I'm doing isn't working, and I can see that Corey's struggling too, so we both veer at right angles into the rock wall, even though it's being battered by waves and is covered with spiky urchins. We find a ledge and hang on, but the accursed *revma* is so fierce that it threatens to sweep our feet out from under us. Still, what a relief to stick our heads above water and to gulp air for a moment! When I ask Corey how he's doing, I see a look of dread on his face—the same look, no doubt, that has come over my own. Then something completely unforeseen happens.

Suddenly, all around us, silver arrows are flashing, colliding with our arms and hair, darting over our shoulders: sardines have been bewildered into flight by the disruption of our lumpy bodies. This sets off a frenzied reaction from above: a gang of hungry seagulls begins dive-bombing the sardines. The gulls plunge so close that I could reach out and grab one by the neck, if I weren't busy hanging onto the rock. It's a giddy, surreal moment (made more so by our oxygen deprivation) that leaves us laughing aloud. I begin to wonder if this is the first in a series of marine hallucinations that will precede my death. It's easy to feel lulled by such comic beauty, exhausted as I am, and I'm tempted to just let go, surrender to the *revma*. But the sardines also leave me feeling like bait: at what point are we going to be raked over the rocks by a wave and ground into grouper food? It's time to move on.

Corey replaces his mask and shoves off back into the *revma*, kicking along close to the cliff, and I follow at a distance, not wanting to shoot him. The dinghy is right there, bobbing in the waves perhaps thirty yards away, but it's impossible to make any progress toward it. We stop once more after several minutes of flailing, wedging our fingers into a seam on the cliff just long enough to fill our lungs with air. I feel my heart racing beneath my rib cage, and my limbs are throbbing with adrenaline. Reluctantly launching myself back into the current yet again, I'm prepared for a bitter struggle, but suddenly the *revma* disappears, and within moments my fingers are around the anchor line of the dinghy, to which Corey is already clinging. We spill ourselves over the boat's now sagging sides, too out of breath to speak. Corey points to my hands, which are covered in blood.

"What the hell just happened?" he asks, "and where the hell is Darrin?"

Corey's gone pale, and judging from the wave of nausea coming over me, I'm also in shock. When I look down, I notice that blood is welling up from gashes on my palms, forearms, and calves: those blessed rocks, which may have saved us from drowning, were covered in razor-sharp barnacles. We spend a moment comparing our wounds, and I remark that I'm happy for the absence of sharks in Greek waters.

Now we see Darrin's fins splashing on the other side of the outcropping— rather than return through the *revma* as we did, he's been clever enough to go around and is coming back diagonally across the sardine pool. He looks annoyingly calm, making slow but gradual progress against the current, and after about ten minutes we pull him back into the dinghy, feeling a little foolish.

"You guys look awful," he remarks.

"And you look just fine—I take it the current wasn't an issue for you?"

"You're kidding, right? I just hoped you guys couldn't see me around the point. I was hanging onto some rocks for the past ten minutes and whimpering like a baby for my mother. When I saw that you hadn't come around the point, I tried to follow. But there's a whirlpool on the other side. A fucking whirlpool."

Tasos, meanwhile, is nowhere to be seen. Darrin (who, we now see, is also bleeding) reports that he last saw Tasos's fins disappear way off the edge of the last outcropping. I know better than to worry—this is Tasos's backyard. He grew up eating *revma* for breakfast.

When Tasos finally does return, we see evidence of what he's been up to: several more *synagrides* and a *melanouri* (saddled bream) glisten on the floor of the dinghy, entwined in the tentacles of a huge octopus. He pulls the dagger from his ankle holster and hands it to me, laughing at the bloody pulp of my palms.

"Show them how to kill the octopus, Christopher."

And though my hands are still quaking, I'm able to steady them just enough to plunge the knife between the beast's glaring eyes, then twist the point until the tentacles begin to relax.

"Well done, *file*," he mutters. "But we have a problem here." He points to the small speargun, which I'd tossed into the dinghy without unloading it. Had I kicked the trigger, I could have sunk the boat. I've never felt so mortified.

"Never mind," he says, patting me on the back. "Let me pump the boat back up and then, what, shall we go for a *real* swim now?"

We stop several more times on the way back to Alyki, but to our relief none of the dives yields the terrors (or bounty) of Bámbouras.

Then we anchor for one final plunge back at Alyki, just off the edge of the marble quarry. Above the water is an acre of what looks like cubist sculpture, formed when huge blocks of marble were hacked away centuries earlier; below water are eerie flights of encrusted marble stairs leading down to nothingness. Tasos clearly knows his way around down there, returning with a haul of urchins and *fouskes*, a local mollusk that looks exactly like a rock.

At long last we return to the beach, very relieved to be back on land. On the way back to the Archontissa, we gather an armful of *kritama*, a delicate green succulent sometimes called rock samphire in English, which is like a cross between seaweed and purslane. It grows between the beach stones and makes an excellent salad.

Back at the Archontissa, Tasos shows us how to halve the urchins—with a specially designed set of pincers—and puts Darrin to work scraping the shells of their yellow roe while he gets busy prying open *fouskes* with a knife. Somehow he locates the mollusks' seams and wedges them open: inside are bright orange lumps of muscle that he scrapes out and hits with lemon juice. I confess to disliking *fouskes*, which taste like very bitter clams, but they're supposedly excellent for one's thyroid gland, and at this point, after my humbling near-death experience, I'm willing to submit to any remedial gestures the sea might have to offer. So I gobble them down, along with the delicious urchins. And Tasos is already at work back in the kitchen, boiling our *kritama* and stewing the octopus with red wine and potatoes. "This is just what you guys need to help you get your strength back," he teases us.

.   .   .

While I'm sipping coffee in the shade the next morning, George Kaltsas pulls up on his motorcycle, having come over from Kavala to spend the day. I've been feeling awful since waking up at dawn, much too early for my own good—once again perplexed at my inability to rest and unsettled by the incident off Bámbouras. But my shoulders loosen when I see George. His years of battling cancer have left him with astonishing clear-sightedness regarding his own life, which puts him in a good position to help others peer into theirs. Considering his illness, it seems absurd to bore him with the vicissitudes of my psyche, not to mention my account of yesterday's "near drowning." I mean, we not only survived our attempt at recreational fishing, but lived to glut ourselves with another night of seafood, friendship, and island alcohol.

"Maybe that's what you needed, Christopher," George suggests without so much as blinking, "to feel yourself being caught up in the sea. But you fought your way free. And look where you are today."

Swallows are inscribing cursive loops in the air over the patio, carving wind with an effortless scissoring of their back feathers. And all three of Alyki's coves are placid—*san ladi*, as the Greeks say, "like oil"—not even a whisper of *revma* this morning. For a moment, there's no need for words. Then George blurts out, "What Kazantzakis said was right: 'Fear nothing, hope for nothing, and you are free.' But you know, there's another Greek saying: 'Fear the sea, fire, and women.'"

And I admit to being afraid.

"Fear can help us. You'll remember the next time you're in the water. Let's go now—we can swim out past the marble quarry together."

It's hard to imagine ever wanting to swim again, though I'm certain I will. It's already getting hot here in the shade. But not yet.

"That reminds me of a tiny poem by Emily Dickinson," I tell him. Though it's hopeless to try to translate it into Greek, at least in my present diminished state, he nods his head when I read it from my journal:

A darting fear—a pomp—a tear—
A waking on a morn
To find that what one waked for,
Inhales the different dawn.

"I don't know what this word *pomp* is," he says seriously, "but with the rest I agree. And it's especially good to wake up here on Thasos. Tonight I will sleep for ten hours so I can have that pleasure."

"And what will you tell me about your health, George?"

"It's nothing, really. I've been doing chemotherapy again, regularly, since last fall. I resist it. They ask me to sit for two hours in a chair every few weeks, but I won't take the full dose. When they aren't looking, I pull the needle from my vein and sneak out of the office after the first hour."

This is ominous news—since it certainly indicates the end of a long period of remission.

"How are you feeling, then?" I ask him through the lump in my throat.

"I feel fine, Christopher. I have my motorcycle. I drink good wine with friends. We will swim today. Yes, this is a difficult period at the hotel—business is down 40 percent. But I can't worry about that now."

I wait for the right words, know any gesture in the direction of sympathy or concern will be rebuffed; all I manage is my best attempt at a hopeful grimace.

An hour later, while I'm gathering things from the clothesline on my balcony, I see the tiny figure of George down at the edge of the water, where he's propped himself on the beach stones. Even at such a distance, I can see he's pulled his knees up to his chest and I wonder what he's thinking, staring out across the wide, flat water, holding still.

.   .   .

Stamatis, on the other hand, has returned from Kavala with a clean bill of health, and he's assured me we'll catch some *barbounia* today. I meet him in the late afternoon at the far cove and must tiptoe across the slippery rocks to climb aboard the *Evanthoula*, the blue-and-white trawler Stamatis has named after his wife.

Figure 8. Stamatis pulls in the *Evanthoula*.

I grew up fishing with a rod and reel—and once even with a bow and arrow—but have always been baffled by net fishing. I've spent hours in the little port of Molyvos, on Lesbos, watching fishermen repair their nets, which they pile in chaotic, impossibly tangled mountains. There are five or six such piles on Stamatis's boat, each covered with a blanket and tarp. The deck is only about twenty feet long, much of it taken up by the engine cabin, and there are rusty buckets and hooks and poles and crooks strewn about. It's all I can do to stay out of Stamatis's way while he attacks the engine with a wrench and screwdriver and drags the nets into position. He's tossed his shirt and shoes into the cabin and has donned a pair of black rubber hip waders with bright orange suspenders.

When I ask him which nets he uses for which fish, he shows us that there are two sizes: those used to catch *barbounia* and other shallow feeders have a

Evanthoula

Figure 9. *Barbounia* at the Modiano market, Thessaloniki. The tag informs customers that these were taken from waters off the Halkidiki Peninsula.

Fish: Tailing Barbounia

mesh size of about one square inch, while those used for larger fish in deeper water have a mesh size about twice that big. Today, Stamatis explains, we're setting the smaller-meshed nets across the entrance to the cove, the aim being to catch whatever swims in at dusk to feed. After a few tries, the stubborn motor awakens in a fit of asthmatic coughing, and I feel an unsteady rumbling beneath me—turns out I'm seated on a piece of plywood just atop the engine. Stamatis doesn't like what he hears and says it's not safe to go far until the mechanic comes tomorrow. But he pulls up anchor anyway, backs expertly away from the rocks, and more or less coasts out to the edge of the marble quarry. While he steers, he keeps his eyes fixed on something inside the cabin, and when I make my way back to investigate I see that in addition to numerous oil cans, cookie containers, beer bottles, pieces of radio equipment, and grimy manuals, there's a full-color radar screen.

Stamatis watches the monitor until the boat is positioned at the right depth—about fifteen meters—then idles the engine and somehow locates the tail of one of the nets (a feat I'd have thought impossible) and ties an orange float to it. Then he fixes a heavy lead weight to the bottom end and with one quick motion tosses both float and weight overboard. The float bobs on the surface while the weight anchors the bottom and causes some drag on the net Stamatis is about to unfurl. He props what looks like a long broom handle horizontally across the stern, and over this he guides the net out in one steady, improbably untangled stream. He looks almost like a circus clown, with his baggy trousers, leaning at a forty-five-degree angle to the water, using an outstretched bare foot to maneuver the rudder while his hands feed out the net in a blur.

To my astonishment, the net keeps on unwinding into the wake behind us—Stamatis says he plans to set out six hundred meters this evening. Heavy red rings, interspersed every two feet or so, sink one edge to the sea floor while the top edge gets pulled taut by our forward motion. Stamatis steers in a kind of zigzag pattern across the bay, and by the time the last few meters of the net are in position, I see it's almost impossible for anything to enter Alyki's shallowest cove without falling into his trap. With the pile of net considerably diminished, Stamatis ties another float to the tail, tosses it out, and then stops to rest, reaching into a small refrigerator to offer me a bottle of Mythos beer—Kouzis hospitality is irrepressible, even on the *Evanthoula*. We drift there a moment or two, the water so still that we can hear music from one of the shorefront *tavernas* and the joyful shrieks of a nearly invisible toddler playing on the beach.

"Tha gyrisoume stis ennia," Stamatis remarks when we've returned to shore and tied the boat up: "We'll return at nine o'clock," to haul in the nets and see what we've caught for dinner.

.   .   .

"Bring my father some good luck, eh?" Tasos shouts at us over his shoulder when I leave the restaurant to meet Stamatis back at the cove.

I make my way out along the rocks, many of them now completely submerged in the tide. Rather than engine noise, however, I hear Stamatis swearing from inside the cabin of the *Evanthoula*. He tries repeatedly to get the motor started, but all it produces is an irritable whine, punctuated with bursts of grating metal. "The starter's shot," he explains when I climb aboard. Never much for words, Stamatis removes his cap and wipes his brow, glancing out at the mouth of the bay where the nets are waiting.

"Avrio to proi," he says finally. "Tomorrow morning."

"But the fish?" I ask.

He says that they'll be lost, eaten by bigger fish overnight. But just when we're about to give up and head back home, another fisherman pulls alongside the *Evanthoula* and offers Stamatis his rowboat. He hesitates for a moment, but decides it would be unwise to pull the nets in by hand, which evidently he could do, albeit with great effort. (Normally hydraulic pulleys would lift the wet, heavy nets for him.)

Fish: Tailing Barbounia

"At night, you need a light to pull in the nets," he says to me in Greek, "because if you snag a scorpion fish and don't see it in time—*po, po, po.*" He holds up his hand and pokes it several times to suggest the wounds a scorpion fish would inflict. "I'll take his rowboat out at six in the morning. You can come and watch me pull in the nets."

.   .   .

I set my alarm, but by the time I've tossed on a sweatshirt and bounded down to the patio, Stamatis has already gone out. Tasos is up too, though his eyes are barely open and he's in serious need of a shave. "Sit and have a coffee," he commands, but I'm eager to learn the fate of our catch. Plus, this morning the muddled feeling in my brain has finally disappeared and my head is empty of everything but light. I would levitate if it weren't for the canopy of grapevines overhead.

When I meet up with him on board the *Evanthoula*, Stamatis reports that he was followed in the rowboat by two dolphins. I'd have been thrilled to see them, though Stamatis makes it clear that dolphins and fishermen are not friends, since they're after the same fish. For the past hour, Stamatis has dragged in his nets hand over fist from the awkward platform of his friend's rowboat, then transferred them to the deck of his own boat, where they now lie in heaps. Except for the low gurgling of waves and the buzzing of the bees that swarm the catch, it's exceptionally quiet.

For the next hour and a half, I perch on the deck and watch Stamatis untangle his nets. He smiles, but doesn't mumble more than a word or two now and then, and I'm content to do the same. There are many fish in the nets, but almost all of them have been decapitated or partially devoured: octopuses and other predators (large enough to avoid being snagged in the net's small mesh) molested the catch overnight. Again, Stamatis has set the broomstick horizontally across the deck, and he uses it to guide one end of the net into a new pile behind him. Next to his bare feet, he positions two plastic buckets into which he tosses anything worth keeping. For every small fish he keeps, he throws perhaps twenty overboard—including the wreckage of a dozen beautiful *barbounia*. This makes him very popular with the gulls, which line up along the ledge next to the boat and wrangle over whatever he discards.

Sorting the catch is gingerly work. Most of Stamatis's time is spent dealing with stones: moving with the *revma* along the seafloor, the nets pick up many sharp, grenade-sized volcanic nuggets, each of which takes a minute or two to pull free. And the fish themselves pose their own challenges.

The very thing that makes gill nets so effective—the fact that they trap fish in their mesh—also makes them labor-intensive, since the victims must be extricated one by one. Stamatis gently pulls the net wide in a circular pattern around each fish until he can see where it's been snagged; if he pulls too hard, he'll wind up with knots. Then he grips the fish and wiggles it until the gills and fins come free. This is an especially delicate operation when it comes to scorpion fish, which must be gripped very securely around the middle to avoid their venomous top and middle fins. Even the gulls seem to hesitate when they are tossed upon the rocks, but the larger ones are either immune to the venom or too hungry to care. I fantasize about turning a pail of these little nasties into a bouillabaisse, but Stamatis considers them too small to bother with.

There's one immature gull (it's been living on the beach for the past few months, Stamatis tells me) who tries to join the fun. It makes a plaintive whistling sound completely unlike the assertive caw of the adult gulls. Stamatis tries several times to toss a small fish in its direction, but the adults won't let it near their breakfast. One of the larger gulls wedges its head beneath the small bird's breast and flips it over in one swift motion, leaving the young upstart to beat a quick retreat.

It's all very fascinating and smelly. A large squid is still moving a little in the net, changing colors now and then in the sunlight while its purple tentacles are nibbled by bees. I've been stung by such bees many times here at Alyki, but Stamatis ignores them completely, even those working furiously to extricate a knob of fish flesh wedged between his toes.

Two fishermen board a small craft docked nearby and prepare to head out to sea. On their way past us, they cut the motor and shout gruff greetings: "Stamatis," one exclaims, "don't catch all the fish, leave some for us!"

"Six hundred meters of net, and nothing in them," he murmurs back without ever looking up.

When Stamatis finishes with the last of the nets, there's not enough in the bucket to justify his four hours of labor. A few *sargós* (bream) have survived intact, as well as a lobster, a spooky flying fish (edible, I'm told), a cuttlefish, and that bee-licked squid. Having seen him return to the restaurant with many wheelbarrows of fish, I recognize this as part of the regular ebb and flow of his difficult occupation, but I can't help feeling obscurely responsible for his bad luck. And since I'm leaving tomorrow, this also means no *barbounia* for our last supper on Thasos.

"Tou chronou," Stamatis mutters with a smile. "Next year." It's a phrase I hear too often when I'm on Thasos, and today it nearly breaks me in two, invoking as it does my imminent departure, reminding me that home is somewhere else. The *barbounia* will stay put. I won't.

.   .   .

After dinner, Tasos and Elpida disappear, then reappear an hour later dressed to impress: Tasos doing his best with a clean shirt and a shower, Elpida doing quite a bit better with a low-cut black dress, makeup, and her hair pulled back elegantly. They are going to Potos, a half hour down the coast, where there are a few fancy cafés in which one can see and be seen. But they agree to stay and have a few drinks with us first.

Before long, many bottles of wine are open, many carafes of *tsipouro* are moving toward empty, and everyone is smoking cigarettes and dancing. Tasos has turned the music up loud: traditional songs revamped by Eleftheria Arvanitaki, whose bright, sexy voice is unmistakable.

What we're all chasing is *kefi*, which is something like merriment or spirit. *Kefi* refers to that moment when the party turns ecstatic, when individual feelings are subsumed into the group's euphoria. You know it's kicked in when someone is spontaneously moved to dance a *zeibekiko*, an improvised solo that is as much flying as dancing. If you don't feel it, you don't dance—in this way, it's like speaking in tongues. George Kaltsas is the first to step forward tonight, and we drop to our knees in a circle around him when he does, clapping syncopation and cheering him on. He's wearing clunky motorcycle boots, but when he closes his eyes and the singer's voice soars, they barely touch the floor. Then he pulls me into the center of the circle, and I've got enough *tsipouro* in me to set aside my American reserve and self-consciousness and shake myself loose through dance.

Greek men have no such inhibitions. For Greeks, there is nothing more macho than a *zeibekiko*, which captures all the hardness and agony of a man's life while also expressing its folly and unexpected joy. Tasos demonstrates this soon enough when I yield to him, high kicking his feet within an inch of Darrin's nose and smashing a shot glass on the floor with his open palm.

Greek women, similarly, keep their inner diva at the ready. Soon enough, Elpida takes over. She is not a small woman, but with a quick lift of her skirts and a leap she's suddenly up on the table, stretching her arms to the rafters and jiggling her generosities every which way. We must hurry to remove the bottles and glassware so she can dance, and then we gather at her feet like rowdy disciples. She eats it up, belly dancing her way through the next two songs, enraptured.

At some point, Stamatis comes down in his underwear to report that the neighbors have called, asking us to turn the music down; our *kefi* is resounding off the temple ruins and marble quarry and can be heard a mile away. So we dim our collective flame a little, and when the others step to the edge of the balcony to cool off, I pull Tasos aside to tell him privately about George's return to chemotherapy. He blanches for a moment and is silent, then drags George over to where we're sitting, embarrassing him by telling him that he knows the bad news.

"You must prepare yourself for autumn, Yorgo," Tasos insists, bunching up a portion of George's shirt in his fist and bringing his face up close, "because Christopher is coming back and we are making big plans."

Even I don't know about these plans yet. I've only told Tasos that I'm hoping to return to Greece for the grape harvest.

"You have never climbed Mount Olympus, have you?" Tasos asks George. George says he hasn't.

"So here's what we must do: I'll pick you up in my truck and we'll get Christopher at the airport in Thessaloniki. He can lead us up the mountain to visit Zeus. And we'll write our names in the little book at Mytikas so no one will forget that we were here on earth. Then we'll climb back down and buy two tons of grapes from a friend of mine who has vineyards in Strymonas. And we'll come back to Thasos and make wine together and go fishing."

"OK, *filoi mou*, then let's," George answers after a short pause, smiling. I see that his teeth are stained with the red wine he's been guzzling.

Tasos's eyes are watering a little and I know I'm also on the verge of too much feeling, but George claps us both hard on the back and raises his glass: "To the autumn, then, and to sharing more wine, my friends."

"And to the future," Tasos says.

"And to *barbounia*," I add.

"And to *barbounia*," they answer.

Kefi

GRILLED OCTOPUS IN THE MODIANO MARKET

The Modiano market in the heart of Thessaloniki spans several blocks adjacent to Aristotelous Square, where in 1943 Nazi troops gathered the city's Jews before sending them off to Poland. Of the forty-five thousand or so Jews who lived in neighborhoods around the Modiano market, only a few returned. Walking through Modiano today, there's no evidence at all of their disappearance, nor is there any way to remember that the language of commerce spoken here for hundreds of years was not Greek, but Ladino (a derivative of Spanish brought here by the Sephardim), and that so many Jews lived here that Thessaloniki was often called "the mother of Israel."

I found out about Myrovolos Smyrni ("Fragrant Smyrna"), a little place tucked into the corner of the fish market, soon after I moved to Greece. But I had no idea that I'd come face to face with the tragedy of the city's Jews while dining there. Back in the early 1990s, Myrovolos Smyrni wasn't much of a restaurant at all. There were only a few stools and little tables strewn about in the alley, or you could opt to rest your elbows on a bar right in front of the kitchen's smoking grill. Hanging just overhead was a long iron meat hook, upon which a bouquet of purple octopuses were suspended in midair. When you requested a portion, the proprietor Thannasis would shout the order across the crowded room to his wife. She'd hack off a tentacle with a huge knife, slap it on the grill, and in minutes a plate of sizzling cephalopod would come sliding down the bar in your direction. The kitchen was about eight steps from the fish market, so all the seafood was perfectly fresh, and the place got raucous on Saturdays, especially when bands of gypsies would stroll through the throng while honking their battered oboes and beating their drums. Then the singing would start, and the breaking of glasses, and now and then an argument and some playful fisticuffs.

I'd try to arrive early enough to claim a stool at the bar, where I'd be in a good position to watch the chef at work and to view the revelry from a position of safety. One such Saturday, I sat next to a broad-shouldered, unshaven, grey-haired creature who looked more like a pirate than a citizen of Greece's sophisticated second-largest city. And like a pirate, he drank hard, *retsina* after *retsina*, and he cackled at all of Thanassis's jokes. We'd exchanged only a few sentences before he poured me a glass from his own carafe. When he did so, his shirtsleeve pulled back across his forearm to reveal a faded blue tattoo—the number he'd been given while a prisoner in Auschwitz. He wouldn't say much about the camps when I asked, and in all honesty I was afraid to pry. He was probably the only member of his extended family, if not his whole neighborhood, to have made it out alive. But he had stories to tell about life as a merchant marine, and he reminisced about the week he'd spent in port at New Orleans. I only saw him at Myrovolos Smyrni once and made a point to pay his tab. To this day, I regret that I never learned his name.

Every time I'm in Thessaloniki, I make sure to have lunch at Myrovolos Smyrni. The restaurant has grown so popular that it now occupies almost the entire alleyway. There's a real table for every patron. I've come to know Thanassis and his family, and I have shared a hundred joyous meals there with friends over the years. But every time I sit down to a plate of their incredibly tender grilled octopus, I think of that old Jew, the survivor, with whom I was lucky to share a carafe of *retsina*.

1 large octopus (about 2 kilos)

1 carrot, shredded

1 small red onion, diced

2 tablespoons flat-leaf parsley, minced

Olive oil, for drizzling

Simple red wine vinegar, for drizzling

Dried oregano, for garnish

Submerge the whole octopus in water and then boil it until very tender, about 1½ hours. Then hang it to dry next to the grill, where it can be cut to order.

Grill each large tentacle a few minutes per side, just long enough to heat it through and to impart a bit of wood smoke to the flesh. Then serve the tentacle whole atop a small mound of carrot, and top it with the red onion and parsley. Drizzle with olive oil and vinegar to moisten the dish before giving it a final dusting of oregano.

Cheese

The Stinky Cheeses of Naxos

Of all the Cycladic Islands, only Naxos is worth visiting for the food alone. Whenever I'm there, my desire to get behind a stove supersedes the temptations of the island's excellent and sophisticated restaurants. So I make sure to have a functional kitchen at the ready, preferably one with large windows in a cottage near Orkos: an unreasonably beautiful stretch of coastline peppered with the kind of small, rocky lagoons my wife and I prefer for swimming over broad, sandy beaches. Nudists—but not of the public variety—we first visited that coast over a decade ago, following its dirt paths in search of coves with a spit of flat stone just wide enough for two towels. There we'd swim and read and do other more private things in naked peace. This all seemed romantically appropriate; after all, it was on one of these remote Naxian beaches that Dionysus encountered the sleeping Ariadne and was mortally wounded by love for her.

One day, while we were splashing about in the water, a bedraggled-looking gentleman stepped out from the brush and stood among our discarded clothing, waving at us urgently. Kerry was too shy to emerge in the buff, but I scampered up to ask him what he wanted. He smelled like a stable and sported a wide straw hat and a goofy grey handlebar mustache. In his hands were two small wicker baskets, and clearly he wanted me to have a look. When I removed the lid from one, I recoiled: inside was the compact brain of a sheep. I did my part, admiring the miniature mountain ranges in the grey matter, and tried to nod approvingly, but it was hardly right for an afternoon snack on the beach. The man grinned at me. I wasn't quite sure how to proceed.

"Mialá?" I asked him, looking as serious as I was able while standing naked before a bumpkin brain salesman. For all I knew he was a serial murderer.

"Oxi, oxi!" he answered, laughing with his mouth wide open, revealing only one or two serviceable teeth. "No, no, not brains, my son, it's cheese!"

With a quick swipe of his pocketknife, he shaved off a crescent and shoved it in my direction. Cheese, indeed, and excellent cheese at that: the curd just barely firm enough to hold the imprint of the wicker mold, and therefore perfect for smearing on the loaf of bread we'd packed for the day. I'd never bought cheese while nude before, but that didn't stop me: I took both baskets for a few coins.

The same day, on a remote stretch of dusty road, we were surprised to discover a minimart stocked with the usual beach supplies, but also with an entire deli case loaded with eight cheeses I'd never seen before, all of them produced by the owner of the shop. He sold his own olive oil, *raki*, potatoes, olives, and wine too. I wondered why this particular island enjoyed such agricultural abundance.

This year, I've come back to Orkos again with my brother Aaron and my friend Corey. They have solemnly promised to help me get to the bottom of this question, and to help me discover the mysteries of Naxian cheese.

.   .   .

We arrive on the island around midnight, having spent four hours on the windward side of the ferry from Athens, scrutinizing passing islands and their "drinkable blue volcanoes," as the poet Odysseus Elytis puts

Figure 10. The Portara of Naxos.

it. When the ship makes its turn beyond the blackened edge of Paros, we get our first glimpse of Naxos in the form of the spectral and spotlit Portara: the remains of an unfinished temple of Apollo begun in the fifth century B.C.E. Few ruins in Greece suggest so much based on so little. Nothing of the

Arrival by Night

temple is upright other than a few foundation stones and what looks like a giant marble doorjamb, a rational rectangular outline of marble—gateway to the invisible sanctuary. "Now surely Apollo knocks / with lovely foot at the door. Do you not see?" Callimachus asks in his Hellenistic hymn to the god.

But archeology will have to wait: on the off chance it's open this late, I'm headed straight for the excellent cheese shop I remember from years ago, located on a whitewashed alley just off the port. Inside we find three long refrigerator cabinets packed with orderly shelves of cheese. And that dairy light illuminates from within a golden phalanx of Naxian honey, jars of which are lined up next to an ancient cash register. I feel sorry for the young man whose misfortune it is to be peddling cheese this late at night, but he's in good spirits. He's a curly-haired, terrifically fragrant giant named George Atsalinos, who knows everything about everything Naxian. When I tell him I've come to Naxos on a cheese pilgrimage, he grins so widely I know I've found my Virgil.

He allows us to try about twenty cheeses, each one more unusual and tasty than the previous, and responds to my endless questions with professorial authority. There's also, he says, some local *raki* to sample (and he's not afraid to refill our cups, and we're not afraid to drink several rounds of samples, even if it smells like kerosene). "Oh, and try this mountain honey," he says, and then we move on to massive, lightly pickled capers, and puckish green olives, and dried tomatoes, and finally some spoon sweets (things begin to get fuzzy here . . . but I know we sampled some candied quince). "And of course you know about the famous potatoes of Naxos," George says, though he hasn't any to offer us. I assure him that I do and promise to see that my friends try them first thing tomorrow. The rest of the evening is a blur of cheese facts and acquisition: when I wake the next morning, sporting a conspicuous headache, I see I've spent every last euro in my wallet and have purchased more cheese than we could safely eat in a week's time. No matter: George has proven invaluable, giving me the names of several shepherds and local producers we can pester over the next week. Somehow, I managed to scratch their names into my notebook in wobbling cursive.

. . .

We don't waste any time before beginning our research. I attack the cheese right away, scrambling eggs and green onions with gratings of a tangy sheep and goat's milk *xinotyro*, which we devour along with a pyramid of cucumbers, olives, and tomatoes. Then we try some goat's-milk feta, drizzling it with honey.

There's also a blinding lagoon to inspect. Swimming out between two shelves of volcanic stone, we find a profusion of marine life: fuchsia anemones, grotesque sea cucumbers, tropical-looking fish of every color. Somewhere, waiting to be found, there are also octopuses and moray eels. This knowledge leads us, inevitably, to lunch at Taverna Paradisos, on the mile-long strand of Agia Anna. We're tempted to occupy a place on the beach itself, where ten tables are positioned, but blasts of wind look to be garnishing the salads of the beachside diners with sand. So we opt for a spot on the restaurant's patio, beneath the shade of a gigantic, gnarled cedar. Right here, five years earlier, I introduced my daughter Sophia to the pleasures of eating octopus. She wasn't a bit put off by the massive grilled tentacle when it landed before her, in part because it rested upon a tower of fried Naxian potatoes. And she was especially fond of the charred suckers, nibbling them delicately between her tiny front teeth.

"This is your second time on Naxos," I told her.

"But Daddy, you're wrong, this is my first time here."

"True, but you were also here before you were born—still hiding out in mama's kangaroo pouch. The two of you went swimming right over there," I told her, motioning across the street to the beach.

That earned me one of those quizzical four-year-old-girl looks that I've learned to translate as: *Dad, you're a moron, but I love you.*

In her honor today, I order us some grilled octopus, plus some stuffed tomatoes, slow-cooked green beans, *yigantes* (gigantic white beans) stewed in tomatoes, a few fried *barbounia*, and roasted potatoes. The potatoes are unnecessary, since nearly every dish comes already garnished with them. But they are great potatoes, and I add them to the list of things we'll need to explore with the Brothers Panteleimonitis, who have agreed to join us on the island tomorrow.

. . .

Both Spyros and his brother Nikolas bear some resemblance to the Charioteer of Delphi. Indeed, like all the members of their family, they wear a classical countenance: chiseled jawbones, sharp noses, and startling blue-grey eyes. I've not met Nikolas before. He's as amiable and well mannered as his brothers, but he doesn't seem to have any of their soft-spoken reserve.

"This guy has CEO written all over his personality," Aaron remarks.

The Panteleimonitis family does brisk agricultural business on Naxos. They peddle farm implements not to mention a host of other kinds of vehicles and industrial equipment. Nikolas comes to Naxos often and cannot walk down the street here without being greeted by some grizzled old farmer at every turn. Within moments of stepping off the ferry, he gets busy working out the sale of a bus to the public transportation authorities while simultaneously talking on his cell phone and setting up meetings out in the island's fertile valleys. When it comes to dairy reconnoitering, I see that we're in very good hands.

Our first stop is Ta Tria Adelphia, a bustling seafood *taverna* in the beach town of Plaka. The restaurant's proprietor—a sunburned, meaty man with battered hands and salt-and-pepper scrub brush hair—speed talks through a mouthful of smooth stones. When I'm summoned over to meet him, he shakes my hand gruffly and unleashes a torrent of gnarled sentences, none of which I understand at all. OK, I understand a tiny bit: he's a potato farmer, which is why I'm making his acquaintance, and he grew up here, and he likes John Deere. Normally I'm pretty confident about my ability to understand and make myself understood in Greek. Not at all, however, with Yorgos Margarites. I honestly have no idea what language he's speaking when he answers my questions about potato farming. Sure, I nod my head and smile, shake his hand in thanks when the conversation hits an end stop at last, then slink back to the table bewildered. I'm embarrassed to ask Spyros and Nikolas for translation. To my relief, Nikolas tells me that it's a running joke in the business that nobody understands a word of the pidgin Greek from Margarites's mouth; all that matters, he says, is that "Margarites grows killer potatoes."

The Brothers P. cannot spend money here—the protocols of Greek hospitality somehow cross wires with the equally complicated rituals governing business in Greece—and not only is our expensive seafood lunch on the house, but the owner is taking us to see his farm. Margarites jumps on his motorcycle and speeds off across the dusty beach road, and we follow him in our cars through a maze of sandy back roads until we are instructed to park next to a beautiful, spit-polished John Deere tractor. There's some showing off here, no doubt, and Aaron and I are duly impressed. Our mother grew up on a dairy farm in Wisconsin, and our grandfather had her driving a John Deere tractor (as kids, we knew it as the "Johnny Popper") by the time she was ten years old. It's very strange to see such an iconic American machine in the middle of a spud field on a Greek island.

Nikolas sold him the tractor, and his potato picker too. Margarites pushes his hired help aside and fires up the John Deere himself, behind which he pulls this fascinating implement: it scoops down into the soil and then bounces the freshly plucked potatoes across a kind of slotted conveyor belt to separate them from the stems and soil. A trail of yellow potatoes emerges in the wake of the tractor and three Albanian farmhands follow, scooping them up with incredible speed and piling them into pyramids. The potatoes are then covered with leafy branches and allowed to dry overnight before being stuffed into red mesh bags. We are only a short walk from the sand dunes along the coast, yet the soil here is so rich and loose that one can't walk in the field without sinking. When I pick up a handful of the black soil and give it a squeeze, it forms a perfect ball and has the rich, chocolaty smell of fertile earth. There's some remarkable farming going on here.

Margarites notices what I'm doing and explains—in words I'm happy to understand, more or less—that it's taken ten years of compost and organic soil conditioning to turn this field around. He beams, picks up one of the potatoes at his feet, and offers it to me. Even nibbled raw, the Naxian potato is a revelation—bursting with milky, mineral sweetness and cool as a cistern in the middle. I've theorized over the years about why Naxian potatoes are so delicious, thinking it must have to do with particularities of the local seed, or the island's volcanic soil, or the plentiful wind and water here. Now that I see the effort Margarites has put into his fields, I think hard labor and good farming practices are, above all, responsible. I'm also shocked to hear that these spuds hail originally from Holland. But that was long ago—now Margarites keeps his crops going by raising seed potatoes, replenishing his stock constantly. The impressive potatoes being picked today are actually for seed: soon they'll be hacked into pieces, sprouted, and replanted in another field. That's heartbreaking, delicious as they are. Luckily Margarites doesn't seem to mind when I fill the pockets of my shorts with the fingerlings too small for the Albanians to bother with.

. . .

It's almost seven in the evening by the time we roll into the village of Biblos for our appointment with Nikos Bernikos, vice mayor of the island and owner of its largest hardware store. Inside a warehouse the size of an average American gas station is crammed an enormous inventory—every farmer, contractor, and painter shops here, and two young women keep busy behind the counter smoking and sorting through a mountain of paperwork and receipts. Bernikos is an important man in these parts, but there's no pretension with him. He jokes with Nikolas and Spyros like he's their cousin. As Nikolas put it to me earlier in the day, "On Naxos, it's quality of production, not quantity," and that ethic seems to guide all human interactions as well, even those involving serious business. Bernikos enlists his brother Manolis to ride along with Spyros and Nikolas so he can guide us to the south of the island. There, we'll meet our shepherd. "If you ever need anything, boys, just tell me," he says to us while we're leaving, "and tomorrow you'll visit a cheese factory on the other end of the spectrum."

The sea is visible from elevated Biblos, and breezes blowing from the coast lift into the village the heady scents of salt water and potato field. But the moment we turn inland, the landscape changes abruptly from dry scrub to pastureland, and the scent of ripe manure gusts through the car's open windows. Suddenly there are cows everywhere, on both sides of the road. We drive over a small ridge and then down into the most fertile valley on the island. Occasionally we pass a cluster of houses or a tidy little church, all of them surrounded by veritable forests of potted geraniums, but for the most part there's grazing land from horizon to horizon. It would be hard to imagine a more a suitable place for a Temple of Demeter, and of course there's one here, beautifully restored and soaking up the last of the day's light. But we speed on, only halting our voyage once on a straightaway when we encounter a large flock of goats on the road, every third one wearing a rusty metal bell around its neck. The old shepherd nods his head in greeting, his dogs staring down our purring Fiats with bared teeth.

In *Don Juan*, Lord Byron writes: "No dirge, except the hollow sea's, / Mourns o'er the beauty of the Cyclades." My companions beg to differ. I've been blasting Greek music from the car's radio ever since we arrived on the island, though we never seem to have good reception for more than about five minutes at a stretch. While I've grown to love the minor-key, melodramatic, and decidedly Eastern style of Greek singing, my brother says it sounds like the "moaning of a wounded man coming out of anesthesia."

"So what's the suicide rate among these Greek singers?" Corey quips tonight.

Many of them do sound miserable. But there's no time to describe this music's noble foundation, built as it is upon folk poetry, ancient pain, and dark passion, because the stream of goats has parted and off we go again, reuniting with the sea just past the village of Ayiassos. In the other car, Nikolas, Spyros, and Manolis turn off down a steep incline onto a dirt road and we follow them, skirting a pebbled beach and fields of bamboo on either side. The ruts in the road are more like canyons, and it's a struggle to keep the car's undercarriage from scraping off on protruding volcanic boulders. But it's worth it to meet Yorgos Babounis and his flock.

As it turns out, we were shown faded photographs of Yorgos and his now dead ancestors back in the cheese shop at the port. The Babounis men are famous cheese makers, real artisans who for generations made just enough cheese to supply their family, with a little extra to sell on the side. These days in Greece, it's unusual for young men to follow in their grandfathers' footsteps. Hooked into the Internet and Euro pop culture, and lured by the promise of money, few willingly accept a farmer's hard living over a cushy job in an Athenian bank. Fortunately, Nikolas explains, the European Union offers subsidies to family farms, giving determined people like Yorgos Babounis as much as half the money they need to bring their facilities in line with the demands of the new millennium.

Normally, to find the Babounis cheese shop, you'd stop in Ayiassos to ask for directions to the *stavlos*, the "stable." But this is no traditional stable: Yorgos has invested in state-of-the-art automated milking machines, not to mention a few sparkling tractors and—much to our delight—a computer-regulated walk-in cheese refrigerator. It's hard to get Yorgos to say much. He's only about thirty and he remains expressionless, with the very heavy eyelids I associate with chronic dope smokers. We are official visitors, I guess, and he doesn't want to seem overly excited to be showing us around his farm.

Until we get to the cheese, that is.

Yorgos points out the old copper vats his grandfather used to heat the sheep's and goat's milk until it was ready to add the rennet and stir the curd; they are now hidden behind the brand-new stainless steel cauldrons, with their gleaming temperature gauges and other bells and whistles. In spite of these hygienic innovations, I'm delighted to see that Yorgos stirs his milk the old-fashioned way, with a whittled branch of *katsalia* wood: the hard roots of the plant are still attached, having dried into a gnarled fist that works like a rustic whisk through the gurgling milk.

We let out a collective sigh when Yorgos opens his walk-in "cave" and for the first time permits himself to crack a smile. Before the door is open wide enough for us to see within, the intoxicating scent of cheese mold fills the room. Eight layers of shelves hold hundreds of small wheels of *kefalotyri* in various states of grace. After we've held and admired several cheeses in the cave, Yorgos gives us permission to purchase some for later. Though we hardly need more cheese, it would be inhospitable not to do so. Then we're led back to the house and made to sit on plastic chairs beneath a grape trellis while Yorgos smokes. His sister and mother scurry into the house and return with armfuls of beer, plates of sliced tomatoes, and some *kefalotyri* so young and fresh it squeaks when we bite into it. The pungency of the goat's milk nearly steals the show, but it is balanced nicely with the tamer sheep's milk creaminess. Yorgos doesn't seem to hear our comments about his excellent product, nor our praise for his stable; he casts inscrutable glances at the hillside. He's so reticent that even the usually voluble Nikolas seems at a loss for words. But when we finally break the silence by rising to leave, we are informed that we were indeed honored guests.

"I think Yorgos is just very shy," Spyros explains to me later that night, "but he pulled me aside as we were leaving to ask me if I really thought you'd write about his cheese."

And so it is: I have. Beautiful cheese it is.

.   .   .

"Damn!" my brother shouts, waking me with a start. I see him standing in his underwear, squinting into the eerie light of the open refrigerator.

"What's the matter?" I mutter, my eyes adjusting. "And what time is it?"

"It's 8:30," Aaron answers, "and I hadn't realized our refrigerator was dying."

The thing is functioning just fine in spite of the heat, but I have managed to set into motion, within the unclean precincts of our cottage refrigerator, a dairy science experiment. There are about thirteen different wheels and wedges of cheese jammed into that very small space—and I added another two last night, those from Yorgos Babounis. Since cheese must breathe, most of them are loosely wrapped in grocery paper, free to compete with one another for dominion over the air. Now that he mentions it, I *can* smell the fridge from across the room. While Yorgos's computerized cave greeted the nose with a beautiful cheese-mold harmony—ripe and definitely "of the farm," but wholly appetizing—the music coming from our fridge, being played by so many cheeses from so many farms with so many contrasting olfactory motives, is pretty awful: an atonal, overripe troglodytic funk, with notes of wet dog, soggy diaper, and rotting Birkenstock. When I pour some peach nectar over ice an hour later, I find that even things from the freezer now taste like cheese.

We invite Spyros and Nikolas over for breakfast. I'm frying the small Naxian potatoes I gathered from the field yesterday, which I'm planning to blanket with poached eggs, mint from the yard, and some of the *xinotyro*. And Corey has meticulously cut and assembled our remaining melon, apricots, and cherries into a smart still life. We even have a strong pot of coffee to

Figure 11. Naxian cheeses, in various states of ripeness.

share. The Panteleimonitis boys step through the open door to say hello, but their smiles disappear immediately and they make a quick exit.

"We've got to go spend a little more time with Bernikos in Biblos," Spyros says, "but give us a call when you're ready to meet over the noon hour."

"You sure you aren't hungry?" Aaron asks.

They say they aren't. When they leave, we know they've been put off by the foul winds blowing from our refrigerator. But they are much too well bred to accuse us of being smelly.

A few hours later, after we've swum off breakfast in our lagoon, Nikolas calls with a suggestion: Bernikos has arranged for us to tour the big Graviera cooperative, and then, he says, "We should really try another island specialty. I know a great place in Halki where they brag about having the best pork in the Cyclades."

So Aaron, Corey, and I pile into our tiny car and head off in the direction of Agios Arsenios, veering away from the beach toward the mountains (which requires some force of will, considering how hot it's become). Everywhere, on both sides of the road, cattle are grazing—or if not, then they're plopped on their haunches chewing Naxian grass. In every other field, potatoes are being gathered. We recognize the red mesh bags we saw yesterday on Margarites's land: here also they're stuffed with spuds, piled into ziggurats, and covered with brush.

Nikolas gave me directions to the Graviera cooperative, and since it's the largest cheese factory on the island I can't imagine it will be hard to find, yet somehow we miss it. Manolis comes to our rescue. We have stopped on the side of the road to study the map and magically he appears on his motorcycle, having been sent by Bernikos to find the lost Americans.

Before we're allowed to enter the factory, we must put on surgical booties, plastic-lined disposable overcoats, and hairnets. Considering it's roughly the temperature of boiling milk inside, we're drenched with sweat immediately. Unlike in Yorgos's stable, the cow's milk here is pumped by giant trucks into gargantuan floor-to-ceiling vats. The famous cow's-milk Graviera of Naxos is a "controlled designation of origin" product, meaning that this is big European business. Big business means big dairy chemistry: everything is computer regulated, sterilized, and meticulously engineered. While Yorgos Babounis's *kefalotyri* will vary from season to season, batch to batch, the Graviera of Naxos is meant to be unvaryingly consistent, and unvaryingly delicious.

It's wonderful cheese—the Greek equivalent of Gruyère, really. Good and plentiful Naxian cow's milk is pasteurized, curdled, and then shaped into large wheels, which are pressed and bathed in brine for a month before being removed from their round molds and allowed to age in the cavernous and blessedly chilly warehouse. There's an overwhelming amount of cheese here—it's stacked so high that elaborate ladders and even forklifts are required

Cheese: The Stinky Cheeses of Naxos

to move it from place to place. The whole facility is without doubt impressive, even though it lacks the traditional charm of last night's stable. But it's good, as Bernikos put it, to have seen both ends of the cheese spectrum. When we discard our soggy gowns and step into the blinding sunlight, it takes a few minutes for our eyes to adjust. Over in the loading dock, some figure in a white gown is using an industrial pressure washer to remove the gorgeous purple mold from a hundred wheels of aged Graviera, which, by tomorrow, will be making their way to grocery stores across the Mediterranean.

Then back into the dusty little cars we go in the direction of the pork palace.

.   .   .

The village of Halki *would* come out of nowhere, since the narrow entrance to the town is located just around a sharp bend in a forest of giant olean-der bushes, but signs proclaiming the wonders of the place have lined the road for the past several kilometers. Halki has just enough going on to lure people away from the soothing breezes of the coast. Located in the center of the island's olive-growing region, the village was once the capital of Naxos, and it boasts some antique churches, picturesque alleyways, and Venetian towers. But today Halki is more famous for its handicrafts. Several shops are crowded with working looms, and the lovely ladies of Halki are so good at hawking their wares that it's hard to leave without a pocketful of doilies you didn't need, or maybe a handmade tablecloth that you did.

More suited to our tastes is the Valindras distillery. The citron fruit (or Mede apple) looks like an obese lemon and is more or less inedible, though its rind can be candied; across Persia and the Middle East, the fruit has been put to medicinal use since ancient times. The Naxians, however, ignore the fruit and coax a potent aperitif from the tree's aromatic leaves. The folks at Valindras have used the same ancient wood-fired still to do this for the past hundred years. Citron liqueur, in its weaker forms, tastes a bit like liquid furniture polish (think Lemon Pledge), but raise the alcohol content high enough and it's less cloying and surprisingly good.

Never mind all that—we've come for pig. And, Nikos explains, we're about to glimpse the social side of agriculture on Naxos. As we've seen for the past few days, everyone here with some remote connection to farming knows Nikolas Panteleimonitis, and since we're traveling in his company, we are guests at Taverna Yannis. The proprietor—a burly, jowly character with a monk's crown of grey curls—motions to the waiter, and we are directed to a table on the patio, in the mottled shade of a giant mimosa tree and some violet bougainvillea. Before we've even broken bread, a beautiful grey-eyed girl (her blonde hair done up for church with smart black ribbons) stops by our table with a basket under her arm. She offers each of us a sesame roll and a wedge of *kefalotyri*, murmuring "Ya to pappou mou" (For my grandfather) as she does.

"It seems like we can't go anywhere without someone giving us cheese," Corey remarks.

Spyros laughs and explains that he's never seen this exact ritual before, but we're to understand that these are gifts—offered to complete strangers— in memory of the girl's grandfather. Today must have been his funeral, or perhaps today was the memorial marking the end of the forty-day grieving period. "You aren't required to eat it," he adds, "but we will take it with us out of respect."

Too late—I've already sampled the delicious cheese, wishing to honor the little girl's bravery and sadness.

When I ask Nikolas why Taverna Yannis is so special—"I mean, surely there are other places with decent pork chops"—he tells me that Yannis himself is maniacal.

"This guy's got a serious reputation around here. In fact, everyone's terrified of him. And he's easily provoked. A friend from Halki told me that last year, when a fight broke out in one of the *tavernas* in town, Yannis disappeared for five minutes only to return with a revolver, which he put on the table in front of him. He pulled out a cigarette, lit it, and asked calmly, 'So who's making trouble around here?' That put an end to the fight right away."

"So he's a bad ass," I interject, "but what about his pig?"

"He makes a very solemn promise that these are the best pork *brizoles* on the island, if not the planet. He's got a few farmers who raise them according to his exact specifications. They're fed like kings. And if the pork is not up to snuff, you can imagine he's not very happy. And the farmers know better than to make Yannis unhappy."

The guy looks harmless enough, like your typical overweight chain-smoker, his shirt unbuttoned to reveal some unruly tufts of white chest hair garlanded with a gold chain or two. He's sitting with his back against the wall of the *taverna* and is surrounded by a trio of much smaller men. They are busy drinking *retsina* and filling a flotilla of ashtrays with butts.

"Rumor has it," Nikolas continues, "that once, a customer—some rich guy off a yacht from Athens—dared to complain that his *brizola* was rubbery. The waitress went and got Yannis, who stormed out of the kitchen, cleaver in hand, to have some choice words with the guest. He called him *malaka* for a few loud minutes, remaining fairly calm, then flew into a serious rage, threatening the man with murder for insulting his restaurant. To Yannis's surprise, the guest didn't back down, insisting that the pork was tough, begging him to try it himself. So Yannis did. And to his shock, the Athenian was right. The pork was rubbery."

"What then?"

"Well, he brought the man a new *brizola*, then left immediately on his motorcycle to beat the living shit out of the man who sold him that pig."

We have no complaints about the pork arriving before us. First, we have the restaurant's "special": a gigantic platter of braised pork with mushrooms, sweet peppers, and tomato gravy, served atop the usual mountain of fried potatoes. We wash that down with ouzo and devour a *choriatiki* salad with fresh *xinotyro*. Then the famous *brizoles* arrive, bringing with them a plume of wood smoke: they are not chops at all, but massive twenty-ounce steaks, each over a foot across, grilled medium rare, and accompanied by another pound of fried potatoes.

"There's no way I could eat all that," Corey says.

"I don't think I'll have any problem," Aaron replies, grinning madly. He's already into his pig high. He drops his knife and fork right away and sets to work with his hands, gnashing his teeth and gnawing at the massive bones, his chin slathered in melted lard and ouzo slobber.

But the *brizoles* win. We must push our chairs back from the table and employ the remaining ouzo as a digestive. I ask Spyros and Nikolas about the reputation of Naxos in the rest of Greece.

"Well," Sypros explains, "Naxos is one of the few Cycladic islands not exclusively dependent on tourism. It's a big island, with enough good land to support a wide variety of agricultural production. Everyone knows about Naxos Graviera. When you buy Graviera in grocery stores all over Greece they'll ask you whether you want Graviera from Naxos or from Crete. Both cheeses are controlled designations of origin by the European Union. And, of course, there are the potatoes."

"It's funny," Corey says, speaking as a chef. "These are great potatoes, but as *french fries* go, they're really lacking."

And he's right. The best fries are blanched a little and then fried twice, so you end up with a crunchy, crusty exterior and an ethereal interior. Here on Naxos the potatoes are coarsely cut and fried only once. But they are fried in extra-virgin olive oil, and that seems to make all the difference.

"And yet," Corey continues, stuffing another wedge of potato into his mouth, "I'm eating about three pounds of these things a day."

. . .

Spyros and Nikolas know another cheese supplier in the port—Emmanuel Koufopoulos, who manages the cooperative we visited yesterday—and they insist on stopping to see him before they catch their afternoon ferry back to Athens.

Up until now, I've tried only young Graviera—most wheels are aged three to nine months before their rind is broken and they are devoured. But here are some rather creepy-looking blocks of aged Graviera, real senior citizens. We try the four-year-old first and find it exquisite, with a rind that has turned the color of dark caramel: all the lush, heady cream of the young Graviera has evaporated away, so now the cheese breaks in jagged hunks flecked with the granular bits one expects to find in Parmigiano-Reggiano. In fact, my tongue thinks *Parmigiano* the moment I taste a piece, but there's a slight twang to the finish that reminds me it's Graviera. The five-year, on the other hand, is really unpleasant: the cheese has turned very dark and in some places is beginning to go blue. It has a sour, burnt flavor I couldn't have expected.

Many of the cheeses here have been marinated in oil and herbs— a treatment more typical of goat's-milk cheese, but very suitable to the task of dressing up the young Gravieras. They are all perfectly delicious. There's even a *skordotyro*—garlic cheese—a simple *kefalotyri* infused with palate-blasting chunks of fairly raw garlic. It was clearly a mistake to taste that cheese last, and I understand that several beers will be required, now, to rinse its intense flavor away. So I allow myself to be dragged from the shop without making a single purchase (luckily Corey bought a hunk of the four-year so we could study it later).

When we emerge from the shop, it's nearly sunset, so we hike up to the Portara to watch the brothers' ferry chug off into the Aegean. The planet cooperates nicely: sun going down through the ancient doorway, our long day ending with a slow smear of color on the horizon, shadowing the sensuous curves of Paros across the strait, while bathing all of Naxos in gold.

.　.　.

According to Herodotus, Naxos "was, in prosperity, way ahead of the rest of the islands." Thus, it was very much worth sacking, being "not very big but beautiful, fertile. . . . There was much property and many slaves." The island's marble was always highly prized (though not as much as Parian marble from just next door), its agricultural productivity noteworthy, its strategic position in the Cyclades desirable. Those virtues have sustained the island since ancient times. So has the mining of emery, the mineral abrasive most famously put to use for manicure boards. By the eighteenth century, Naxos was the only supplier of the desirable substance in Europe. Business boomed enough that, in 1923, the world's first aerial railway (imagine clunky iron cable cars strung up like Christmas ornaments along an impossibly steep mountainside) was constructed here. When we cross over the top of the island today, we see what an incredible feat of engineering this entailed. But this story doesn't end well for the island. Some ingenious American invented an artificial replacement for emery, causing the industry to die overnight. And the cables seized up long ago, leaving the cars to hang rusty and forlorn.

We're headed to Moutsouna, a spot on the eastern half of the island. There's a good *psarotaverna* there, I remember, perched right on the edge of the sea with a view of neighboring Amorgos. But to get there we must first cross Mount Zas. It was either there or on Mount Ida in Crete that baby Zeus was reared in a cave (the two islands feud over this mythological claim). In any case, the drive is hair raising, all switchbacks and not a decent guardrail anywhere. Just as you finish your ascent from the village of Apeiranthos and cross over the mountain's crest, you glimpse a possible fate: over the edge some poor sucker rolled his truck, and the mangled, oxidized carcass is still wedged upside down in a crevice half a mile below, a memento to bad driving.

The table promised to me by memory is still here at Taverna Dychti, so we lay claim to it, order a round of drinks, and since it's sweltering, work our way into the water. Aaron locates a good-sized octopus beneath a stone just off the dock. We take turns diving down to harass it. I also see an old fisherman cleaning a half dozen just-caught *barbounia* at the water's edge.

I've lured Corey and Aaron here with the promise of seafood, and the sight of *barbounia* inspires me to head back toward the kitchen. I stroll cheerfully beneath the mottled shade of a grape arbor and peer through the French doors, where, I'm delighted to find, three people have stretched a thin plateau of dough atop a long table and are assembling what look to be ravioli, or savory pies of some kind. I've been itching to fashion some pasta here as a way to use up some of our unwieldy cheese supply. Even with limited kitchen resources, I proved some years ago that this was possible by flattening sheets of dough using an empty wine bottle as a rolling pin, then ripping them by hand into jagged pappardelle to support a ragu of braised lamb shoulder, rosemary, and orange. Seeing these cooks' meticulous work today leaves me grinning and a little jealous.

"Ti mageirevete simera?" I ask the man closest to me, though his back is turned in my direction. "What are you cooking today?" It's a simple question, one asked out of culinary curiosity, and I ask it with a friendly grin.

To my astonishment, rather than the smile and greeting I expect (hell, I expect to be motioned into the kitchen to have a look at what they're doing; this is Greece, after all, and normally one is welcomed at every turn), a sweaty, cross-eyed man in a grubby white T-shirt turns on his heel and barks, "What do you want?"

When I tell him I'm only looking, and that I've come to ask about the fish, he slams the door in my face, shouting, "No— *don't* look! The fish is over there."

I'm flabbergasted and, within a few more seconds, very angry. Treatment of a guest in this manner is befitting of a cyclops, not a Naxian restaurateur. I ponder Homeric retaliations, then storm back to the table (which the waitress has already set with silverware, plates, and a basket of bread) to inform

Corey and Aaron that we're leaving. When I tell them what's happened, they are surprised, but unconcerned—they don't budge an inch. Clearly I'm guilty of romanticizing my expectations for Greek hospitality.

Never mind. The old fisherman motions me over to the fish cooler, which is right next to the grill he tends along with his other son. Thankfully, they are smiling. The just-caught *barbounia* would be an obvious choice, but instead I order us a plate of grilled sardines and choose a perfect two-pound *melanouri* (saddled bream), which I'm sure they'll treat nicely on the coals. The food is as simple and fresh as I remembered it. They add lightly cured anchovies and capers to the usual *choriatiki* salad, and along with that we devour a plate of expertly fried zucchini. I even order some of the accursedly delicious pies they were assembling in the kitchen—which are stuffed with wild greens, fresh *xinotyro*, and dill. While we're eating, I see the grumpy pie maker emerge from the kitchen in his filthy shirt. He sits off in a corner by himself under the grapes, smoking with great urgency and trembling a little, his feet tapping violently. I see now that he's a little touched, not quite right in the noodle. Surely I can forgive the village idiot for his rudeness to foreigners? The fish arrives with its attendant lemon halves, and it's just what we needed. Well, I also order a plate of potatoes, just for good measure.

.   .   .

When it's time to return to Athens the next morning, I must see to the problem of the refrigerator. I can't abandon so much cheese, and we haven't yet had a chance to sit down with the proper wine and concentration to make tasting notes. I want to remember each one. Two of the fresh cheeses have gone south and must be pitched. I know from experience (two summers ago on Serifos) that fresh *myzithra* or *xinotyro* is good only for a few days; eating it later than that might mean a week of explosive guts. But every other nubbin of cheese is coming along on the ferry ride.

"We'll taste them on the ship," I tell Aaron and Corey. "I'll pick up some bread and olives in town and we'll make it a picnic."

We set up camp at a table on the upper deck of our ferry and watch the Portara of Naxos fade into the distance behind us as we cruise across the strait toward Paros. My friend Natalie has been at a writers' colony on the neighboring island, and it turns out our ferry is stopping there on the way back to Piraeus, so we add another friend to our cheese party. Natalie was up late drinking with her literary friends and looks a bit green around the gills. But when the sun begins pounding down an hour into our voyage, she's the one who suggests a cold beer—and we agree. She's terrified, however, when I begin unloading the massive bag of cheese onto the table. The bag's been sitting in the sun for the past hour and that's concentrated the aromas; a skanky cloud of dairy gas unfurls when I untie the knot at the top of the bag.

Nevertheless, there's service to be performed on behalf of cheese lovers everywhere. As G. K. Chesterton announced in 1910, "The poets have been mysteriously silent on the subject of cheese." It's time to break that silence. So I line up the wedges and pull out my notebook (which must be held down with a beer bottle, since the wind is whipping). Here, with a little help from my poetic friends, are the impressions I record:

• *Graviera* (cow's milk, aged about eight months): Though the name "Graviera" indicates some familial relationship to Gruyère, in the Naxian cheese there's much less of the piquant after-twang I associate with its Swiss cousin. Now that the cheese is quite warm, the texture is very smooth and voluptuous with milk fat, with just the slightest flavor of pistachio at the finish. Justifiably famous.

• *Xinotyro the Infant* (scooped from a bucket in the cave of Yorgos Babounis): We had to abandon this one back at our beach house, but I ask us to pause for a moment of silence in remembrance of it. The sheep's and goat's milk curds are skimmed and drained slightly, but are not yet pressed into baskets to be molded; this results in a loose cheese with the texture of ricotta, but with a flavor that is much more pungent. It proffers a wild mixture of sour fruit, tongue-startling acid, and butterfat. Highly perishable, as I've said.

+ *Xinotyro the Younger* (farmer unknown: purchased at the original cheese shop just off the harbor): A mixture of sheep's and goat's milk, aged about six months. The rind is pale yellow and the cheese hits the palate with the definitive flavor of goat's milk, but Aaron swears the very soft texture and the fruitiness of this cheese (not to mention the color of the rind) remind him of banana. He told us this the first night when he'd had a lot to drink and we thought it was a joke. But today, when he is relatively sober, he claims it once again—and we all agree, the cheese finishes with the flavor of banana. It is oddly appealing.

+ *Xinotyro the Elder* (also an unknown farmer, from the harbor shop): This one is aged about one year. Now the rind is much darker and the cheese has a firmer, dry texture. We find it surprisingly mild and creamy, but the finish leaves us thirsty. The aggressive flavor of the goat's milk has receded into the background during the aging process, and the milder flavor of sheep's milk now has the last word.

+ *Kefalotyri* (from Yorgos Babounis): Again a mixture of sheep's and goat's milk, but this one aged about eighteen months. The cheese is very sharp, riddled with delicate little holes, and has a sour, almost bitter finish. But that's followed with an earthy flavor that reminds us of Asiago. And the cheese keeps giving. Out of nowhere another flavor emerges: it has what we all agree is some "funk," either from the moldy, almost alcoholic notes we remember from his cave, or from the pungency of the milk he uses. His animals do graze in some forbidding territory.

+ *Irseniko* (a.k.a. "The Manly," farmer unknown, from the cheese shop on the port): A mixture of sheep's and goat's milk, aged about one year. A firm, moldy white rind opens to reveal a somewhat crumbly cheese riddled with the tiniest of holes. The finish is very dry and nutty, reminiscent of Romano.

+ *Anthotiro* (also from the cheese shop on the port): Nearly identical in preparation to the *kefalotyri* above (a mixture of sheep's and goat's milk, aged about eighteen months), but this one has an almost purple, moldy rind. The cheese has a uniform, milk-white interior, but it isn't as moist on the palate as it looks. Very nice balance of piquancy and cream. Though there's some sheep and goat manure on the nose (which sounds awful but is actually intriguing), this cheese has absolutely none of the "funk" of the *kefalotyri* of Babounis.

As dessert, we take one last stab at the four-year-old Graviera, which we declare the finest cheese on Naxos. I wish I had the courage to smuggle a wheel of it back through customs, but I reconsider that wish by the time our ferry has pulled into port in Piraeus. There's the usual mad rush of humanity and dogs in the direction of the taxi stand, with lots of pushing and shoving and ornery behavior. The cool breeze we enjoyed on the island is nowhere to be found, and sinister waves of heat emanate from the melting sidewalks. Our bags suddenly feel very heavy.

I propose splurging on a taxi to our hotel in Monastiraki, but every driver we approach quotes us a price so ridiculous I don't even bother haggling. So we line up with all the other sweaty specimens of humanity and wait for the metro. I've got my small rolling duffel in one hand and my big bag of cheese in the other. Corey and Aaron suggested I leave the cheese behind on the ship, but I didn't have the strength to part with it so callously. Someone should inherit the spoils of our labor. Though we're leaving Greece tomorrow morning, Natalie is going to dinner with a mutual friend of ours tonight and—problem solved—I've asked her to deliver the remains of our beautiful cheese as a gift. She agrees—out of weariness and hungover politeness, no doubt. It helps that I offer to carry it until we part ways in the city center.

The new metro is a state-of-the-art, super-efficient addition to Athenian life. When Athens hosted the 2004 Olympics, there was a massive push to complete the lines running between the airport and the port of Piraeus, and miraculously the city did complete them, making travel in Athens much

In a Station of the Metro

cheaper and more pleasant. I've read estimates suggesting that improvements for the Olympics cost every Greek man, woman, and child about one thousand euros; much of the expense was put on the equivalent of a national credit card, leading in part to the country's current crisis. Money wasn't the only problem. Completing the metro also meant navigating the precious layer of archeology underneath the modern city. You can't dig in Athens—anywhere—without unearthing something ancient, and several of the subway stations exhibit charming discoveries from the underworld. There's no subway in the world I'd rather ride, usually. Today is another matter.

We pile into a crowded car, clinging to our belongings and looking in vain for anything to hang onto when the train lurches into motion. After a few stops, though, the car clears out enough so we can see one another again. At last, the air-conditioning stands a chance. Aaron has secured a spot right next to the door where he can almost sit on his suitcase, but a dripping man is clutching the safety strap above him with both of his hands, thrusting his sweaty armpits into Aaron's face. Whether Aaron's pretending to gag for laughs, or is actually gagging, we can't quite tell.

Natalie is definitely gagging. I've tied a knot in the top of my cheese bag, but when I set it down on the floor next to my suitcase, all the rarefied air inside comes blasting out of a vent hole in her direction. She's turned pale. The bag is really hot and fragile after six hours marinating in the sun, and it's beginning to leak—I notice a slick of slimy oil on the floor of the subway car. When I try to push it away from Natalie with my foot, I only make it worse—another vent hole opens in the side, dispatching another cloud. Even the smelly Greek woman next to me is outdone—I see her turn up her nose (surely she thinks these repulsive vapors are emanating from my body) and she lurches across the moving car to get upwind.

When we step off the escalator into the blinding light of the Monastiraki station, I realize that no Mercedes-driving taxi man is going to let Natalie into his car with a torn bag of Naxian fondue. "I guess this is it, friends," I announce to the others. "It's time to say goodbye to our cheese. It has served us well."

I look around for a garbage can, but due to fears of terrorist bombs, none are allowed inside the station. Thankfully, there's a janitorial cart parked next to the men's room.

"Do you think the cleaning lady might want this cheese?" I ask, but even I know the sad answer to that ridiculous question. Into the garbage goes my dairy fortune—making a hearty thud at the bottom of the can—and out into the Athenian heat go we.

According to the opening strains of his *Theogony*, one day while he "tended his sheep at the foothills of god-haunted Helikon," the Muses taught Hesiod a "beautiful song" of the world's origins.

Following Hesiod's lead, I spend much of my time in Greece waiting around for the Muses, but I've never found much time for shepherding. Instead, I get inspiration by *eating* lamb, which is readily available and easy to find in island restaurants. But I tire of dining out, and given the abundance of excellent meat and produce available in local markets, and after long days of writing, the urge to cook soon takes over. Sure, the kitchens of rental houses are almost always insufficient, but with a few lousy burners and a functional pan or two I can always make something delicious.

I begin by visiting a local butcher, seeking out those less expensive cuts—like lamb shoulder, used here—which make for excellent slow food on a slow-moving island day. And island eggs are typically very fresh and never refrigerated; their yolks are preternaturally orange, as egg yolks should be, which means they deserve to be transformed into saffron-colored pasta.

Of course, I can't bring my battered old stainless steel Imperia pasta roller with me while traveling (I did go so far as loading it into my suitcase one year, but it was way too heavy). So I improvise upon arrival. An empty wine bottle works fine as a rolling pin, I discovered one summer. I had a wonderfully smooth marble countertop in my cottage near Orkos Beach and I sipped cold ouzo while assembling the pasta sheets for the ravioli featured here.

The additions of orange and cinnamon give the filling a decidedly Levantine flavor. Greece is in the East, not the West, I like to remind people. At home, I serve such ravioli with sage butter, but though wild sage grows all over Greece, I couldn't find any in my Naxian backyard. But rosemary grew everywhere there (in giant bushes), and its resinous, dusky notes paired nicely with island lamb.

Salt and pepper

A 2-pound lamb shoulder roast, preferably bone-in, cut into 4 large pieces

3 tablespoons extra-virgin olive oil

1 medium onion, diced

1 stalk celery, diced

1 carrot, diced

2 cloves garlic, smashed

1 cup red wine

1 large, ripe tomato, diced

2 cups lamb, beef, or chicken stock

2 six-inch stalks of fresh rosemary

1 cinnamon stick

¾ cup grated dry *anthotiro*, plus more for garnish

2 tablespoons minced flat-leaf parsley

1 teaspoon grated orange rind, plus more for garnish

½ teaspoon sugar

½ teaspoon cracked red pepper

3 very fresh island eggs

2½ cups yellow, hard durum flour, plus more as needed

5 tablespoons butter

To prepare the ravioli filling:

Heat a heavy-bottomed stew pot or Dutch oven over medium heat. Generously salt and pepper the pieces of lamb. Add 2 tablespoons of the olive oil to the pan. Just before the oil begins to smoke, place the lamb pieces into the pan and brown them on all sides (resisting constantly the urge to turn and move the pieces) until they are uniformly dark (like the color of well-cooked bacon)—perhaps 5 minutes per side. Don't worry if the meat sticks a little, but turn the heat down slightly if the oil begins to blacken. Remove the browned pieces of lamb to a plate and set aside.

Drain off any fat that's collected in the bottom of the pan, then return the pan to the heat and add another tablespoon of olive oil. Add the onion, celery, carrot, and garlic; season the vegetables with a pinch of salt and pepper and sauté for 2 to 3 minutes, until the onions just begin to soften, then add the red wine and diced tomato and scrape the bottom of the pan to deglaze any bits that have stuck. Return the lamb pieces to the pan along with the stock, 1 stalk of the rosemary, and the cinnamon stick. Bring up to a simmer, then cover the pan with a tight-fitting lid and adjust the heat to very low. Cook for 2 to 3 hours, turning the pieces of lamb occasionally (adding a little water if the liquid completely cooks off), until the lamb comes apart easily when pressed with the back of a fork.

Remove the lamb from the pot and discard the cinnamon and rosemary stalk, reserving the vegetables. When the meat is cool enough to handle, pull it apart into small pieces or shred it, discarding the bones and any large pieces of fat. Then place the shredded meat and braising vegetables on a cutting board. Run a knife through the mixture until you've achieved a more or less uniform, rustic consistency. Transfer the mixture to a bowl and incorporate the grated cheese, parsley, orange rind, sugar, and cracked red pepper. Refrigerate until ready to fill the ravioli.

To make the dough and assemble the ravioli:

Combine the eggs and almost all of the flour and knead until you have a pliable, uniform dough, adding more flour as needed. Wrap the dough and allow it to rest for at least 30 minutes, then cut the dough into 6 pieces. Using an empty wine bottle or rolling pin, roll long (5- to 6-inch wide) sheets of pasta until they are thin enough that you can just see the outline of your hand through the dough. Place rounded tablespoons of the filling in rows down the middle of the first (of the six) pasta sheets, leaving about an inch between each mound. Then place another sheet of pasta on top of the other and seal them together carefully, pressing gently down around each mound of filling. Trim off any rough edges and then separate the ravioli by cutting them apart between the mounds. Transfer the finished ravioli to a towel-lined baking sheet until ready to cook.

To finish the dish:

Bring a large pot of salted water to a boil. Before dropping the ravioli in the water, begin the sauce: heat a deep skillet over medium. Add the butter along with the remaining stalk of rosemary and allow to heat until the rosemary leaves just start to sizzle, and then turn off the heat.

Add the ravioli to the boiling water and cook just until tender, about five minutes; they should be al dente. Drain well, then add the ravioli to the skillet along with the rosemary butter. Transfer the ravioli to a serving platter, drizzling with any remaining butter and the rosemary sprigs from the pan. Garnish with generous gratings of dry *anthotiro* and a little additional grated orange rind.

CHAPTER FIVE

Meat

Goats in the Ghost Towns of Chios

During the long winter months in western Pennsylvania—when it snows all day, every day, and low clouds suffocate our valley—I feel most intensely my longing for Greece. The distance is vast and painful and the offerings of the Greek table, all freshness and ripeness, seem inconceivable. By January, I'm starving for the place, having run out of supplies I brought home from the previous summer's visit: sour cherry preserves, bags of *throumbes*, jars of Kythirian honey, and even the precious bottles of *tsipouro* and olive oil, which I've rationed for months, since in them I horde reminders of the Greek sun.

When I can bear it no longer, I shovel out my driveway and skid down my town's equivalent of Main Street to Otter's Pub, a smoky dive bar with sticky floors and an irritable, redneck clientele. There, Yannis Fekos grumbles Greek to me through the thickets of his grey beard while we sip glasses of the Lesbian ouzo he keeps in stock on my behalf. I feel some relief in exercising my Greek conjugations with Yannis, and in the welcome heat of the anise, and in meandering, as our conversations always do, back to the obscure corners of Greece we remember for each other. I tell him stories about the Greco-Turkish settlements of Thrace, which I visited twenty years earlier, or of an octopus I snagged at Horefto on Pelion one year, or of a meal of *paximadia*, goat cheese, and *raki* I once shared with a polyglot priest on the southern coast of Crete. Yannis reciprocates with stories from his childhood in Pityos, on Chios, where his family still owns a house or two beneath one of the village's (now defunct) windmills. When he speaks about Chios, his eyes brighten with sad happiness and the claustrophobic atmosphere of the midwestern bar evaporates like a bad mirage.

Though I have visited Chios three times before and have always been attracted to the island's fascinating history and excellent food, somehow I've failed to visit its most important destination: Taverna Makellos, an outpost of artisanal Greek cuisine in Yannis's own village. He's reminded me of this each time we've spoken for several years, one caterpillar eyebrow raised incredulously. "How could you expect to know the food of my island unless you visit Pityos?" he asked again last winter.

"Listen. You will go into the center of the village and utter the name Fekos and you will be greeted everywhere you go. Take some photos of my family there. They will remember me. And you must bring me back some *hourmades*—oh, *Panayia mou*, the olives!—and also a portion of *kopanisti*, the cheese they ferment for forty days. It will make hair grow on your feet. Then sit for a while and eat goat and *makaronia* at Makellos. Then you will know."

I'd be happy to visit Chios on an ambassadorial mission for Yannis Fekos, but I also have my own reasons for going. First, I'm obsessed with handmade pasta; I have been since my raids upon the kitchens of Tuscany and Umbria decades ago. But I know very little about Greek takes on the noodle. The Greeks eat a lot of factory-made pasta—nearly as much as the Italians, in fact—but most of it isn't worth writing home about: spaghetti *me kima* (literally, with "ground meat," a pale approximation of ragu alla Bolognese) is a staple in many cafeterias, and of course there's *salsa domata* to be found on any tourist menu. *Pastitsio*, a sublime mongrel of a dish in the right chef's hands, is built upon a base of *bucatini:* atop that goes a layer of a nutmeg-and-cinnamon-brightened meat sauce, then a crowning inch of béchamel. Sure, there's excellent *spaghetti frutti di mare* to be had on the seaside now and then. But in almost all of these dishes one feels the echo of something imported and Italian. The fact of this debt is evident in an excellent demotic insult: ever since Mussolini and a painful Axis occupation, Greeks have derisively referred to Italians as *makaronades*.

As for hand-fashioned pasta in Greece, I know only *hilopites*—wide egg noodles featured in mountain places like Arahova above Delphi. But Yannis tells me there are at least four kinds of pasta made on the island of Chios alone, and I'm curious about the importance of the noodle there, of all the remote places in Greece.

On top of that, I wish to return to the ghost towns on the northern half of the island. Ten years ago, I set off from the castle-crowned village of Volissos with some friends in search of lunch, or at the very least a coffee. Several times we pulled the car off the narrow, unkempt roads into absolutely silent settlements. On hundreds of derelict stone dwellings, doors and windows had rotted off their hinges, allowing us a glimpse inside the literal demise of village culture. Plates and cups were still set out upon dust-covered tables; collapsed boxes of food remained in the cupboards, dotted with rodent droppings; sheets were still tangled in heaps atop water-soaked mattresses. Only the mourning doves, roosting atop old bedposts and exposed rafters, seemed content. It was as if, sometime around 1975, the entire population of these villages decided—right there in the middle of breakfast—to leave Chios and never come back.

In Kéramos, the last of the villages we visited that day, we found one lonesome chicken scratching for grubs in the shadow of a fig tree. A chicken seemed to imply human habitation, but there wasn't a soul around. Half an hour later, just when we'd given up all hope of meeting anyone, we heard a voice and saw an old woman's tiny head emerge out from behind the shutters of her blue door. Who were we and what did we want? *Xenoi* (foreigners), I told her, looking for a café. At that, she abruptly pulled the door shut with a clatter. But then we heard the dead bolt loosen and at last the whole door swung wide open: she stood there in her flowered apron, waving us inside. She was Kyria Maria Haralambous and she lived with her husband, Ilias, in a crowded but immaculate two-room cottage. The dark foyer and bedroom, where pictures of their son in his army uniform were exhibited to us ceremoniously, were separated from a narrow kitchen by a white curtain. Equal in size to the house itself was their broad balcony, from which one peered into a violent cleft in the mountain. The entire floor there was covered in giant green and brown pods: they'd been busy drying and shelling *koukia* (the local variety of fava bean) when they heard our commotion outside. Awkward as it was to take anything from them, since they were very poor, we accepted their offering of coffee and *kourabiedes* (almond cookies) from a tin container. Only five people still lived in Kéramos, Ilias told me when I asked, and all of them were over seventy. But it had been several weeks, he added, while removing his glasses to clean them with the tail of his shirt, since they'd seen any of the others. That seemed impossible in a village no larger than a flyspeck on the map.

"But we have *many* people here in Kéramos," Maria joked, waving her index finger toward the opposite mountain. "In the village over there only one person lives. She's an old crone of ninety-something. Each night she climbs with her cane to the top of the hill just to turn on the switch for the village's one streetlamp. So she won't feel too lonely."

Now, preparing to return to Chios after all these years, I thought back to our encounter. Was there any possibility old Ilias and Maria were still there in Kéramos, shucking *koukia* and watching the village disintegrate around them?

. . .

Tourism is never enough to sustain real culture of any kind, and certainly not the delicate social balance of a traditional Greek village, which is based around isolation and shared necessity. Typically, a village would have its

Ghost Town Philoxenia

own olive press, wood oven, and butcher shop, not to mention a population with the inherited knowledge and skills to harvest, process, and transform raw materials into edible sustenance. There would be regular traffic out into the local groves, orchards, and gardens, of course, and occasional excursions to neighboring villages, but it was possible (and for many, desirable) to live a whole life without ever leaving the immediate vicinity of one's birthplace. In many such places, the inhabitants of neighboring villages were referred to as *xenoi*—the word can mean "strangers" or "foreigners"—and they'd be trusted about as much as someone from Montana or Mongolia.

The moment island roads were paved, however, the world came knocking, and within a generation the villages cleared out, young residents bolting for the mainland, leaving only the very old to persist in the traditional ways. Slow, labor-intensive production couldn't compete for long with cheap goods and services coming in by truck. This familiar story of village decline was inevitable in most of Greece, but it was never a foregone conclusion on Chios, since for almost a thousand years this was the richest of all the Greek islands. Even its smallest villages offered lives of relative comfort and affluence. And the reasons behind this wealth are crucial to any investigation of the island's cuisine.

. . .

If Asia Minor is a giant, then Chios is his severed left ear, floating just five miles from Çeşme and the Karaburun Peninsula. A caïque sailing into the Aegean from the port of Smyrna (once a great Greek city, scene of the infamous massacre of Greeks in 1912, and now the overpopulated Turkish city of Izmir) would pass the northern coast of Chios on her port side before making the turn south toward the Mediterranean. Therefore, since ancient times Chios always looked to the east, benefitting from the gastronomic riches of the continent (including steady supplies of grain) and the cultural riches of its cosmopolitan centers. In addition to Smyrna, the rich cities of Pergamum and Ephesus were just a short sail away. And in the archaic period, Herodotus reminds us, the Chians were allied with Miletus—that famous boot camp for philosophers. But Chians have also benefited from looking west, toward the great sea. Trade up and down the Aegean coast meant the island was an important outpost and a very desirable piece of real estate.

It's always been a place of poetry and food. "The blind man of rocky Chios," a.k.a. Homer, was born here (well, and in at least six other places). Just twenty steps from my friend's house in Volissos, in fact, a rusted sign reading "Birth House of Homer" hung on the threshold of a ruined cottage that had to be at least four hundred years old. Such absurdities aside, it's easy to see that Chios would have been a desirable gig for any traveling bard, as it was strategically located to receive sophisticated visitors from land and sea. Given that, it's not surprising that the cooks of Chios have had a good reputation through the ages. Other islands would have struggled to offer wanderers much more than a respectable barley loaf and a mug of diluted vinegar, but according to food historian Andrew Dalby, the Chians established a culinary tradition very early.

We have to guess about what the ancients ate there, but we know that Chian wine was universally celebrated. In one of his fragments, Aristophanes lists it in a catalog of naughty vices:

> He didn't learn these things when I sent him to school
> but rather drinking, bad singing, Syracusan cuisine,
> Sybaritic feasting, "Chian from Spartan bowls,"
> drinking well and unsparingly. . . .

And as late as Horace, the "black wines" of Chios seem to have enjoyed as much prestige as the Falernian of Campania—that famous, favorite wine of wealthy Romans.

But the real secrets behind Chian prosperity and cuisine extend beyond geography, springing from two odd sources: the mastic tree and the imperialistic acumen of Genoa. *Pistacia lentiscus*, cousin of the pistachio tree, grows everywhere in the Mediterranean, but only on the island of Chios does it weep. Only here will incisions cut into the shrub's ragged bark make it drip a precious amber resin called mastic: chewing gum of the Byzantines, breath freshener of the Turkish harem, and lauded medicine and culinary delicacy since ancient times. The flavor of mastic is unmistakable; it's sweetly floral, not unlike myrrh, with a little of the piney twang one would expect from an evergreen. Added to cakes or *loukoumia* (Turkish delight), not to mention alcohol, it makes an excellent digestive. Some Chians even insist that it will enkindle one's sexy bits (curious how many weird edibles are credited with aphrodisiac powers).

Why the microclimate of southern Chios encourages the tree to weep has never been explained. In any case, the presence of mastic on the island has been both a blessing and a curse. A gloriously wealthy cluster of mastic villages (the Mastichochoria) sprung up in the island's southern Cambos region, each of them lightly fortified and arranged in pirate-baffling labyrinths of alleys and archways. Still, the pirates did to Chios what pirates do, and the great empires have behaved toward the island predictably too: thanks to mastic, the island was always someone's crown jewel, endlessly pillaged and sacked and occupied as a result.

By far its most successful colonists were the Genoese. The Byzantines granted Genoa control of Lesbos and Chios by 1275, and remnants of three hundred years of Italian residence can still be observed in the hilltop castles and observation towers scattered across both islands. In addition to using these islands as commercial stations, on Chios (which the Italians called Scio) there grew up an important center for nautical training and shipbuilding. A young Genoese man named Christopher Columbus visited the island several times (as with Homer, some conspiracy theorists assert that he was actually born there). He likely came to earn his nautical chops, or at the very least to escort loads of mastic west to Spain and Portugal. Giving some credence to these historical rumors is the fact that, to this day, a fairly common surname on Chios is Kouloumbis. Could these be the ancestors of that famous sailor?

. . .

As befits the home of mastic, Chios freshens its own breath: the heady perfume of citrus is in its air, orange and lemon notes capering on the salt breezes that stir every tree in Chios Town, the most fragrant port of any Greek island. That's fortunate, since the town itself is homely, full of concrete buildings plopped carelessly along the shore road. Neither the harbor's picturesque windmills nor the occasional mansion, with its garden of palm trees and pomegranates, can disguise the general shoddiness of Chios Town. A devastating earthquake flattened most of the island's best architecture in 1881, and its grandeur was never restored. But its shipping industry has helped to keep the island prosperous, even during the current economic crisis—each morning, men in fussy suits buzz their Vespas back and forth from the port while doing business by cell phone.

When I visit Chios, I try to depart this island Babylon as soon as possible, especially if I'm hungry, but I've got a bit of my own business today. Michalis Makellos, in addition to overseeing his restaurant in the hinterlands, owns a café on Chios harbor—the only place in town, I'm not surprised to find out, where one can get a Greek coffee prepared the old-fashioned way: in a bronze *briki* brought to boil in a pile of heated sand. Since the Chians I know in Pennsylvania are all tall and burly, and because he's famous and his name is clotted with noisy consonants, I had imagined Makellos would be intimidating and Cyclopean. So I'm surprised to find that he's about my height (which is to say: short), compact and muscular, with thinning, slicked-back black hair. He's been courteous, if a bit curt, on the telephone, which I now understand is only because of shyness. Yes, I can certainly work *makaronia* at the restaurant, but it appears I'll have to wait until tomorrow. Feeble as the Greek

Weeping Trees and the Famous Genoese

economy is, Makellos can afford to open his restaurant only on the weekends. He must work long, more-profitable hours here at the café to make ends meet.

Driving from Chios Town toward the northern half of the island requires me to switchback up the side of a precipice for almost ten terrifying minutes. As my car grinds its way higher, mansions, parks, and beachside hotels gradually shrink. All outward evidence of Chian prosperity disappears for good the moment I pass inland over the cliff edge, where the asphalt dips and curves a few minutes before it straightens toward the summit of Marathóvounos—a spooky lunar plateau spiked with slate-colored boulders and thistly shrub. While the rest of Chios is relatively green, here along the island's spine there's a mournful barrenness.

The silence of the place is frequently broken, however, by a festive jingling of bells and the clamor of cloven hooves: this is a place only the goat could love. The first herd I encounter is so big it takes them a full five minutes to cross the road. I quickly lose count of their dreadlocked brown-and-black hides and peculiar antlered heads, but there must be at least a hundred in the herd, many of them heavy with milk. A few are exhausted—or impertinent—enough to plop down in the middle of the road, all four feet tucked in beneath them, oblivious to the frenetic skittering of the herd. One bleat of my horn gets them moving again.

Unlike delicate sheep, which require at least a modicum of tender pasture and some protection from predators, goats require almost nothing. Once the prime milking season ends in the late spring (goats are capable of lactating for up to two hundred days), they may be left to their own devices in a forbidding landscape such as this, in which they'll scavenge things few other beasts would be able to eat, carousing from bluff to bluff until midsummer. Then they are gathered and the herds are culled of their weakest members: meat for places like Taverna Makellos.

This seasonal routine, like all cycles of husbandry and harvest, follows the dictates of nature—not to mention the human palate—and was codified long before Hesiod put it into the dactylic hexameter of his *Works and Days:*

> When the thistle blooms and the chirping cicada
> sits on trees and pours down shrill song
> from frenzied quivering wings in the toilsome summer,
> then goats are fatter than ever and wine is at its best;
> women's lust knows no bounds and men are all dried up,
> because the dog star parches their heads and knees
> and the heat sears their skin. Then, ah then,
> I wish you a shady ledge and your choice wine,
> bread baked in the dusk and mid-August's goat milk
> and meat from a free-roving heifer that has never calved—
> and from firstling kids.

Once upon a time, Chios was called Pityoussa, or "the place having *pitys*," or pines. Pityos, located right in the heart of the island's northern half, is devoid of pine trees now, but it seems fitting that the place clings to this ancient title—no valley on the island could be more hospitable to human settlement. Whether approached from north or south, the village rises from the landscape unexpectedly. Upon the highest outcrop, a Byzantine tower broods, much higher than the windmills, which are themselves higher than the humped Orthodox steeples of the Agios Yiorgios and Agios Dimitrios churches. Ripples of elevation rise gradually on every side, so Pityos has the advantage of near concealment in the bottom of a green bowl, on the edge of a steep little canyon carved by a million years of spring torrents. It's easy to imagine goatherds climbing up from the village with their hungry herds to exploit rich grazing land in every direction. Unlike the barren crest of the island, here is a pastoral world dominated by water-loving chestnut and plane trees, fruit orchards, olive trees, and grapevines. The contours of the terrain, which funneled water into town, also encouraged the goats back home again: every ridge in the surrounding mountains seems to spill downward.

I expect to find Taverna Makellos in the town's *plateia*, or main square, but instead there's only a little café and the charmingly named Oinopanto-poleion, the "wine and everything shop," which looks like it's been closed for at least a decade. So I wander at random down one of the alleys radiating from the square, where I find a silver-haired woman sorting through a heap of wild greens in her tiny courtyard. Sure enough, she knew Yannis Fekos as a boy, and she stops her work to insert her bony feet into a pair of slippers so she can rise and clutch my hands in hers. She is Amalia Kostalas. "Wait here a second," she says, before ducking into her stone house. I hear a refrigerator open and close, followed by a rattling of silverware, and then she is back with a fork and a massive jar of orange spoon sweets. Spearing a wedge of candied orange with her fork, she hands it over. I struggle to chew and swallow the enormous treat, syrup running from the corners of my mouth, and no sooner have I done so than she plunges the fork back into the jar and hands me another.

The oranges are sweet and refreshingly cold, and I'm both hot and hungry. But I've been waiting years to eat at Taverna Makellos and don't want to spoil my appetite now. Of course the old woman knows where the *taverna* is, and when I tell her I'm going to learn about its famous *makaronia* she laughs, rubbing her palms together in a gesture I don't yet understand. Somehow I manage to evade another forkful of orange and her offer to bring out some coffee, thanking her with a flurry of kisses and handshakes, not to mention one quick snapshot of her beneath her roses, "for Yannis." I promise to return for coffee another time, and sincerely hope I will.

.   .   .

The *taverna* turns out to be on the edge of the village, adjacent to a dry riverbed and in the shade of a gargantuan plane tree, whose trunk has been buttressed with concrete and stone to keep it from crushing the restaurant. In an old photo hung near the kitchen, a group is gathered beneath this same tree, their attention focused on a well that still sits nearby.

Meat: Goats in the Ghost Towns of Chios

Two long-faced women in head scarves and woolen dresses balance ampho-rae on their shoulders, while two others heave a rope up from the bottom of the well. A skeptical gentleman in a black vest leans on his cane, looking sideways at the proceedings. The tree, I'm told, has been here since at least the fifteenth century. Thousands of customers have feasted in its shade since the restaurant opened around 1970, and it gives me pause to consider all this gluttony in light of the decades of famine and war earlier in the century, a period called to mind by the sight of these hooded, emaciated, witchlike women in sepia, laboriously drawing their water.

There's nothing witchy about Maria Mavrianou, the restaurant's head cook. Her vigorous brown hair, brushed off to one side, is peppered with grey around her ears, in which she wears smart gold earrings. She moves through the kitchen with the stately confidence of a traditional French chef in his whites, but her uniform consists of a sequined brown blouse, a well-ironed black skirt, and fashionable wedge sandals.

Maria takes me on a tour of the massive Makellos kitchen, gleaming with polished stainless steel tables and stoves. It's clear that they need so much room: fifty people can be seated in a little chalet-like hall indoors, and there's a series of broad patios encircling the tree where about a hundred guests could fit on a busy night. While Makellos is obviously a very capable host and proprietor, it's immediately apparent that the real force in the kitchen is Maria Mavrianou.

I stand speechless before her pasta cupboard: at least two hundred por-tions of freshly made pasta are drying in twenty trays, arranged in racks. "This morning's work," she says with a bashful shrug, neglecting to mention that she's already broken down and braised several goats and made batter for three different kinds of croquettes as well.

One of things I like most about Greek cooks is their ease around food. This is especially true of the women of Maria's generation: they cook the way their grandmothers taught them, with cheerful nonchalance and

Figure 12. *Cherisia makaronia* at Taverna Makellos, Chios.

simplicity, as though preparing a meal for their family, not an anonymous clientele. I don't seek out places like Taverna Makellos for refinement or luxury, but for the unfussy perfection of their local specialties—only on this island, in this village, beneath this plane tree, will one find the *cherisia makaronia* of Maria Mavrianou. Follow the branchings of her family tree—from her nineteenth-century ancestors, who saw the violent end of Turkish occupation, up to those faded old women by the well, and on to the latest generation—and you'll arrive at this exact spot, where Maria is now bearing a pitcher of tepid water, a bowl of coarse yellow flour, a soufflé cup of olive oil, and an ouzo glass filled with odd little skewers, ready to show a hungry American poet how she makes her famous noodles.

The first steps are familiar and simple enough. She dumps an unmeasured heap of flour into a large plastic bowl. "Is it semolina?" I ask. She merely tips her chin backward, the Greek way of saying "nope." It's just coarse, unbleached durum flour. She mixes in a glug of water with her fingertips and then pounds the dough with her fist, kneading in extra dashes of flour until the texture is right. Finally, she rubs a small piece of dough back and forth between her palms to make a thick pasta snake, its head and tail squirming out from between her hands, and then she cuts the poor snake into uniform little pieces, each one about the size of a chickpea.

What follows leaves me absolutely flummoxed. Maria shapes the first macaroni so quickly I barely realize how difficult it will be until she makes the second one in slow motion, for my benefit. First, she places a tiny ball of dough between her thumb and index finger and with one quick motion smears it into a flattened oval with her thumb, as if making a long *oriechietta*. She then dabs her fingers with a droplet of olive oil and just barely touches one of the skewers. She wraps the dough oval around a skewer and rubs her palms back and forth at lightning speed, so it stretches out along its length (these skewers look like segments of young bamboo, but she explains that they are actually dried stalks of *spartoxylos*, a local reed that hardens into a tough, semiflexible wand about the thickness of spaghetti).

Once Maria demonstrates all this, it seems easy enough. But removing the dough proves nearly impossible: my first attempts either tear apart on the skewer or flatten completely between my palms and wind up looking like trampled night crawlers. Maria does it with the merest flick of her fingertips and off the pasta comes in one clean swipe, looking like tender six-inch *bucatini*, or thin *pici* with a hole running through the middle. She makes the macaroni with astonishing speed and arranges them on a towel in neat rows. Those of mine that aren't entirely crushed or mangled are still of uneven length and thickness, which means they won't cook evenly. Maria elbows me in the bicep and tells me not to worry: "They'll be fed to the dog." She likes her joke so much that she collapses into a fit of giggles, pressing a floury finger across her lips. I may know the recipe, but it's going to take a

Maria's Macaroni

lot of practice to master *cherisia makaronia*—in the meantime, I'm happy to order a portion of it from the waiters, who've been watching me from the sidelines and have now decided to join in with Maria's laughter.

I ask Maria, belatedly, if these *makaronia* have a name. She doesn't understand my question. "Indeed, they are *cherisia makaronia*." But this term— "handmade pasta"—seems too generic. Impossible. There must be another local name for the noodle. A quick lecture by Maria yields this explanation: Of the four pastas made on Chios, this is the only one that actually bears the imprint of one's hand. It is, therefore, "hand pasta." In other villages, she explains, one can find *koulouridia*, short flat noodles like tagliatelle, fashioned with a rolling pin. Again, the dough is simply water and flour (the same thing, a friend reminds me, that one uses to make papier-mâché); eggs are never used in pasta dough here, which surprises me since they are cheap and plentiful. There's a version of the porridge-like *trahanas* too, in which a dough fortified with goat's milk, yogurt, and salt is pressed through a wire mesh and cooked like pastina or couscous. And last, there are *skouloukaki* ("little worms"). Maria grabs another chickpea of dough and shows me how these come into being. Using the same back-and-forth motion of her palms, but without a wand of *spartoxylos* this time, she makes an extremely thin snake— not even the width of angel hair—then rips it into inch-long squiggles that would be dropped into soups or just some rich meat broth. They are vermicelli, of course, as the *makaronades* across the Adriatic call their little worms.

But then Maria explains that there's another, somewhat older name for these little noodles: *fides*. Her evocation of this beautiful word leaves my head bursting with pasta theories. First, in Genoa today, one still finds Ligurian *fidelini*. Second, *fidia* is the Greek word for "snakes": not much of an aural leap from *fides*, of course, nor much of a visual leap from worms.

A glance at Oretta Zanini De Vita's invaluable *Encyclopedia of Pasta* stokes the fire of these fascinating connections. By the fourteenth century, a pasta called *fidej*—or *fideus*—was being made in Genoa. Eventually, this popular delicacy was packed into barrels and loaded onto ships bound for ports scattered across the wine-dark sea. Zanini De Vita writes: "The merchants of Genoa, above all, were responsible for the spread of pasta from the Mediterranean into Europe, and the pasta produced in Liguria quickly became one of the most sought after in international markets." Furthermore, Zanini De Vita quotes documents testifying that Genoese sailors were traveling (and fortifying themselves) with *fidej* right around the time when Chios was handed over to Genoese control by a weary Byzantine emperor.

Did Chian cooks, with their distinguished and ancient history of guest accommodation, learn to please their Genoese visitors with plates of assimilated island *fidej*? *Fidej, fides, fidia*. If so, imagine the possibilities of this culinary pun: those Italian sailors thought they were just eating pasta, while wily Greek chefs had the pleasure of serving their effeminate invaders bowls of oily snakes.

Never mind such excursions fueled by poetic license: Maria has invited me back into the kitchen by now, where her *cherisia makaronia* are boiling for my lunch. Being rather thick, the noodles must roll in a cauldron of boiling salt water for about fifteen minutes before they are dressed with a very simple tomato sauce and a finely grated dry goat cheese. The goat itself was cut into large pieces and braised in an aromatic base of red onion, white wine, and crushed tomato for about two and a half hours: just long enough so it loosens from the bone, but not so long that the subtle, musky flavor of free-range goat—which tastes just slightly, I swear, of the wild thyme and sage I can smell on the Pityos breeze—is cooked away. Sometimes sun-dried tomatoes are added to the braise; Chios is one of the only places in Greece where these are incorporated into traditional cuisine. Some recipes even call for mastic. But such distractions aren't necessary at Makellos. The simplicity of this dish is its main virtue, allowing the goat to take center stage.

I also make sure to order a small portion of *kopanisti*, since Yannis Fekos begged me to try it. It's some of the strongest Greek cheese I've ever tasted.

A fresh goat's-milk *myzithra* is packed into a clay pot and topped with an inch of olive oil, then allowed to ferment for about forty days, unrefrigerated. All the unwelcome microbes are released and absorbed by the antiseptic oil, which is poured off before the cheese is eaten. Though it remains more or less white—or perhaps slightly grey—when I close my eyes I swear I'm eating something moldy. Then the unusual flavor of goat cheese announces itself, reminding me that we are not anywhere near the pampered, hay-loving cows of Denmark or Roquefort. On top of this Chian delicacy, my hosts offer me a good Greek salad, some just-steamed *dolmades*, and a pitcher of slightly chilled red wine. It's a beautiful lot of staggeringly good food.

A Basque shepherd famous for his enormous appetite was once asked by an interviewer whether he thought he could eat an entire goat in one sitting. After a moment's thoughtful silence, he gave this matter-of-fact answer: "Well, sure, but only if I had enough bread." Today, I think I could eat a whole goat, and there's plenty of bread. In fact, it was made by a cousin of Yannis Fekos in an old wood oven right here in Pityos.

Several times during my meal I'm startled by the sounds of gunshots: one every ten minutes or so. I can't help thinking ('tis the season, and the restaurant is about to open for the weekend) that I'm hearing the not-so-distant execution of additional goats. "Of course not," Makellos responds when I ask him if that's the case. "That would be a waste of bullets." Anyway, just across the stream from where I'm dining, I can see a goatherd napping in the shade of an olive tree, his crook leaned up against the trunk while his beasts gnaw weeds and caper in a semicircle around him. It's a very short journey from the pasture to the table here on Chios.

.   .   .

"All the ideas which poetic fancy can form of an earthly paradise seem here realized," the traveler Peter Edmund Laurent wrote of his visit to Chios in 1818. "The face of the country, itself most fruitful, is cultivated with the greatest assiduity; everywhere you ramble through rich vineyards, intermingled with fig trees, loaded with fruit. The valleys are intersected with paths, shaded by trees, spreading over the traveller's head branches bending under the weight of lemons, oranges, and pomegranates. The inhabitants seem willing to join their efforts to add to the charms of their island; by all the foreigner is welcomed, and with delight the traveller hears the peasant's salute. . . ."

Though I receive a similarly warm welcome everywhere I go, and can attest that my own poetic fancy has always been titillated by the island's charms, I fear that Laurent's book captures Chios in what might be its last moment of greatness. Mention the island to any Greek today, and you'll likely get an indignant reminder about what happened here under the Turks in 1822, just a few years after Laurent's account was written.

Thanks to the sultan's liking for mastic, the island enjoyed tremendous privilege for hundreds of years of Ottoman rule. This came to a violent end during the Greek War of Independence in the spring of 1822, when some ornery rebels from the neighboring island of Samos inspired the Chians to take up arms against the Turks. Retaliation was swift and brutal—so brutal, in fact, that it awakened unprecedented public sympathy across Europe, thanks to the rhetoric of writers like Lord Byron and a famous, sickening canvas by Delacroix. In the space of half a year, at least twenty thousand of the island's citizens were slaughtered and three times that many were enslaved.

Nowhere is this history more spookily evident than at Anavatos, a dead village south of Pityos. In a perfect strategic setting, since it straddles a terrifying bluff that's ringed by deep canyons on all sides, Anavatos thrived during the late Byzantine and Ottoman periods: remote, self-sufficient, and intimidating, with a school, church, olive press, and myriad stone houses built atop one another in the classic defensive posture. While the Turks slaughtered and burned everything along the coast, the inhabitants of Anavatos battened down and waited for the siege they knew would come. The men fought for a few days until their ammunition ran out and they surrendered. The four hundred remaining souls—most of them women and children—had to take matters into their own hands. First, the distraught mothers threw their children over the jagged cliffs. Then they followed suit themselves, choosing suicide over lives of servitude in Asia Minor.

.   .   .

I set off early from Volissos in hope of circling all of Mount Amani (and thus, the entire northwest corner of Chios and its necklace of tiny villages) before noon. But I don't get beyond Nea Potamia, the first village, before stopping. A very old man is bent over in the middle of the road, waving his hand up and down, as if patting the head of an invisible boy. At first I think I might be driving too fast, but in fact he's beckoning me. So I pull up beside him and shut off the engine—around us, the village is so quiet I can hear the seconds ticking by on my cooling radiator. The man is wearing a thick wool sweater in spite of the heat and is leaning upon a twisted walking stick the color of dried bone. When he puts his hand on the forearm I'm hanging out the window and leans his face close to mine, all the hairs on the back of my neck rise. I'm sure he's a ghost, for it is impossible how much he resembles my Norwegian grandfather, already dead fifteen years.

I'm even more spooked when he opens his nearly toothless mouth to speak. While his lips spell out "Apo pou eiste?" (Where are you from?), no sound comes except a wheezing rasp from his chest. Then I see: a white mesh bandage has been taped across his larynx. Throat cancer, I suppose. He smiles when I tell him "America," then pats my arm a few times and tells me I'm a "good boy." I smile back, of course, not really sure what else to say, so I compliment his village in a few sentences and ask the way to Hálandra. It's an idiotic question, since it's only a few kilometers up the road, as any moron with a map would know, but his answer is beautiful.

After a deep breath, and with considerable effort, sweeping his arm in a wide circular gesture, he slowly rasps: "Hálandra. Kéramos. Aphrodisia.

Kourounia. Nenitouria. Agia Gala. Melanios. Tripes. Parparia. Pírama. Volissos." There couldn't be a more haunting litany, this catalog of dying places I'll pass on the road today, each name rattling in his perforated throat. After a moment's pause, so he can catch his breath, he lifts the tip of his cane in the direction I'm headed, and whispers: "It was once a very long way by foot. May your road be good."

It's a Tuesday morning. There's not a child in sight in Kéramos, and the courtyard of the school is ankle-deep in eucalyptus trash. It's not been swept since winter. Could there be any surer sign of a village's death? I duck down some stairs beneath the school's empty playground (tiny saplings have grown up around the motionless swing set) and find the ruins of the olive press, its roof collapsed and its machinery rusted black. I'm encouraged, turning down another alley, to find some brightly painted feta tins—now geranium and carnation planters—outside a silent house. To my surprise, I see a nanny goat nibbling weeds beneath a chestnut tree. Her legs have been tied together to keep her from wandering. Someone must water the flowers and tend the lonely goat, but where have they gone? There's no sound at all except the humming of some bees in the flowers and a few noisy crows. Turning back along the upper road, I find the blue door where Ilias and Maria used to live, but it appears to have been shut a long time. Some fallen bougainvillea blossoms, dried to a dark purple, have gathered on the threshold in a pile of dust. I walk around the house to see if anyone's on the balcony. Nothing. I've come back too late.

In Nenitouria, three villages later, I finally find a living being. There, a *kafenion* has just opened its doors and the proprietor (who seems impossibly young for these parts, perhaps only fifty) is sweeping up and futzing around in the kitchen. While she boils my coffee, I circle the room and study the photographs hung about. One in particular draws my attention: about thirty people, all of them dressed for the occasion, are grouped around what looks like an old school bus. A large wreath of flowers has been set upon its hood, and a soldier in uniform stands at attention beside the right front tire. Five

The Lonely Goat of Kéramos

boys have climbed up on the roof and others are gathering in the bus's path on the dirt road. Only one person looks directly into the lens: a little boy wearing a beret and a jacket two sizes too big, who smiles at the camera angelically, as if he's just witnessed a miracle and wants to tell someone about it.

When she brings me my coffee, the proprietor deciphers the image for me: this was the first bus ever to arrive in the village, a few years after the German occupation. What promise! With years of stagnation and hardship behind them, the outside world had arrived at last in the form of this magnificent machine. No wonder all their faces are lit with awe. The attractions of Chios Town would be available now—not to mention the port, its ships, and the cosmopolitan wonders of Athens. This much they understand: the bus has brought them the future. What they don't know is that within a few short decades this same bus—or one just like it—will bear their offspring away, never to return, leaving villages like this one in its dust.

.   .   .

I wake the next day feeling foolish. Why didn't I knock on the door at Ilias and Maria's house in Kéramos? Was I too afraid to find them gone? I decide to drive back up the slopes of Amani one more time to check on them. Kéramos is just as silent as yesterday, but there's no sign of the goat. That's encouraging, since someone must have moved it. But when I find the same pile of blossoms and dust in front of the blue door, I know it can't have been opened since yesterday and my stomach sinks. Since I've come this far, however, I take a deep breath and rap my knuckles on the metal shutters. My knocks echo within the house and no answer comes. Then, just as I've turned to walk back to my car, I hear the door open behind me. When I spin on my heel I see Ilias, squinting in the bright light, one hand shadowing his eyes.

There's no way to tell if he remembers me. When I remind him of his wife's kindness and the *koukia*, however, he nods his head in a way that indicates he might. Ilias is now eighty-seven. His wife's absence is palpable,

Meat: Goats in the Ghost Towns of Chios

and I hesitate to ask after her. When I finally do, he takes her picture from the shelf. "She passed last August," he tells me, "a very good woman." I lack the proper vocabulary to express my sympathies. "My daughter checks in on me, and I work when I can," Ilias continues, "and so my life runs on." Though I'm confident he's not left the house since yesterday, I'm happy to see that he's put himself together in an ironed plaid shirt, some blue jeans, and a knit cap. He's very robust for his age.

By coming, I've obliged his *philoxenia* (literally, "friendship to strangers"— or what we call hospitality, and which all Greeks take very seriously) and thus I regret my stupidity: I should have brought him a gift from town, some small offering at least. If only I'd had more hope that he'd still be here. My heart sinks further when he leads me out to the patio, has me sit in a wicker chair, and then apologizes: he regrets he has nothing to offer me.

"No, wait," he says after a moment, rising from his chair to step back into the kitchen. He brings me a bottle of water, having poured a glass from the tap for himself, and then he unwraps a few morsels of cheese and bread from a towel and sets them on a plate before me. "From yesterday," he says, "but still good."

Piled on tables around us are sheets of tin and some thick dowels. Out of these, he crafts *farasia*—little dust pans—"something to keep my hands busy," he says. He creases the tin and fastens it to brightly painted handles with decorative silver rivets. There's no way he will allow me to buy one, of course, no matter how much I protest. I promise to use it proudly in my wood-burning *fournos* back in the United States.

"Sto kalo," he says when I stand to leave. "Go with the good." Before I climb back into my car at the top of the village, I turn one last time to wave good-bye. He's waited there on the threshold, the blue door ajar behind him, one motionless hand raised in a friendly salute. From where I stand, I can take in all that remains of Kéramos in one glance, and it appears to be swallowing Ilias up, and the lush green crags of Mount Amani behind him too, slowly closing in.

Sto Kalo

REVÍTHOKEFTEDES

The Greeks inherited their word *keftés* from the Turkish *köfta*, which the Turks themselves borrowed from the Persian *köfte*. Across the Levant, that's your go-to phrase when you want minced meat. But the Greeks take that abstract idea and run with it. Every Greek grandmother has her recipe for *keftedes*— simple beef or lamb meatballs that are fried up and devoured by hungry grandchildren. But she also knows that almost any edible thing can be pulverized, seasoned, bound with flour, rolled into a ball, and fried. Once they become vegetable- or seafood-based, it seems a little strange to still call them "balls" (my daughter was revolted by the idea of eating "octopus balls," for instance, and "green balls" didn't sound much better), so I'm going with "croquettes" instead.

Most common are *kolokythokeftedes* (zucchini croquettes seasoned with onion and mint), *hortokeftedes* (wild green croquettes), and *domatokeftedes* (tomato croquettes). Octopus and salt cod croquettes are excellent too. Once, Tasos of Thasos even made me croquettes out of some sea anemone. They were slightly poisonous when raw, he told us, but wouldn't be after they'd been cooked. That's fortunate, since they were delicious.

Looking toward the East, as their menu often does, the Chians make *revíthokeftedes*, or chickpea croquettes, laced with mint and cumin. They resemble falafel only superficially, but like their Levantine cousins, these chickpea patties (from the village of Avgonyma on Chios) pack a lot of healthy vegetarian protein.

  1 pound dried chickpeas

  1 teaspoon baking soda

  1 red onion, minced

  ¼ cup cornmeal

  3 tablespoons fresh mint, finely chopped

  1 teaspoon dried oregano

1 teaspoon ground cumin

2 teaspoons sea salt

2 teaspoons ground pepper

All-purpose flour, for dredging

Olive oil, for frying

Soak the dried chickpeas overnight, then rinse them well and toss them in a bowl of fresh water with the baking soda. Let the soda go to work for 10 minutes, then rinse the chickpeas again. Now bring them to a simmer in a deep pot of water. Boil for 1 to 2 hours, or until they are just a little beyond al dente. Drain well and allow to cool.

Combine the cooked chickpeas along with the red onion, cornmeal, mint, oregano, cumin, salt, and pepper in a food processor, or smash until very smooth with a mortar and pestle. The resulting batter must be thick enough to shape into small patties—add some additional cornmeal if necessary.

Make small, round patties that are about 1/2-inch thick and toss them on a plate of all-purpose flour, tapping off any excess flour before frying them. Heat about 1/4 inch of olive oil in a deep skillet and fry the fritters about 3 minutes per side, until very hot and slightly golden. Remove to drain on paper towels and serve while still hot.

CHAPTER SIX

Beans

Chasing Chickpeas at Plati Yialós

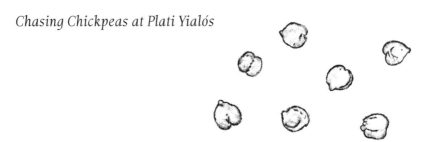

I can't believe Vitos remembers me. I mean, we had only one conversation, about vegetables, three years ago. But he grabs my hand enthusiastically and welcomes me back to Serifos with a gap-toothed grin. I'm just finishing my first lunch back on the island, nibbling a few *mezedes* at one of the mediocre joints on the port, when he stops in to do some business with its proprietor. The name of Vitos's own restaurant, Akroyiali, is splashed across the side of his pickup truck. It's on the list of places I want to visit as soon as I have a chance to venture beyond these hit-or-miss restaurants in the port town of Livadi, where I'll be participating in a series of literary seminars for several weeks. It's still the off-season, and Serifos is generally quite sleepy no matter what the time of year, so our presence on the island (there are about forty writers here) constitutes something close to an invasion. But we are welcome invaders: Greece is about to default on its loans and the future looks bleak. There's some desperation legible on the faces of the shop owners along the waterfront this summer; they can certainly use our business.

Vitos, on the other hand, couldn't care less for the vicissitudes of economic policy. For him, it's all about the food. He looks disapprovingly at the plates I've been served, cocks his cap mischievously, and says I must come to see him soon. By way of reminding me why I should, he rummages around in the back of his truck and fills a plastic bag with about twenty just-picked cucumbers, which he thumps down on my table, refusing payment. Vitos is known across the island for his produce, which he grows in a fertile little watershed outside the remote seaside hamlet of Sikamya.

The last time I was on Serifos, a friend directed me to Akroyiali and I had an excellent meal there, made up mostly of things that had been pulled from the earth a few hundred yards away. When I went inside the kitchen to give my compliments to the chef, she accepted one or two sentences of praise and then pointed out a farmer on the patio, who she said deserved the real credit. Vitos was wearing a felt cap and a filthy denim shirt and was seated at a corner table with some other, drowsy-looking old men. Empty demitasses and a shared ashtray littered their table. After introducing myself and extolling the food I'd just been served (singling out the perfectly crisp, sweet cucumbers in my salad), I made the mistake of asking Vitos if he farmed organically. "Ohi!" he replied, stamping a dusty boot on the marble floor. "No, *much more* than organic! They grow right here!" A pretentious concept like "organic" is foolish, he intimated, since no other kind of farming makes any sense at all. You weren't going to find me arguing with him on that point.

Vitos said I knew a lot about farming "for an American." I'm not sure I do, but since I run a produce cooperative out of my garage in Pennsylvania, I've spent a lot of time standing in fields (along with the Amish farmer who supplies us with vegetables) chatting about the habits of arugula and heirloom tomatoes. Such talk is dear to farmers on every continent, and Vitos seemed happy to rehearse his love for agriculture, even with total strangers like me.

Places like Akroyiali represent an archetype of Greek dining. The cook buys fish off the boat (if she hasn't caught it herself), harvests produce from her own gardens, buys meat from her neighbors or hunts it in the hills, and serves a "menu" that changes according to seasonal availability. No, I'm not describing Chez Panisse, though Alice Waters often takes her cues from these idyllic mom-and-pop joints in the Mediterranean. As Vitos made clear with his proud indignation, fashionable concepts like "local" and "organic" and "sustainable" have always been a priori facts of existence in much of Greece.

Printed menus are almost completely useless in such places. Typically, if they have a hardbound menu, it's there only to present a theoretical overview of the dishes that the restaurant *might* offer on a given day. What's actually available *today* is another matter, and you'll find that out when the waiter tells you, or when you walk into the kitchen yourself to have a look. Go ahead—customers are usually welcome to stroll in and ask questions about the food.

These delightful culinary outposts are, however, becoming increasingly hard to find in the Greek islands. The more accessible an island is, the more likely it is to be "developed"—which implies competing restaurants with written menus one is actually meant to follow. Since most of the food served at these places comes out of the freezer, their menus are predictable and their food stale. In such pits, one is sometimes served wedges of an insipid tomato grown in Germany or Denmark, right in the middle of tomato season in Greece. Such are the culinary blasphemies of the Eurozone.

But you'll find nothing of that sort on Serifos, at least once you get off the beaten path. You can't even get to Serifos via the usual Cycladic ferry routes (which connect more fashionable places like Mykonos and Santorini). Rather, Serifos is linked by ferry to a chain of islands that few tourists have ever heard of: Siphnos, Milos, Kimolos, and Folegrandos. Even during high season, Serifos is rarely mobbed, which means that the frozen food and restaurant supply purveyors aren't as likely to come by ship from Athens to peddle their homogenous garbage.

Furthermore, on Serifos, as if by tacit agreement among island elders, most of the spectacular beaches have just one restaurant, and each of them is fairly self-sustaining. This fact shapes human behavior in delightful ways, since one often chooses a beach for its restaurant, or a restaurant for its beach. The question *What are we hungry for?* needs to be answered in tandem with the equally compelling question *Where do we want to swim?* Granted, at times the choice is dictated by the gods. Patrick Leigh Fermor declared Serifos the "windiest of the Cyclades," and most days on the island begin like this: if the wind is blowing sand in your face while you sip your coffee, then you make plans to retreat to the opposite side of the island, where the water will be calm; if the wind is blowing at your back, sending napkins skittering off the patio in the direction of the sea, you choose a *taverna* and a cove closer to home.

Akroyiali has everything to recommend it on the days when the wind is in your face, and the wide, sandy beach at Sikamya isn't unappealing at all (I've spent many hours there hunting *barbounia* with a speargun). But my sentimental favorite on that side of the island is actually Taverna Nikoúlias, where I had my first encounter with Serifosian chickpeas. The restaurant's patio is perched on the arid headland above the double lagoons of Plati Yialós. My wife and I went there when our kids were still very small, and we found it perfectly suited to our needs. Running parallel to the larger beach is an outcropping of marl with a tide pool that is perpetually refilled with warm water and hermit crabs—a perfect kiddie pool, in other words. That meant we could relax on our beach towels without having to jump up and rescue our offspring from the waves every few seconds. My daughter and son would spend hours romping in the shallow water, capturing crabs and fashioning habitats for them in the bottoms of their garish plastic buckets. Then, all of a sudden, they would be famished and on the verge of hunger tantrums. We'd make them return their pets to the sea (these were difficult, tearful liberations) and then we'd hike up to the restaurant on the hill.

There, a young man named Aris Monovasios ran his parents' sparklingly clean, well-organized kitchen. The service and the food were always so good, and the view from the restaurant's balcony so lovely, that we were a little sad to find that we were often the restaurant's only customers (when we came back one Saturday afternoon and found the place packed with locals, we understood that they weren't dependent on tourism at all). The kids would guzzle ice water, devour roasted potatoes and garlic-and-mint-seasoned *keftedes*, and then pass out on their beach towels on the cool stones of the shaded patio. My wife and I would order three or four *mezedes* to share—typically a salad, some real *taramosalata* (a fish roe spread that is often artificially pink in tourist restaurants, but was left its natural off-white color here), a few marinated anchovies, and the pièce de résistance: a bowl of *revithia*, or stewed chickpeas.

It seemed impossible that a bowl of beans could be so delicious. Normally, I have little trouble puzzling out a dish's ingredients and preparation; I taught myself to cook by mouth the way others learn to play piano by ear. But the chickpeas at Taverna Nikoúlias stumped me. It was obvious that they'd been simmered for a long time in liquid—presumably in meat stock—but not so long that they'd fallen apart. They were swimming in a dark tan gravy that was earthy, voluptuous, and appealingly sweet. I extracted a large bay leaf from one bowl, but I couldn't seem to pinpoint the flavor that held the dish together. So I asked the waitress if I might have a word in the kitchen. Maria, Aris's mother, was sheepish at first, but at last she gave in, murmuring that the chickpeas were cooked "in water, with olive oil, rosemary, bay leaves, and many onions."

"How many onions?" I asked, but she only pursed her lips and waved her fingers in a little circle, as if splashing herself with water from a bowl, which is how Greeks indicate abundance.

"For how many hours?" I pleaded.

"Until they are done," she replied, as if bewildered by the stupidity of my question.

I pushed her a little: "Three, four, five hours? And do you cook them on the stove or in the oven?"

"*Entaxi*, my boy," she said after another pause. "In the oven. Until they become chocolaty."

So that was it: the "many" onions had completely disintegrated, imparting to the finished dish something of the dusky warmth and sweetness of chocolate. Her use of such a perfect, poetic description made me forgive her reticence. Still, it was hard to fathom how such complexity could come from such simple ingredients. Could onions really be transformed into chocolate? One day, I vowed to my wife, I'd get to the bottom of this island alchemy.

. . .

While very easy on the eye, much of the landscape of Greece is incompatible with agriculture, being dry, rocky, and at times completely barren. For thousands of years, Greeks have had to rely on their wits and tenacity to fend off starvation. In addition to surviving, of course, they also found time to cook up philosophy, mathematics, astronomy, athletics, and a beautiful system of mythology. And they did all this while constantly trying (and sometimes failing) to parry invaders. The Greeks, of all people, have learned that war and hunger almost always go hand in hand. No wonder, then, that the Greek love affair with the bean is ancient and passionate.

Because they are a rich source of protein and can be dried and stored indefinitely, and because they are not only capable of thriving in thin, sandy soil, but add nitrogen to the soil rather than leach it away, beans—by which I really mean pulses, or the seeds of legumes—are the perfect crop for this part of the world. According to food historian Andrew Dalby, the cultivation of pulses accompanied the development of civilization: lentils were already a staple in prehistoric times, and chickpeas and broad beans arrived a little later, being cultivated in Thessaly (the breadbasket of Greece) by 4000 B.C.

It is no surprise, then, that pulses have left their mark on the Greek literary record. In the *Iliad*, Homer describes how the arrows of the minor hero Helenus glance off the breastplate of Atrides as harmlessly as "black-skin beans and chickpeas bounce and leap / from a big bladed shovel, flying across the threshing floor." In Plato's *Republic*, Socrates and Glaukon include chickpeas in the list of things that should be available for maintaining health and peace in the ideal city. Hippocrates himself lauds their nutritional value. Such praise is partially tempered by Aristophanes (the John Belushi of ancient dramatists), who seasoned many of his plays with fart jokes. Theocritus, meanwhile, seemed to associate bean eating with bucolic decadence. In his seventh Idyll he writes:

> I by the fire shall quaff Ptelean wine,
> And one shall roast me beans, while I recline
> Luxurious, lying on a fragrant heap
> Of asphodel and parsley, elbow-deep. . . .

Like the Italians, who celebrate the virtues of *la cucina povera*, the Greeks take pride in a cuisine that has been shaped by scarcity and consequent frugality. "We ate bread and salt together," runs a common Greek saying, used when one wishes to express a sense of shared hardship, and a survivalist streak informs the ethos of the Greek table, though that ethos may be eroding. Since joining the European Union in 1981, Greeks have enjoyed a period of enormous prosperity, and the youngest generation has never had to contend with the hunger their grandparents (and maybe even their parents) remember too well. Could this be the first generation of Greeks to take food for granted? The older generation certainly doesn't. When I lived in Thessaloniki in the 1990s, I'd often see elderly men and women foraging for weeds on the hillsides outside the affluent suburb of Panórama. They'd do this out of habit, not necessity, finding it illogical to buy pricey "wild greens" at the supermarket when they could be picked for free within walking distance.

With the Greek economy in shambles, such practices may soon become necessary again. When I recently asked my friend Adrianne Kalfopoulou (who, as the author of a book called *Wild Greens*, knows wherof she speaks)

Beans: Chasing Chickpeas at Plati Yialós

what she thought about the "food of the poor," she sardonically replied, "Oh, yes, we'll be eating *to fai ton ftochon* for the next decade."

Along with rugged barley (a hardier grain than wheat) and olives, the humble bean is a cornerstone of Greek cuisine. If the country has a national dish, it's probably *fasolada*, a simple white bean soup dressed with olive oil and eaten with moistened *paximadia*. Few dishes are more sustaining, nutritious, and evocative of antiquity. Barley, olives, and beans: these same three crops sustained the armies of Alexander the Great.

In addition to *fasolada*, several other bean dishes frequently appear at the Greek table. The white broad beans charmingly called *yigantes* are stewed with a bit of tomato and fresh herbs. Another popular bean dish is ordered as *fava pandremeni:* yellow split peas "married" with onions and cooked down to a delicious mash resembling Indian dal. Black-eyed peas, too, can be found when in season (they are typically eaten fresh). And stewed lentils are not uncommon in winter.

Hummus, on the other hand, is almost never found on Greek tables, to the astonishment of many travelers who've only eaten "Greek" food in restaurants outside Greece. The Greeks prefer their chickpeas—or *revithia*—boiled or made into soup. On Lesbos and Chios, one finds *revithokeftedes:* falafel-like chickpea croquettes held together with cornmeal and flavored with red onion, oregano, and mint. In Macedonia and Thrace, among the last parts of Greece to throw off the Ottoman yoke, bars will serve you dry-roasted chickpeas, which the Turks call *leblebie* and eat obsessively. (To me, they have the texture and flavor of burnt sand, but they do induce thirst, and perhaps that's the point.) Like all the other beans, chickpeas have come to the rescue during tough times: Yannis Fekos from Chios tells me that when coffee disappeared during the German occupation, chickpeas were toasted in a pan, ground, and then brewed as a surprisingly good substitute.

But the tastiest preparation for chickpeas in all of Greece was developed on Serifos and its sister island, Siphnos (the two are separated by a narrow

Humble Beans

strait). Pottery has something to do with it. The clay on Siphnos can with-stand unusually high temperatures, and one of the most famous pottery workshops of ancient Greece was located there (the island is still the home to some of the most skilled potters in the archipelago). When the potters of Siphnos weren't fashioning art objects, they were throwing more utilitarian vessels for the kitchen, including *skepastariá*: decoratively painted, potbel-lied casseroles with tight-fitting lids. Since nobody wants to sit around a fire pit to keep a pot boiling for five or six hours, most of the casserole dishes in Greece were designed to be used in a wood oven. After the day's bread was baked in the communal *fournos*, families would arrive with their *skepastariá* filled with chickpeas, onions, herbs, and water. These would be pushed into the vault so that the beans would cook slowly, absorbing all the residual heat from the bricks. A casserole full of rich, hunger-slaying *revithia* would be ready by the time families gathered for their evening meal.

. . .

In addition to its famous chickpeas, Serifos has two famous sons: Perseus and Polyphemos. According to local legend, the former brought the decapi-tated head of Medusa to the island and pitched it in a deep hole beneath the old town, the Chora (Pausanias suggests that he took the head to Argos, but who knows). The latter raised sheep in a Serifosian cave and is best known as the violent and dunderheaded Cyclops of Homer's *Odyssey*. At Koutalas, one of the best beaches on the island, you can swim in the glorious turquoise lagoon where an indignant Polyphemos heaved that boulder at Odysseus and his men.

. . .

On my first free day on the island, I have a difficult decision to make: with the wind blowing in my face, should I head for Plati Yialós or Sikamya? My leguminous longings win out, and I lead a troop of hungry writers over the

Figure 13. Chora, the whitewashed capital of Serifos.

mountain to Aris's place. I'm itching to see if his chickpeas are as delicious and chocolaty as I remember them. I'm hoping, too, that he'll be willing to give me a more detailed account of how they're made.

Aris seems pleased to see me and asks politely after my wife and children. They'll join me here in a few weeks, and I promise to bring them for lunch. As for his news: his mother has put him in charge of the restaurant at last. I like his perfunctory manner and fine-featured face, behind which he shows very little emotion. He's as inscrutable as they come, but a wizard behind the stove.

My friends and I are happy to hear that Aris has a dozen just-caught *barbounia* in his refrigerator, and we vow to eat them all after we swim in the lagoon below the restaurant. Even in June, the Cyclades can be sweltering, but the weather is perfect today: warm enough for swimming, but not so hot that one broils while taking a siesta on the beach's fine brown sand. As we hoped, the water is almost completely calm on this side of the island. Occasionally, a colorful toy ship churns across the strait, causing waves to chatter along the edges of the lagoon minutes later. Beyond that, not much happens. My friend Scott hunts for big fish with his harpoon. Pam swims out far, until she's just a blonde head bobbing in the blue distance, leaving her companion Greg to cast worried glances in her direction. In the shade of a tamarisk, Joanna teaches Carolyn Greek by walking her through a George Seferis poem; they are charming and unobtrusive scholars. Marcia wades in the shallows. And I cruise the lagoon with my mask and snorkel, looking for octopus dens and building my appetite.

After we dry off and hike back uphill to the restaurant, the meal begins. First come *pantzaria* (beets boiled with their greens), served with a dollop of stinky *skordalia* (a garlic paste held together by olive oil and moistened bread), and some excellent steamed *horta*. We also order several bowls of *choriatiki salata*, the classic Greek salad of tomatoes, cucumbers, peppers, and onions. But on Serifos, rather than the usual slab of feta on top, you get some fresh, tart *myzithra*, which melts into the salad's olive oil and coats every ingredient. Since capers grow like weeds across the island, you get those as well, their briny acid counterbalancing the dairy fat of the cheese.

Next comes *revithia* and a portion of the sublime baked eggplant dish called *imam bayildi*. Carolyn saw one of the waiters eating *imam* on his break; it's her favorite offering on the Greek table and she insists that we order it. In fact, she loves the dish so much that we've eaten *imam* at every possible occasion. Aris's version is particularly good, and I vow to ask him about it later.

The *barbounia* come out last. They are sweet and fresh, just as they should be, and we swiftly dismantle them, transforming the beautiful rosy fish into a pile of delicate, very clean bones.

Finally, Aris emerges from the kitchen to offer us cold beers on the house and to ask if we're satisfied. I assure him that we are, and that we'll be returning for more meals over the coming weeks. I also ask him whether I might join him some morning in the kitchen to learn the secrets of Serifosian chickpeas—purely for research purposes, I add.

"OK," he says without any pause. "Come early tomorrow morning. We'll make *revithia* and *imam bayildi.*"

I love this about Greek cooks. They are not guarded or secretive about what they do, and their recipes, being traditional, don't allow for a lot of creative variation.

This, at any rate, is my general experience. But I was about to be confronted by an alarming exception to the rule.

.   .   .

Aris is already hard at work when we arrive back at Plati Yialós early the next morning, but he stops what he's doing to welcome us and offer us coffee. Fortunately, he seems unperturbed by my literary beach-rat entourage. My writer friends couldn't get enough of Plati Yialós yesterday and have crossed the mountain with me once again. They're firing their cameras like paparazzi and crowding the kitchen, but Aris doesn't seem to mind.

Someone else in the kitchen seems less pleased by our presence. He's a nervous kid named Marios, dressed in full chef whites. Frankly, he seems a little out of place. Aris recently brought him over from Athens, where he completed three years of culinary school. It remains to be seen whether that attention to kitchen hierarchy and knife skills will serve him well in a family kitchen out here in the middle of nowhere. Either way, I'm sure the last thing he wants is to have a bunch of Americans poking around and watching his every move.

He's certainly capable, but perhaps too meticulous. He's peeled at least twenty onions and is now slicing them with his very large and very fancy knife. Aris, meanwhile, removes the lid from a deep kettle to show us the two kilos of *revithia* he's soaked overnight. At this point, some Serifosians add a bit of baking soda, which is thought to tenderize the chickpeas and make them more digestible. Aris looks incredulous when we ask him about this; he thinks soda ruins the chickpeas' texture. No, he merely gives them a rinse before transferring them to a pressure cooker with a drink of fresh water, where they'll precook for thirty minutes.

By the time Aris locks down the lid, Marios has reduced his mountain of onions by only a few, so Aris grabs a handful and goes to work, hacking the onions into perfectly thin, uniform slices about three times as fast as his apprentice.

"The secret to this dish is in the quantity of onions," Aris says, making eye contact with his audience while his knife flashes through another onion. "For two kilos of *revithia* I'll probably use all twenty of these, even if that seems like a lot."

It's not a complicated dish. Besides water and oil, it has only three ingredients: chickpeas, onions, and rosemary. But of course all the ingredients are of very high quality. The onions have the perfect balance of sharpness and sweetness. The rosemary is wonderfully pungent, having been cut from a bush that remains vigorously green in spite of the intensity of this desert landscape. Aris dries the rosemary a little before use, which tames some of its turpentine without altogether subduing its rich, minty essence. He knows it's dry enough when it falls off the stalk with a light sweep of the fingers. As for the tiny, dried chickpeas—well, today these come from the Peloponnese. I'm not surprised to hear that few people bother growing legumes on Serifos anymore, since the crops are so meager. But I *am* surprised when Aris tells me that nowadays Greece imports a lot of chickpeas from Canada. That seems like an awfully long way for a bean to travel. But I'm in no position to judge, having come just as far chasing the chickpeas of Plati Yialós.

In addition to the quantity of onions, what's crucial here is technique. Aris heats a massive, short-sided cauldron over a wide blue ring of flame, adds a substantial amount of olive oil, and then throws in all the onions at once. They fill the kitchen with a cinnamon sweetness as they begin to caramelize. He lets them develop a rich brown color, which gives the finished dish its chocolaty hue. After popping the lid on the pressure cooker, which has sped up the cooking process by several hours, Aris pours the chickpeas, along with their cooking liquid, on top of the onions. Then he tosses in a handful of rosemary and tops the dish off with more water and another glug of olive oil. Into a four-hundred-degree oven the uncovered cauldron goes. When I ask Aris about the absence of bay leaves, he confesses that he doesn't always include them—though his mother usually does.

"That's it?" I ask.

"Nothing more," he replies. "Heat is the other ingredient. We must let it do the rest of the work."

So, Serifosian *revithia* are essentially chickpeas flavored with lilies and trees: onions being a member of the lily family, and forests of rosemary being some of the island's most hearty vegetation. Aris chooses not to add laurel, or "bay," whose leaves do grow on trees all over Greece (where they're called *daphne*, after the girl who saved herself from Apollo by turning into a laurel). Other cooks on Serifos forgo the rosemary and use six to eight *daphne* leaves instead. It's up to the cook to choose her tree.

With the chickpeas in the oven, the chefs turn to a pile of small eggplants, splitting them in half lengthwise. I notice that Carolyn is front and center, as eager as I am to see how Aris puts his spin on this famous dish. Few things on the Greek menu embody history as fully as *imam bayildi*—a Turkish dish that can be found anywhere from Athens to Armenia. The story of its origins, which Greeks repeat with as much fascination as Turks, is told in many versions, but they all end in the same punch line: "the imam fainted," or *imam bayildi*. My favorite version goes like this: an imam commands his chef (more patriarchal versions have him commanding his wife) to invent the best eggplant dish he can. The chef succeeds so well that the imam faints after eating it, *either* because it was so rich and delicious, or because he's learned how much expensive olive oil was used in its preparation. Because not that much olive oil goes into the dish, and because olive oil is plentiful in this part of the world, I tend to side with delicious.

Aris begins by submerging the split eggplants in a bowl of very salty water, where their bitterness dissipates and the flesh contracts slightly, so that it will soak up less oil in the next stage of cooking (eggplant flesh is like a sponge and will otherwise drink as much oil as you offer). After removing the eggplants from the water and drying them off with a towel, he fries them flesh side down until they begin to soften and take on color, and then drains them on paper towels. Next he thinly slices six or seven green peppers, while Marios slices more onions (beyond this repetitive and unpleasant task, I've not seen him do much else this morning). These are sautéed together.

"No garlic?" I ask Aris, since other versions I know include it. Once again he just tips back his chin by way of saying "less is more."

Aris puts the eggplants on their backs in a large, round vessel, piles the limp onions and peppers on top, and adds sliced fresh tomatoes on top of those. Then he dissolves about a half cup of tomato paste in warm water and pours it around the dressed eggplants. After an hour of roasting, what results is a rich nightshade broth—the person holding the last crust of bread at the meal's end gets to mop this up.

At home, when I make *imam bayildi*, I add parsley, garlic, and a dash of cinnamon to the onion mixture. On Thasos, Tasos bakes his *imam* in a wood oven, which gives a caramelized sweetness to the onion and pepper topping. In Aris's more austere version, the flavor of the eggplant predominates.

With the *imam* and *revithia* gurgling away in the oven, we realize that we should probably clear out of the kitchen: class dismissed, at least until lunchtime. We head back down to the lagoon to rinse the scent of onions from our skin. Just as I'm about to dive in, however, I hear someone calling me from the restaurant. It's Marios. I see the arms of his white uniform waving in my direction. So I return to the patio, where Marios is seated with the matriarch, Maria.

She's not happy. In her view, I'm an American cookbook writer who's come to Serifos to steal recipes from the island's venerable restaurants, which I'll sell at an *enormous* profit. My friends are not writers, but a camera crew in disguise, here to document my cooking lesson for an American magazine or television show. Didn't someone have a video camera out for a little while? In short, Maria is accusing me of culinary piracy. The idea makes me laugh out loud on behalf of my compatriots, who are innocent of everything but curiosity (and, in Carolyn's case, an obsession with *imam bayildi*).

But Maria's mainly interested in her own cut. What percentage of the profits will she get? When I protest that I'm not writing a cookbook exactly but am eating my way around the island, she refuses to be convinced.

"Sas parakalo kyrie . . . ," she says, using the most formal possible address. "Please, Sir, print here your full name, passport number, and the name of your hotel. I would like to call them to verify your identity."

Her next move, I think, is to summon the island's one policeman and have him escort me to the brig. Then my friends will be asked to surrender their cameras. My notebooks (full of subversive lines of verse) will be confiscated and we'll all be booted off the island.

I'm completely bewildered and also angry, having been a loyal customer here for several summers. In over two decades of living and traveling in Greece, I've rarely encountered anything but kindness and generosity. The ancients welcomed strangers in the name of Zeus, I want to remind Maria. But her accusation has thrown me off kilter, and I'm left speechless and blushing.

Fuming, I stare off at the horizon, where another toy ferry is passing through the strait. It must be full of greedy foreigners like me, I think, a wave of guilt washing over me. Maybe I *am* a kitchen imperialist, an overcurious barbarian nosing around in other people's gustatory business. Wasn't I exploiting Aris's generosity (though I note that Aris isn't here making these accusations himself) and wasn't it presumptuous to think of his recipes as communal property? True, every grandmother on the island knows how to make *revithia*, but I'd come here because it was beautiful and because Plati Yialós's *revithia* were so damn good. And, yes, because here I could have my octopus hunting and eat lunch too.

But, but, but. I know what really brought me here: love for this rugged island, its small population of survivalists, and this country, whose customs, manners, and table I adore. I remind myself that times are hard in Greece. Maria looks much older and sadder than I remember her, and I can only guess at the depth of her anxieties.

"Maria, Maria," I say. "Forgive me for liking your *revithia* so much." At that, her shoulders loosen a little. I do my best to look charming, in spite of the fact that I'm gritting my teeth.

"There is nothing I want to take from you, or your family. If you wish, I promise never to mention your chickpeas in my book." I look into her eyes when I say this, and I mean it. Marios is shifting uncomfortably now, and I wonder whether he's an innocent bystander in this business or its instigator. To him, I offer only a manly and perhaps too aggressive nod of my head. Then I square my shoulders and continue.

"Or, Kyria Maria, I will do what I'd hoped to do when I came here this morning. I wished to learn from your son Aris what you taught him about making the chickpeas of Plati Yialós, and I wanted to include a description of them in my book. Then people would know that Maria Monovasios makes the best *revithia* on the island. If they know what's good for them, they'll find their way here to Serifos and try them for themselves."

That heartfelt sentiment seems to win her over.

"Now please, Kyria, write your own address here so I can send you a copy of my book, in case it ever gets published."

She spends a long time writing out her address very neatly, and even Marios scribbles his. But this is a Pyrrhic victory. I leave them feeling like a real creep. I stop halfway down the stairs to rip a sprig of rosemary from a bush and thrust it into my mouth. I want something on my tongue to match the unexpected bitterness I've just experienced.

When I return to settle my bill later that afternoon, Maria is nowhere to be seen. But Aris comes out to shake my hand. "I'm so sorry if we were any trouble," I tell him. "Thank you for the cooking lesson."

"Don't think of it again," he replies, to my relief. "I welcome you here every day. Tomorrow I am fixing some beautiful *yigantes*."

. . .

Even in midsummer, the winds of Serifos can begin howling and the temperature will suddenly drop. This is a pan-Cycladic phenomenon, but the wind seems to be especially intense on Serifos. When it starts up this year, everyone gets depressed, complaining of headaches and sore throats. Nothing tastes as it should, all writing comes to a standstill, and we're visited by bizarre dreams. Villagers claim that vampires are flushed from their hiding places in such weather. "Everyone / on this island," my friend Aliki Barnstone writes of Serifos, "knows the wind carries the voices / of ghosts."

One night I dream I'm dining in a restaurant in Pennsylvania, but for some reason Maria is there. When she hands me the menu, I'm horrified to find only burgers and fries on it—no *revithia* or *imam bayildi* in sight. While Maria describes the revolting soup of the day (whose main ingredient seems to be American cheese), her hair coils into snakes, which writhe in a halo around her head. She's smiling at me, but even in my dream I know to look away, avoiding her petrifying gaze.

When things get this bad, *rakomelo* is the only thing that helps, even if that means ascending the mountain and diving right into the heart of the wind, which pits all of its force against the ancient whitewashed buildings of the old town, the Chora. It's worth climbing one hundred stairs to get to Strato's Café, where they have the best *rakomelo* on the island. The drink, which consists of strong island *raki* mulled with honey and spices, is served warm in little glass carafes, and you sip it while clutching your cup, huddled with your friends against the wind. *Rakomelo* warms your insides and takes the edge off your madness.

After a few glasses I find I have to pee. The men's room at Strato's is completely dark, and through a hidden air vent the wind is shrieking and clanging. I feel around the doorjamb and run my hands along the walls, hoping to find the light switch. At last, when I step forward into the darkness, the light flickers on. Seen in the bathroom mirror, I look vaguely Medusa-like myself, my wind-whipped hair sticking out every which way. Beneath the mirror, a handwritten sign explains in Greek that the light is activated by a motion detector. There's also an English translation: "MOVEMENT IS REQUIRED FOR ILLUMINATION." Given the extra meanings of the word *movement* in a lavatory setting, I find this hilarious. But I take heart in the sign's unintentional profundity too.

Most days on the island, it's easy to forget we're moving at all. Once the wind dies down, we settle into a blissful and slothful routine. There are morning visits to the market and bakery, some seminar activity and writing time, and then long afternoons spent swimming and eating with my wife and kids, who join me for the second half of the month. We divide most of our free time between Sikamya (where a litter of kittens scampers about the garden, to the delight of Sophia and Alexander) and Plati Yialós (where I have no more run-ins with Maria). These are the places I'll miss most when I leave.

. . .

Among all that pleasure and slow movement, there's only one frustration. On my return trip from the market every day I drive past a sign advertising "local traditional cheese," but I can't seem to make contact with the cheese maker, Rita Paraskevopoulou. I've dialed her number every day for a week, but the phone just rings and rings.

Finally, near the end of my stay, I try the number again, and this time Rita picks up right away. Following her directions, I drive to an industrial area outside Livadi. At last I find the little blue arrow she promised I'd see on a concrete slab at her property's edge. She waves from the top step when I pull in.

Rita is the most cheerful person I've ever met. When she laughs, she throws her whole body into it, scrunching her shoulders forward, clenching her fists, and nodding her unnaturally reddish curls up and down, all the while emitting a high-pitched whinny. She has a prodigious nose and thick arms strengthened by years of farmwork, and I have to suppress an urge to hug her (we've only just met).

She leads me into a foyer lined with shelves of homemade delicacies: salted caper berries, dried tomatoes, *limoncello*, *raki*, and spoon sweets made from figs, quince, tangerines, and green walnuts. There's also a refrigerator full of cheese. Rita has eighty goats and a hundred sheep, which she milks in a pen adjacent to her kitchen.

Since I haven't seen Rita's products in the local markets, I wonder how she moves the stuff. Mostly, she explains, she sells her wheels of *kefalogra-viera* to her neighbors, though she also supplies a few restaurants with fresh *myzithra*. But only those she trusts.

"Everyone will say they buy their *myzithra* from me, but that's not true. Much of it is frozen and some of it even arrives by boat. I only sell to restaurants who promise to serve it the same day, when it's still sweet. After that, it's too late." She pauses for a moment before bursting into laughter again, at the absurdity of cheese fraud, I guess.

While we nibble her cheeses, she tells stories about her four-year-old grandson, who recently told her that he wants to be a shepherd or a politician when he grows up. "Either way," Rita says, her giggle rising in anticipation of the punch line, "I told him he'd spend his life yelling, but at least if he's a shepherd he'll be able to keep his flock in order." At that, she cackles and bobs up and down until she's completely out of breath. The joke *is* much funnier given the current chaos of Greek politics.

The same grandson, she continues, was recently told he'll be inheriting this farm one day. He looked up at his grandfather to see if he was joking, then stretched out his arms imperiously and declared, "It's all mine!" That sets off another fit of laughter in us both. Rita has to wipe tears away with the back of her hand in order to write up my bill for all the stuff I'm buying.

Just then, her husband Yorgos walks in. My nose tells me he's been working. He's a jowly fellow with bags under his eyes. When we shake hands, mine feels tiny compared to his calloused bear paw. Then I ask him about the large red barrels in the corner (which I expect are full of oil or wine). At that, he smiles nervously. Rita interjects that they're "for the French." When I press her, she explains that several years ago some *fromagiers* made a pilgrimage here to "make reservations" for an almost forgotten Cycladic cheese. The project is now in its final stages.

"This is a very special product, whose history goes back many centuries on the island," Yorgos tells me. "Before we had refrigeration, our ancestors found ways to make cheese survive. Inside these barrels is *lakotyro*. I may be the only one still making it on the island."

Now, *lakkos* can mean "cesspool" in certain contexts, so any translation of *lakotyro* will come out sounding pretty revolting, but "hole cheese," "pit cheese," or "trench cheese" are all near the mark. In the old days, wheels of *kefalograviera* would be placed between layers of *tsigouri* (an herb resembling wild thyme) in an earthen pit, which was then sealed for two years. Today, Yorgos uses plastic barrels instead of earthen pits; these he keeps at room temperature and never opens. But he agrees to unscrew one of the heavy lids for me. After two years without refrigeration, the cheese will, I expect, stink to high heaven. Instead, it's as if Yorgos has opened a barrel of Serifosian hillside air: warm vegetation, dry soil, salt breeze. He reaches his arm down into the shadows to lift out what looks like a moth-eaten wig of grey dreadlocks. The herbs have almost entirely disintegrated and are now inextricable from the wheel of cheese they enclose. Their function, Yorgos explains, is to draw out the moisture (my guess is that their essential oils must have antibacterial properties as well). What results is something desirable to the French, and to me: a hideous, crumbly, extremely dry cheese. "It's much better than Parmigiano or Roquefort," Yorgos crows.

To my disappointment, he says I won't be able to taste any. The French reserved these cheeses and they'll return at the summer's end to fetch them, having already waited a long time. But I'm not to be deterred, and not only because I really want to try this cheese (I also love the idea of stealing from the French, who will no doubt sell puny morsels of this cheese at enormous profit to fussy Parisian ladies with yappy little dogs). Invoking my research into local foodways, including the chickpeas of Plati Yialós and the cucumbers of Vitos of Sikamya, not to mention my own dairy-farming American grandfathers, I eventually win out. Rita shrugs her shoulders and says, "Why not?" Yorgos agrees to sell me a wheel as long as I promise never to put it anywhere near a refrigerator. "It fears the cold," he tells me sternly.

The wheel is worth every euro, and it's the best souvenir I could hope to buy. The cheese has an unearthly flavor that bewilders everyone who tastes it over the next few days. I'm in a hurry to force it on people and use it up before flying home. In the end, I mummify the last wedge of it in paper towels and smuggle it through customs at JFK, wanting as always to bring the flavor of the islands back home with me.

.   .   .

That's easier said than done. Back in Pennsylvania, I line up all the ingredients for *revithia* on a table beside my roaring wood oven in the backyard: caramelized onions, rosemary, olive oil, water, and some chickpeas I've parboiled for several hours. Since Canadian chickpeas sometimes cross the

Atlantic to be transformed into Serifosian *revithia*, I feel should be able to transport Greek chickpeas back to North America and do the same thing (I picked up a kilo of Peleponessian beans at a grocery store in Athens). Even the cooking vessel came home in my suitcase: at the same store where I bought my chickpeas, I found one of the short-sided stainless steel braising dishes that Greeks use in their wood ovens.

If I were making pizza today, I'd have gotten the oven temperature up to at least seven hundred degrees. That's about the ideal temperature for pizza (which no ordinary gas or electric oven can safely reach in the confines of an indoor kitchen), but it's much too hot for chickpeas. So I let the first flames die down, then remove almost all of the hot embers, leaving just a few branches burning. Those I push off to the side of the oven. I'll continue to add a little wood to keep the heat consistent, and the flames will lick the top of the dome, hopefully imparting some wood smoke to the finished dish. As Aris said, heat is the other important ingredient.

I layer the onions into the braising dish and add the chickpeas, rosemary, and water. Then I drizzle in a generous amount of oil. It swirls atop the water for a minute before dispersing into little pools of oil that look, I'm pleased to note, like golden islands floating atop a seabed of sand-colored chickpeas. Then I push the dish back into the oven, where I leave it for the next three hours.

My kids are on the swing set, flying so high their feet nearly brush the leaves of our neighbor's apple tree, whose branches hang over our back fence. And the dogs (a young black Lab and an ancient chocolate Lab) make their rounds, sniffing at the wood oven, harassing the kids, and marking their territory in the herb garden. The scent of cooking chickpeas is on the air. A glass of ouzo is working hard to melt the ice cube I've plunked into it. My wife brings out the remaining morsel of Rita's *lakotyro* and some *throumbes* for us to snack on while we wait. Though it's lost some of its funky luster, the cheese is still good. There's no view of the Aegean here, but it's still summer, and the crickets are chirping their legs off as if to prove it.

Periodically, I pull the *revithia* from the oven to check on their progress. The onions, I notice, break down after about two hours and then dissolve completely. The dish is achieving the dark color I was aiming for, and it smells like the *revithia* I ate on Serifos too.

But the end results are disappointing. The chickpeas are entirely edible and even, my son declares, "yummy." There's nothing missing from the dish, and yet there's something not quite there. Are the onions to blame? (The ones I used were less pungent than their Greek counterparts). Or was my rosemary not dry enough? Ultimately, the thing that's missing, I know, is Greece.

Home Fires

MARATHÓTIGANÍTES

Every good Greek cook is a closet botanist. The landscape may seem like a barren dustbowl in midsummer, but for someone with a trained eye, a good appetite, and a propensity for weed gathering, there are culinary riches to be discovered at every turn. Hundreds of herbs grow wild in the hills, not to mention all the varieties of *horta*, which can be boiled for a healthy lunch. Tisanes and other healing concoctions are brewed from the leaves and roots and berries of myriad obscure plants. Hedges of rosemary serve as fence lines, and most every kitchen garden has a small field of flat-leaf parsley.

On Serifos, there's an abundance of wild fennel, which seems to line all the roadsides. The plant never really forms the round root base you find in domesticated fennel, but it's easy to pluck a whole bouquet of its fragrant green tops as you walk home from the sea. They are featured in a traditional Cycladic *meze*. Along with some of the most succulent *kontosouvli* I've ever eaten (formidable wedges of pork, slow cooked on a massive skewer until crisp and tender), Restaurant Aloni near the Chora serves these remarkable fennel fritters. They are a lesson in simplicity. I didn't believe *how* simple, in fact, until the restaurant's owner, Marietta, took me back into the kitchen to show me how to make the batter. The trick is to use a huge amount of green fennel fronds. Since most people toss these in the trash after exploiting the fennel bulb, the recipe is also an ingenious way to salvage an otherwise underexploited ingredient back home.

Strip the branches of the wispy green fronds and then chop the fronds finely, along with some of the thinnest green branches. Then proceed with the batter.

1½ cups all-purpose flour

Sea salt and black pepper

1 cup finely chopped fennel fronds

Approximately ⅔ cup room-temperature water, plus more as needed

½ cup minced red onion

Olive oil, for frying

Add the flour to a deep bowl along with a generous pinch of salt, some grinds of pepper, and the fennel fronds. Begin adding the water to the flour mixture slowly, whisking all the while, just until you have a rather thin batter (about the consistency of pancake batter). Then fold in the minced red onion.

Heat a thin layer of good olive oil in a skillet until glistening, but not smoking. Drop in heaping tablespoons of the batter, taking care to not let them overlap, and fry until golden on both sides. Season the fritters with an additional pinch of sea salt just as they come hot from the oil.

CHAPTER SEVEN

Wine

Another Carafe at Prionia

One afternoon, as I'm about to toss on a blazer and stroll down the hall to teach my poetry seminar, this astounding specimen of Thasian English lands in my e-mail inbox:

Gia su aderfe,

i know that we have only 20 days befor seeing each ather, and i have many thinks to tell whats hapen to me the last 10 days. i tell you only one think maybe i will come in America . . . the ather i explein in 20 days when you will be here.

i whant a feivor i need somethink from America because thear is cheper, cald, TRI-TRONICS TRASHBREAKER G2

i do not know if you know about this is somethink you youse for horce and dogs to teaching them not doing bud thinks.

this think you put it in the nek of the animal and you have one tilecontrol in your hand so if you push the botm then from this think comes elektik and stop the animal, and it has range 3 kiliometers.

this think you can use it for difrent work like to know were is the dog.

if you can not anderstand call me so i call you back for speaking, no problem the time.

i waite your news
gretings to all
Tasos

It's the unmistakable voice of my Greek brother from across the waters. His poetic mangling of the language leaves me grinning, and an hour later (in the middle of a discussion of Paul Celan and postwar Germany) that phrase "bud thinks" pops back into my head and I begin giggling uncontrollably, to the bewilderment of my very serious students. And Tasos of Thasos might be coming to America?

.　.　.

It's madness to fly off to Greece in the middle of the semester, since by the time I return my courses will be speeding toward their frenzied finish, and that means an avalanche of papers and meetings. But the grapes of Greece ripen when they ripen. If I want to join the harvest, it's now or never. Having spent some time last summer touring massive, state-of-the-art wineries in the Nemea region of the Peloponnese (epicenter of the viticultural revolution in Greece), I want to see the other end of the wine spectrum on Thasos. I'm also overdue for a beaker full of the warm South.

Then there's the issue of the mountain. Snow is about to close Olympus for the season, and Tasos and I are determined to get George Kaltsas up it. So with my wife's blessing, I am off. In tow: a new pair of hiking boots for me and an expensive training device for Tasos's hunting dogs.

.　.　.

I consider taking the old road from Thessaloniki to Kavala. It zigs across the olive groves and grain fields of Halkidiki and then zags slowly along the coast. I'm curious about what's happening out in the groves and fields this time of year, but I also know there'll be agricultural traffic to contend with, and I'm too jet-lagged to spend the next three hours trying to pass slow-moving farm vehicles on hairpin turns. Luckily, the northern Greek harvest is also on full display along the new superhighway. Both times I stop for coffee at a rest area, beautiful table grapes are for sale at prices that make them almost free. There are massive apples and golden quince, too, not to mention varieties of wild greens I never see during the summer. In the fertile Strymonas River delta, vineyards stretching all the way from the mountain to the sea are ready: vines sag with the weight of ripe fruit and the once green grape leaves are flecked with autumnal yellow and rust. When I roll my window down a crack, I swear I can smell wine—that, or the earth itself fermenting.

While most of the top Greek winemakers are now headquartered down south, the country's modern winemaking business actually got its start here in Macedonia, in vineyards much like these. Credit for this goes to Yannis Boutaris, who in the late nineteenth century established plantings of *xino-mavro* grapes near the city of Naoussa, then bottled and sometimes even exported the very respectable red he produced. Ancient and noble *xinomavro* ("sour black") was the right and obvious choice—its heavy tannins make it suitable for slow maturation, and in the right hands it yields very dry, full-bodied wines. For a long time, it was one of the only good retail wines available in Greece.

When I first lived in Thessaloniki twenty years ago, wine buying was a sad but clear-cut enterprise. The first option was to take your own jug to the farmer's market and have it filled with the "two-drachma chuck" someone's grandfather produced out in the hills. This wine could be drinkable, and sometimes even good, but it was too often effervescent or cloying. As Hemingway put it in *A Farewell to Arms*, "The wine was bad but not dull. It took the enamel off your teeth and left it on the roof of your mouth." The second option was to splurge on bottles of Naoussa Boutaris at the grocery store. This wine was dark, spicy, and reliable, despite the fact that most of it had been terribly abused: room temperature at midsummer in most Greek grocery stores rivals that of the Sahara. I'd toss several bottles of it in my backpack before I boarded ferries for weekend excursions to the islands. Along with a hunk of feta, some bread, a tomato, and a bag of olives, it made for a perfect picnic. I have the Boutaris family to thank for some very enter-taining bacchanals at sea.

By the late nineties, Boutaris also began pushing a clear-headed and citrusy white wine made from *assyrtiko* grapes grown in the volcanic soil of Santorini. Like the Naoussa red, this *assyrtiko* was marketed to the nouveaux riches who emerged after the country entered the Euro-pean Union. As soon as beach season began in May, billboards across the countryside would feature half-naked models in sybaritic tableaux, sipping their Boutaris white. (Always conscious of their image, actual well-dressed Greeks on actual beaches would reenact these scenes all summer long at fashionable hangouts on the Halkidiki peninsula.) Santorini Boutaris even enjoyed modest success as an export; in fact, it was the first Greek wine I ever saw on a wine list in the United States. Eventually, some Greek wines like these wound up in the glass of Robert Parker, who scored them favorably in his *Wine Advocate*. By the year 2000, a serious wine revolution was under way.

But I'm getting ahead of myself. Until recently, there wasn't really much of a retail Greek wine "industry" at all. Sure, huge amounts of wine have been produced in Greece for thousands of years, much of it of exemplary quality. It was the ancient Greeks, after all, who introduced wine growing to the fertile places we now call Italy and France. But while the wines of Bordeaux and Tuscany were slowly perfected over time, those of impover-ished and oft-conquered Greece nearly died away. This atrophy was most profound under the teetotaling Ottomans, who largely forbade private wine production and ripped up many ancient vineyards. Luckily, the Ottomans did allow monasteries to keep their vines, and we have monks to thank for the survival of hundreds of native grapes.

There are over three hundred indigenous varietals in the tiny country of Greece, many of them found only on one island or in a niche valley. Not that anyone outside of Greece was at all interested in these obscure grapes, of course, but for generations Greek families have nurtured them for household use and have kept them from disappearing.

Then there's *retsina*. On the one hand, nothing has done as much to damage the reputation of Greek viticulture as this ubiquitous white table wine spiked with pine resin. On the other hand, cheap *retsina* and its heady buzz have fueled a billion festive, half-remembered vacations— for Greeks and foreigners alike. What exactly is it? Well, the ancients used sap from the Aleppo pine to seal their amphorae for storage and transport. Some of the adhesive would trickle down and inform the flavor of the wine. Drinkers grew used to the flavor and even began to desire it—and they still do. This fact has not been lost on modern producers, who encourage consumers to have turpentine with their wine, as the ancients did. Some clever advertisers even hint that *retsina* (as with Guinness in Ireland) is good for you. The famous logo of the Malamatina company in Macedonia suggests as much: a little, doughy green man tips himself backward while downing a giant mug of *retsina*. He would fall on his back, in fact, if it weren't for the massive skeleton key (the key to health?) that's been inserted into his potbelly. Yes, pine resin: the key to balance and upright behavior.

Neither the beverage's nastiness nor its virtues have been lost on me over the years. While I am appalled by the common practice of mixing *retsina* and Coca-Cola, I also admit to enjoying *retsina*'s strangeness now and then. Its sour-bitter twang really does complement the unctuous, fried, garlicky offerings of cheap *tavernas*. I think with particular fondness of a student hangout in one of Thessaloniki's seedy alleyways. There, on every table, was a small wooden barrel of *retsina*, affixed to which was a chalkboard and a nubbin of chalk on a string. Each time you filled your battered tin carafe, you were supposed to put a hash mark on the chalkboard. Someone would strum a bouzouki, encouraging merriment and dancing, and fried squid and *skordalia* and grilled hot peppers would keep arriving at your table whether you ordered them or not. At night's end, the owner would "accidentally" erase half the marks on the chalkboard with a brush of his elbow and then charge you a pittance for the rest.

But turpentine wine? No wonder a renaissance of the grape in Greece seemed so unlikely. It has arrived nevertheless, to the extent that when I enter grocery stores where just fifteen years ago I found only Naoussa Boutaris, I now find two or three whole aisles dedicated to Greek wine, much of it outside my price range. For decades I've been calling Greek cuisine the most underappreciated in Europe. Now I'm inclined to make the same claim about Greek wine.

So how did this happen? Patriotism, money, and technique have all played roles. While some Greek winemakers switched over to growing French grapes, others saw the virtue of working with Greece's indigenous varietals. The European Union gave subsidies to create jobs in the industry, which allowed vintners to send their sons and daughters to study enology in France and California. Many of these have returned to Greece to experiment with their native grapes, applying their sophisticated knowledge of wine chemistry and technology. What happens when you mix the soft *ayiorgitiko* with a muscular Greek-grown Cabernet, for instance? What happens when you apply oak to the jazzy white *malagouzia*, a grape that had almost become extinct? Well, excellent things happen, that's what. And the world is beginning to pay attention.

. . .

George Kaltsas approaches this revolution in Greek wine with his usual skepticism and philosophical detachment. He's been drinking good Greek wine all his life, since he makes it himself each year from the hardy *georgina* grapes he grows organically on his own land. Also, it's part of George's business at the hotel to make food and drink recommendations to his guests, so he always knows who's serving the good stuff.

Within minutes of my arrival at Hotel Oceanis in Kavala tonight, he puts a glass of *ayiorgitiko* before me. The *ayiorgitiko* grape (which the Greeks often call "Saint George") is very suitable for producing rosé, but it also makes a nice light-bodied red, and that's what George serves me.

As usual, he brushes off all questions about his health with a smile. I do get this much out of him: he's finished his most recent round of chemotherapy and is coming back to himself slowly.

"In fact," he tells me, "I've been training for Olympus for over a month. You see these?"

George lifts up one of his pant legs to show me the thick ankle weights he's wearing.

"I walk up and down the stairs of the hotel all day long, Christopher, and this way nobody knows I'm working and going to the gym at the same time. I suggest we have dinner up in the old town, but I'm going to change out of my suit and put on my hiking boots first."

Since my own boots still need to be broken in, I follow suit. It's a short but strenuous climb to the old city: a steep cobblestone road snakes its way up from the harbor past a gorgeously restored imaret (a massive Ottoman-era hospice) and concludes on the doorstep of the palatial birthplace of Mehmet Ali Pasha, who was born here in Thrace but went on to found the last Egyptian dynasty. His equestrian statue—featuring Ali Pasha in a robe and turban, caught in the act of unsheathing a scimitar—dominates the main square at the top of the hill. We stop to catch our breath for a few minutes and stare across the water at the darkened outline of Thasos, where I'll be headed tomorrow.

Then we stroll into a sleepy little restaurant. When the owners see George, they snap to attention. In honor of the adventure ahead of us, George suggests we drink something from Rapsani, a tiny appellation at the foothills of Olympus. A bottle is uncorked by the proprietor within seconds of our ordering it, and I couldn't be happier, since this is one of my favorite Greek

Wine: Another Carafe at Prionia

wines. In fact, after Naoussa Boutaris, it was the first one to challenge my preconceptions about Greek wine. Its backbone is *xinomavro*, as with many Macedonian wines, but two other grapes grown only in Rapsani—*krassato* and *stavroto*—are added in equal parts to round it out. Treating that blend to a year in oak barrels results in an almost black, full-bodied wine that sells for under ten euros a bottle in Greece (though you'd pay triple that in the United States).

My brain has been dulled by the long journey from Pennsylvania, but when the wine's delirium comes I feel wildly awake in spite of myself. Wine's "gentle discipline," Horace reminds us, causes "the dull to be less dull than usual" and brings

> courage to the poor man, so
> He's neither scared of tyrants in their crowns
> Nor soldiers brandishing their scary weapons.

George is never dull to begin with, and he has enormous reserves of courage, but I credit the second bottle of Rapsani for inspiring in my philosopher friend an animated soliloquy. For fifteen minutes he ranges eloquently from politics to poetry to Eros and Thanatos. Though he doesn't speak about his health directly, I know that what he isn't saying is at the heart of his monologue. We're not climbing Olympus for any ceremonial purpose, he insists, but he does reveal that he'd planned to climb it once before, with a now dead friend, and squandered the chance. He won't let that happen again.

"We live in a sphere, not on a line," George tells me, while hoisting an invisible orb toward the ceiling, "and we must find a way to fill it. Only fools worry about what's coming. We are here, after all, swirling black wine in our glasses like a couple of emperors."

It's true. We've conquered our dinner and a lot of wine: the bones of about twenty *koutsomoura* (the 'lame-faced' cousins of *barbounia*), a few lonesome beans, two empty bottles, and a heel of bread are evidence of that.

When my eyelids begin to get heavy, George motions for the bill and rouses me with a challenge.

"Christopher, on the way back to the hotel we must race. I know the perfect spot."

George leads me to a place singularly unsuitable for drunken sprinting, especially in heavy mountain footgear: a steep, pitch-black alleyway just off the main square. I'm not even sure how cars manage the ascent, though there are a few parked along the sidewalk at the top. But off we go, running, our boots kicking up a racket on the cobblestones. George passes me halfway up the hill. While I'm wheezing at the top, he lifts one leg of his jeans to remind me that the cancer patient who's just beaten me has done so while wearing ankle weights.

On the square behind us, eerily spotlit by a half-moon, the Pasha Ali is still wielding his scimitar, as if ready to disembowel the sky itself.

.   .   .

I've never seen Tasos of Thasos so rattled. Though it's only eleven in the morning when I arrive at Pension Archontissa, he's already filled us each a glass of *tsipouro* at one of the stone tables on the patio. Hanging just out of reach overhead are the dark clusters of grapes I'll be picking. Some have already fallen—the flagstones are stained with what look like spatters of blood and bees are lazily raiding the devastated booty.

Tasos grins in welcome through the first glass, but his expression changes when I ask him why he might be coming to America. He looks me square in the eye and speaks with severe pathos. Elpida, the bookish belly dancer from Thessaloniki, is out. She had tried to weave herself into the family business, but her controlling and jealous nature clashed with Eva's culinary and maternal authority, and things ended badly.

Before I have a chance to respond to this news, he pulls a wad of yellow paper out of his pocket and waves it in the air.

"What's this?" I ask him.

"A letter," he says. "But I don't know what to do with it."

No wonder Tasos is flummoxed. Some weeks after Elpida left the island, a van load of Turkish Armenian women arrived at the pension for a week's holiday. All of them were fluent in their own folk dances, but they wanted to spend their holiday drinking wine and learning some Greek dances on Thasos. One of them, named Karolin, caught Tasos's eye. She'd left her home in Istanbul years earlier to follow the money to Los Angeles, where she sells diamonds for a living. She and Tasos fell instantly in love. Faced with the disapproval of Eva and Stamatis, they had to carry on in the shadows and in the wee hours. At the end of the week, Karolin piled into the van with the rest of her group and left for Istanbul.

Three hours into the journey, she commanded the driver to stop, jumped out of the van with her luggage, and took a taxi all the way back to Keramoti, where Tasos, unbeknownst to his parents, came to fetch her. There followed two weeks of secret bliss: Tasos would work fifteen hours a day in the restaurant, then sneak off to spend the night with Karolin at her hiding place in a posh hotel up the coast.

And the letter? Karolin has written to tell Tasos that she's willing to quit her job, sell her Porsche and her chic LA apartment, and relocate to Thasos, just to be with him.

"But what kind of life can she have here?" Tasos asks despairingly.

It's a good question. Life on Thasos may seem idyllic, but it can be a hard and isolated place. There's little time for glamour, given the relentless demands of rural labor—and the winters are chilly and dismal. So Tasos has a lot to think about. He's making plans to fly to California to see Karolin's corner of the globe. It's hard to imagine Tasos of Thasos in LA, since I've never met a person more tied to his birthplace. Nevertheless, I congratulate him on having turned his life into a Hollywood romantic comedy.

At that he laughs, downs the rest of his glass, and then rises to fetch a small ladder from the other end of the patio.

"I've already picked our other grapes," he tells me, "but these I've left for you. They are *georgina*. Tomorrow you can fill those crates over there and then we'll smash them."

This afternoon, however, there's a bigger task to attend to: removing Stamatis's boat from the sea. It's sunny and headed toward seventy degrees on this October day, but when the *Evanthoula* is put to sleep, summer on Thasos is officially over. It takes a team of men to get her out of the water: Tasos and Stamatis do all the heavy lifting, while the rest of us (some of Tasos's friends have come for the event) pace on the beach, shouting out unhelpful suggestions.

First the nets must be unloaded; otherwise the boat will be too heavy for the trailer. After Stamatis inches the *Evanthoula* as close as he can to shore and anchors it, Tasos strips down to his underwear and wades out so Stamatis can heave nets onto his back. I know these nets are heavy, since I had to move one a few summers ago; even wrapped into a tight bundle, they are unwieldy as boulders. Tasos is bent double by the first of them and works his way slowly toward shore. He staggers a little across the slick, algae-covered rocks and then stops, trying to reposition the net on his shoulder. There's an awkward moment when he nearly tips forward, and several of us are about to jump in to help, since we know that the net will be even heavier if wet. But Tasos gets one hand loose from the bundle and pushes back against the seafloor to right himself. Then, to our amazement, we see that he hasn't been struggling at all. When he stands up again, he's gripping a large octopus, which he tosses to us before wading the rest of the way in. I'm stunned by this feat of dexterity, but his island buddies just shake their heads in amusement. They've known Tasos a long time and don't seem very surprised.

Once the rest of the nets have been unloaded, we all grab hold of ropes tied to the *Evanthoula* and help to pull it into position. Stamatis revs the engine on his truck, and the boat creaks and glides her way up the ramp, headed for hibernation. Then we turn to the business of the octopus, which is going to be dinner.

.   .   .

I'd planned to be up by daybreak to harvest those grapes, but I oversleep and don't manage to step out of my room until after nine. It's a beautifully clear morning and I can see the outline of Samothrace on the eastern horizon.

Tasos has been out rabbit hunting with his dogs, testing the electric collars I brought him. But he's returned empty handed.

"I see and I shoot," he says, "but I didn't take."

The instruction booklet for the collars is a hundred pages long, and I promise to help him make sense of it before we leave for Olympus. But first I have a job to do. After a bowl of strong coffee, I set to work on the patio.

Just three days ago I was pushing a pen in my office at the college, so it's wonderfully disorienting to be standing on the top rung of a ladder harvesting grapes on a Greek island. Now and then, I poke my head up through the leafy canopy to bask in the sun. Did I really suggest a moment ago that this was a hard and isolated place? No, today it's the beautiful axis mundi of the wine-dark world.

As with olive picking, the repetitive motion—from hand to vine to crate and back again—inspires an expansive calm in me. I find myself thinking of Keats's "To Autumn":

Season of mists and mellow fruitfulness,
Close bosom-friend of the maturing sun;
Conspiring with him how to load and bless
With fruit the vines that round the thatch-eves run. . . .

Off in the hills, someone is going nuts with a chain saw. Tasos's dogs are barking gleefully beneath the olives. And I can hear the sea below, raking the beach stones. Sweet labor, this.

In fact, it's a pity I finish my task so quickly. Before long, I've stripped all the vines of their fruit and have filled four-and-a-half olive crates with *georgina*. I'm prepared to stomp them, but instead Tasos dumps them into a mechanical grape crusher, which drains the blood of my paltry harvest in less than five minutes. We add this juice to a huge plastic barrel of crushed grapes, which are already beginning to ferment: bubbles crawl along the surface and the crimson liquid exudes that sweet, yeasty scent that was blowing through my car's windows the other day.

When I ask Tasos if we can get a head start on distilling the *tsipouro* this week, he tells me that that's impossible, since they fire up the still only after the olives have been picked. I'm tempted to skip the rest of the semester, shrug off every responsibility, and stay in this timeless place, working until winter. As Emerson puts it, riffing on the Persian of Hafiz, "Bring me wine to wash me clean / Of the weather-stains of care."

But just as soon as I climb Olympus, I'll have to rush back to Thessaloniki for my flight home, with a big watch strapped to my wrist.

. . .

At dinner, Tasos lets me taste the wine he made last year, as "an experiment," using a few hundred kilos of Cabernet grapes he bought in Strymonas. Though it's very young, I'm impressed. He's "determined to make new and better wine each year," so he listens intently when I tell him about Domaine Skouras, a vineyard on the Peloponnese that I toured last summer. I went there to investigate their Megas Oenos, a gigantic red I'd heard about in American magazines (the 2007 scored an 89 in *Wine Spectator*), but had rarely seen in Greece.

Domaine Skouras, which in 2009 was named "winery of the year" by *Wine & Spirits Magazine*, lived up to its hype and is, hands down, the slickest winery in Greece. The grapes run right up to the imposing rosé-colored chateau, which George Skouras built to be ready for the hordes of the 2004 Olympics (many busloads of foreigners have gotten their first taste of high-end Greek wine here). Vine rows lead off behind the chateau, too, in the direction of some low mountains, one of which is crowned with the castle of ancient Argos. The monumental ruins of Mycenae are also just a few miles up the road, which means we're in the heart of the Argolid, where they've been making "the blood of Herakles" for at least three thousand years.

The French-trained Skouras was probably the first winemaker to blend native Greek varietals with "cosmopolitan" (that is, foreign) grapes. Case in point: Megas Oenos. The somewhat wispy *ayiorgitiko* that George Kaltsas poured for me in Kavala is barely recognizable in this bottle. Skouras matures 80 percent *ayiorgitiko* and 20 percent Cabernet Sauvignon in French oak for a year and a half, resulting in an elegant wine with lots of body, bursting with fruit and dark chocolate. When I took my first sip, I was blown away, but also confused. Was this Nemea or Sonoma? Never mind, my palate decided: it's delicious. But I see the point of those critics who worry that the use of foreign grapes is doomed to failure; the future of the Greek wine industry will, they argue, ultimately depend on developing native varietals, these being better suited to the extremities of the Greek climate.

I loved the continental blends I was poured at Domaine Skouras, including an almost tropical-tasting Viognier called Eclectique and a very wild Syrah, in which I thought I detected the limestone and chalk of the Peloponnese. But terroir? I felt the essence of Greek soil and Greek soul to be more present in the winery's *moschofilero*, which had touched no oak, and in the *ayiorgitiko* of their "Saint George Nemea."

In the years to come, smart winemakers like Skouras will continue churning out their cosmopolitan blends while others tweak native varietals to compete with them. Only about 10 percent of Greek wine is exported right now, so there's not much danger that the dictates of the foreign palate will entirely carry the day. Provided the wine revolutionaries of Greece can survive the collapse of their country's economy, this ongoing debate will encourage them to make even better wines in the coming years. That means it's a really good time to be thirsty in Greece.

.   .   .

Except, I should say, when climbing Greece's tallest mountain. As expedition leader, I should know better, but when Tasos wedges two bottles of *tsipouro* into his backpack, "for the mountain," my survivalist instincts are no match for my thirst for anise-laced rotgut.

We fetch George from the hotel in Kavala hours behind schedule, which means we're rushing and have skipped breakfast and lunch. It's about a four-hour drive from Kavala to the mountain, even with Tasos at the wheel, since we must get past traffic-snarled Thessaloniki, not to mention a lot of trucks hauling grapes. We should have boots on the trail by three in the afternoon, I keep saying, or we'll be caught by darkness during the ascent. But it's clear we're not going to make it by then.

We begin at the trailhead of Prionia, parking the car in a lot next to a mountain stream. There's a rustic *taverna* there, with fragrant smoke pouring out of its chimney, but we don't have time to sit—the chocolate bars and peanuts in my backpack will have to suffice. Climbing with Tasos of the Greek Special Forces and George of the Ankle Weights, I figure we can make up for our lateness and reach our overnight destination by dusk.

We're aiming for Spilios Agapitos Refuge (which everyone calls "Zolotas Lodge"), an attractive but Spartan chalet located at 2,000 meters. There, we'll be rewarded with wine, bowls of braised meat with rice, and bunk beds with heavy wool blankets. It'll be "lights out" by ten o'clock. Just before daybreak tomorrow the generator will be switched back on, and at that point we'll set out for the summit, another two or three hours beyond the refuge.

That's when things get hairy. Above the tree line, there's no longer any clear-cut path, just an endless slope of loose, traction-defying shale. Finally we'll reach Kakia Skala ("Bad Staircase"), which leads up to the peak—Mytikas—at 3,000 meters. There waits Zeus. The final 200 meters of elevation must be navigated with great care, crab walking the mountain's spine one person at a time, then hitching gingerly up some loose rubble. Plenty of people have died there after being struck by rock slides triggered by other climbers in front of them.

But there's really no real danger between Prionia and the refuge, I assure my companions. We're all giddy with anticipation, and George is beaming. Within five minutes, however, two bad things happen. The first I cannot control: it begins to rain, hard. (I've got a flimsy plastic poncho and Tasos and George both have waterproof coats, so we won't get totally soaked.) The second is pure stupidity, and I'm furious with myself about it: my boots still aren't properly broken in and my heels begin to blister almost immediately. I didn't even need them—the first time I tackled Olympus, in 1992, I reached the summit in a pair of Converse high-tops. There's nothing to do now but trudge on, hoping for the best.

When Tasos offers me a glug of *tsipouro* about forty minutes into the climb, my feet hurt too much to refuse it. The three of us hunker down in the shelter of a cliff and pass the bottle back and forth. By the time we begin to climb again, it's pouring so hard we can barely see the trail.

But our spirits remain high. At times, Zeus relents a little and the rain slows to a trickle. There are preternaturally green chasms to be taken in, along with splotches of brightly colored moss and profusions of late-blooming wildflowers. Now and then we encounter beautiful and enormous black slugs with waggling optic tentacles.

Like the slugs, unfortunately, we make very slow progress. We haven't eaten all day and keep stopping to drink *tsipouro*. There's a sloshing inside my boots that I suspect involves a good deal of blood, and by the third hour of climbing I have to try hard not to look defeated. Tasos looks crestfallen and exhausted; George is ashen. Little rivers are now forming on the trail and the rocks are becoming slippery, even icy in spots, since the temperature is dropping.

It's an hour after dusk when we finally arrive at the refuge. When I remove my poncho just outside the threshold, a waterfall pours from my shoulders.

. . .

Maria Zolotas has been waiting for us. She and her husband, Dionysios, are descendants of the inimitable Kostas Zolotas, one of the first climbers to summit Olympus and map out the various paths of ascent in the 1940s and '50s. Kostas himself has retired, but Maria and Dionysios have taken over in his place, living at the refuge four or five months each year, acting as restaurateurs, guides, and, if necessary, an emergency crew. They are fluent in Greek, English, and German and are willing to rescue you in any language. Maria scolds me with a clicking of her tongue when I tell her about my boots. "You've been here many times," she says, "and really should have known better."

There are only a few other climbers in the refuge tonight, and they all arrived much earlier in the day, before the rain. Already asleep in the bunkhouse is a trio from Kyoto. Still awake are two girls from Frankfurt, but they seem to want nothing to do with us. After we spread our gear out to dry in front of the hearth and I bandage my feet, Tasos and I pile into steaming bowls of stew and begin guzzling red wine. George refuses to eat, which worries me, but he agrees to have a sip of wine, and a little color comes back into his cheeks.

"It's good wine, Christopher," he says. "To think that it had to be hauled up here on the backs of mules."

He's right. Even if the wine's a bit too sweet, served in mugs at mountain temperature it couldn't taste better. But we're still in shock from the climb.

My hands tremble each time I raise the mug to my lips, and it's all I can do to lift my arm for the next sip.

We do our best to stay awake, rotating our steaming clothes in front of the fire. The Frankfurt ladies warm up to us enough to join us for a carafe. After they tell us they ran up the mountain in tennis shoes before noon, we're too embarrassed to say much about our own climb. They hope to summit with us in the morning, if we're up for some company.

Soon, the generator is cut, and we finish our wine by candlelight. Then we collapse in our bunks.

.　.　.

At daybreak, my feet aren't putting up with any shenanigans—the left heel begins bleeding again the moment I pull on my boot. But when we step out to the refuge's patio, we see that the clouds have parted and the serrated outline of Mytikas is clearly visible. At least for the moment, the conditions are right for summiting. George, however, says that getting to Zolotas Lodge was enough for him. One of his knees is badly swollen and he prefers to wait for us here. Since he's already deep in conversation (in some combination of English and French) with one of the Japanese climbers, I know he'll be fine. I'm tempted to heed my instinct to stay with him, but decide to continue anyway.

Simply ignoring my blisters works for about an hour, until the switchbacks become steeper and the wind starts howling. Then my boot slips on some wet stone and I feel my bandages come loose. When a massive gust of wind hits me square in the chest, my resolve finally crumbles. I begin to panic, thinking about having to make the descent with shredded feet, and I know it would be foolish to continue. Tasos offers to return to the refuge with me, but I insist that he keep going. "So that George can take his time," I tell him, "we'll get a head start." Tasos agrees to meet us down at Prionia, if he doesn't catch up to us on the trail.

Mytikas in Sight

When I get back to the refuge, however, George has disappeared. Maria says she encouraged him to start down ahead of me and sent him off with a walking stick, to help with his knee.

"You should get going too," she says, "with those ugly feet. And it's going to rain now."

Indeed, it starts pouring the moment she says so.

I catch up with George about an hour and a half later. He's taken shelter in a stand of black pines, leaning on his walking stick and meditating, apparently. I'm pleased to find him in a good mood, and he seems energized by my offer to buy him a carafe of wine down at Prionia. We spend the next hours hobbling down the mountain in the rain, reciting poetry and singing. I know we've probably pushed George harder than his doctor would have liked, but it all seems worth it as the trail begins to level out into the final mile.

Alas, the gods have one more trick to play on us. As the trail curves around a huge boulder, we hear rushing water in one of the chasms below. It grows louder as we descend, and I feel a knot of real apprehension in my gut when it turns to a roar. A lot of rain has fallen in the past day, and though I've never heard of trails being washed out, it doesn't seem impossible. As we come into a clearing, we see, just below the trail, a plume of water blasting from beneath a heap of Volkswagen-sized boulders, hitting trees with enough force to bend them almost sideways. It seems, in short, that an underground river has erupted. The water is deafening and we can feel its power under our boot soles. We scurry across the trail above it while we still can—the earth there seems unsteady and could, I worry, liquefy at any moment. Once we've crossed and moved down the trail a bit, George smiles wickedly and lets out a barbaric victory howl. I join in, though we can't really hear ourselves over the cascade.

These underground rivers are part of the mythology of the mountain. Pausanias tells us that Orpheus, after being dismembered by the

wine-frenzied Bacchae, was laid to rest near one of them—but I'd never seen
one let loose before. It's a spectacle of raw, brute power, and I'm reminded
that the mountain is a tectonic and sublime place, where gods have much
more business than puny human beings like us. Based on the violent demise
of Orpheus, not to mention the past day's misadventures, I'm beginning to
think the mountain is especially unsafe for poets. I've never been more eager
to get off it.

By the time we arrive at Prionia, the rain is coming down even harder
than it has all day. At the *taverna*, we choose a table next to a radiator and
peel off our dripping rain gear. "Never mind," the grizzled proprietor says
when George apologizes for the pool of water forming at our feet.

"Bring us your best red wine," I implore him. He seems to find this
funny, to judge from his cockeyed expression. He pours me a sample from a
box of wine on the counter. It's the usual, mass-produced red from Limnos,
that windy pile of rock out in the middle of the northern Aegean. The island
is known for its ancient strain of muscat, but in the past few decades there's
been a revival of interest in its hardy red *limnio*, which has been grown there
long enough for Aristotle to have recommended it. Some genius on Limnos
saw a gap in the box wine industry, and now *limnio* is the default table wine
of most *tavernas* in Greece. I down my sip and nod "yes" to the proprietor,
who returns with a chipped glass carafe filled to the brim. Though almost as
light as rosé, the wine's got some assertive acidity, a high alcohol content,
and a finish that reminds me of bitter herbs. There's nothing subtle about it,
but the first glass seems to reignite the pilot light in my chest. I don't think
I've ever earned the right to love a glass of mediocre wine more.

Of course, we're also famished. We start with a tomato salad decorated
with some hard green olives and a pile of searing red onions. I don't particularly like raw red onion, but I'd be willing to eat matches today. More fire is
to be found in the large slivers of raw garlic decorating our five anchovies.
We press slabs of bread into the fishy oil, then lay whole anchovies across

An Orphic River

them, along with some garlic. By the time the salad and our improvised crostini are gone, so is our wine. It seems like bad form to eat or drink any more without Tasos, whose face we expect to see peering through the foggy panes of the door at any moment.

"This is Circe's wine," I tell George. "And don't you see what's happening here? The mountain has bewitched us and we'll never be able to leave."

"Yes, I know, Christopher," he replies. "But we are helpless men, and since men are pigs, there's no shame in surrender. Let's have another carafe."

"But what will we tell Tasos? By the time he gets here, there won't be much time left for feasting and we'll be in a hurry to hit the road. He's the poor bastard who has to drive us pigs back to Thessaloniki so I can make my flight."

The question stops George midchew.

"Simple," he says at last. "We won't tell him. Watch me destroy the evidence." At that, he takes the empty carafe and places it on an empty table across the room, then walks over to the owner and places another order.

The second carafe arrives along with two massive bowls of *fasolada*, the most beloved comfort food in Greece. The restaurant has made an excellent version of the soup, adding to the tender white beans some diced carrot and onion. George spikes his with a few dashes of red wine vinegar, and since he always seems to know what he's doing, I follow suit. Ignoring the fact that it's too hot, I begin shoveling it down anyway. Never has a dish been more satisfying. I can feel it filling my weary, hollow legs and swelling my chest with steam.

Just as we reach the bottoms of the bowls, Tasos comes in from the rain at last, the two soggy German girls right behind him. It turns out they were turned around by high winds and cloud cover at Skala, but they seem overjoyed to have gotten that far. We order another carafe and three more *fasolades*, and then we raise our glasses through beany steam in the name of friendship, and the gods, and their rainy mountain.

. . .

As usual, I'm doomed to leave Greece almost as soon as I've arrived. By the middle of the next morning, I'm already at Fiumicino airport outside Rome, killing time and an espresso before the second leg of my journey. I'm exhausted and my feet are in terrible shape, so I'm looking forward to collapsing into a window seat on the trans-Atlantic flight. I'm also praying the passenger next to me will be mute.

Instead, my seatmate is a gregarious Greek American who wears a Rolex and looks like he's just leapt from the pages of a Banana Republic catalog. He seems thrilled to find himself seated next to a fellow oenophile. I learn that he makes wine in California, where he owns several plots of old-vine Zinfandel. Our conversation begins in Greek, but he says he'd rather speak English, since for the past few weeks he's done nothing but speak "peasant Greek" in his family's village in Arcadia. We exchange impressions of this year's grape harvest. His village is populated, he declares, by "hicks of the first order."

"They're all ignorant and paranoid. They can't see beyond the edge of their own village, even the young ones. All they care about is stabbing one another in the back and fighting over property lines and evading taxes and trying to work their new cell phones. No wonder the Greek economy is going to shit and the Germans are taking over again."

It's often like this with Greek Americans, who either display a fanatical devotion to everything Greek or write off their ancestral home completely. I know he's right about the backwardness of village life, since I grew up in a village myself—even if it was in Wisconsin. Still, his snobbishness puts me off, and I'm happy when our conversation turns away from Greece to the world of California Zinfandel. He started with one tiny vineyard in

Lodi, which his father bought in the 1960s on a whim, but his holdings have gradually expanded. These days he sets aside the best of his crop for private bottling, then sells the rest to big wineries. He's a New World capitalist of the first order, bragging about his recent purchase of a warehouse and scoffing at the idea of organic wine when I bring it up.

Really, he's a pretty nice guy. Under different circumstances I might enjoy his feisty opinions and quick wit, not to mention his descriptions of village life (which is, I admit, too easy to romanticize). But his scornful pronouncements about Greek wine put my hackles up.

"The Greeks don't know anything about wine," he remarks between sips of his gin and tonic, "and nobody there is interested in embracing modern technology. Not that it matters, since most of the Greek grapes aren't worth thinking about anyway."

I've spent the last several years drawing exactly the opposite set of conclusions, but I'm too weary to offer a rebuttal. So I'm relieved when he disappears at last into his sleeping pill and noise-canceling headphones.

Given the state of the economy, Greece's wine renaissance may very well be over. I wonder how many vintners who threw their fortunes into grapes back in the boom time will go belly up. And I worry about all those shelves of good Greek wine in sweltering island grocery stores, now gathering dust thanks to their high price tags; the Greeks, I fear, won't be able to drink their own best wine. In the meantime, come spring, the lattice over the patio at Pension Archontissa will fill with green leaves again and the *georgina* will come on.

MAÏNTAINOSALATA

If you're driving down the mountain from Mitata to the secluded paradise of Kaladi Beach on Kythira, it's best to fortify yourself in advance: there's nothing at Kaladi but bees, blue water, and stone, and you must descend a small precipice to get there. Hit Taverna Skandeia first. It's located beside a dry riverbed and the ruins of the ancient port (destroyed by a massive earthquake and tsunami around 350 B.C.) and is shaded by huge poplar trees, beneath which you can devour *mezedes* prepared by the ebullient Evantheia Protopsaltis.

Always on the lookout for local dishes I haven't seen before, I spied something strange on Evantheia's menu called *maïntanosalata*, or "parsley salad."

In addition to composed salads built around a foundation of greens, cabbage, tomatoes, or other raw vegetables, many Greek "salates" are actually smears and may not contain vegetables at all: common offerings include *melitzanasalata* (an eggplant mash vaguely resembling baba ghanoush, but more typically made with roasted eggplant and brightened with lemon, garlic, and parsley), *tyrosalata* (feta smashed with olive oil and often some hot pepper), and *taramosalata* (a fish roe spread held together with potato or, more commonly, yesterday's dampened bread).

Maïntainosalata turned out to be one of these. And no wonder I'd never heard of it before, since Evantheia invented it. Like so many Greek dishes, it came into being at the intersection of health and frugality. When she visited her herb garden one day and saw that flat-leaf parsley had taken over the entire bed, Evantheia set to work deforesting the plot, extracting a lot of parsley she didn't want to go to waste. Her family suffers from genetic anemia, and so she's always scheming to get her kids to eat iron-rich dishes: on the spot, she found this delicious solution. Turns out parsley—the most popular herb in the Greek kitchen—is rich in iron, not to mention vitamin C. Her kids never suspected that the *meze* she created, which they devoured with abandon, contained a dose of powerful maternal medicine.

8 cups stale bread, crusts removed, cubed

2 large bunches flat-leaf parsley, larger stems discarded

2 small red onions, quartered

3 garlic cloves

2 teaspoons red wine vinegar

Juice of 1 lemon

Salt and pepper

½ cup extra-virgin olive oil, plus more for serving

Soak the bread in warm water for 10 minutes, then drain and squeeze out most of the water. Place the parsley, red onions, and garlic in a food processor and pulse until finely minced, and then add the bread slowly, with the blade running, until well combined. Add the vinegar and lemon juice along with a healthy pinch of salt and ground pepper. Then, with the blade running on low, slowly add the olive oil until the mixture loosens slightly. Serve on small plates with an extra drizzle of very good oil.

CHAPTER EIGHT

Honey

The Thyme Honey of Aphrodite

It's not easy to get to Kythira. In fact, I didn't know anyone who'd actually been there, in spite of the fact that Greeks speak of the island's thyme honey with such reverence. But no one I asked could account for why it was so good, and so expensive, and it was about time someone went there to find out.

The island is located *between:* out where the Aegean and Ionian Seas dissolve into each other, along the invisible line connecting Monemvasia and Chania, five miles off the tip of Lakonia, the easternmost leg of the Peloponnese. Another fifty miles of salt water separate it from Crete. Even Pausanias, the ancient geographer whose directions are usually reliable, is a little vague about how to get there: "Kythira lies opposite Boiai, but to the Plane-trees, where the crossing to the island is shortest, that is to the cape called the Plane-trees from the cape on the mainland coast called the Donkey's Jaw is a distance of five miles sailing."

If you can't locate the Donkey's Jaw these days, you could come by plane: a little airport on Kythira permits overpriced flights from Athens. But most everyone crosses on the ferry from Neapolis, a homely port town at the end of the Peloponnesian road. The impossibly twisted course between Sparta and Neapolis is both beautiful and monotonous, and even if you manage to keep from falling asleep and running your car into the vineyards along both sides of the road, there's a chance the ferry won't be running when you arrive. The sea off Cape Malea likes to devour ships.

No wonder Dimitris Mitropanos croons "We will never find Kythira" in the chorus of a famous Greek love song. The place feels out of reach. Bureaucrats (by definition illogical) have tended to group Kythira with Ionian islands like Corfu and Zakynthos, though that is silly, geographically speaking. Its closer neighbors are Cycladic. But there's nothing Cycladic about Kythira except its propensity for tectonic disaster: portions of it are demolished by an earthquake once every hundred years. "You could set your watch by it," one shop owner said. "And when the last one came, it was so strong you could see the mountains dance." Both of the recent big ones, in 1903 and 2006, registered in the upper sevens or low eights on the Richter scale and could be felt as far away as Sicily and Trieste.

Adding to the island's mystery is the fact that love was born here: Aphrodite rose out of some sea foam that gathered around the severed genitals of Sky, which were cast upon a Kythirian beach by Time the Castrator. The island is an idea as much as it is a place: temperamental, bittersweet, remote, crowded with bees, and as elusive as the love Mitropanos and company may never find.

. . .

I'd been wanting to find Kythira for a while, thanks to my friend Titos Patrikios. He's not a man prone to excess, but he reserves almost hyperbolic praise for Kythirian honey and always has a jar in his kitchen. I remember the first time I joined Titos and his wife, Renna, for breakfast in Athens. He set the honey alongside some Cretan barley rusks, a hunk of ripe feta, and a pot of strong coffee—a simple repast we set upon while chatting and gazing through the sliding glass doors at Mount Lykavitos. Now, I'm not big

Honey: The Thyme Honey of Aphrodite

on sweet things in general, and at the time I didn't really think that much about honey, but I was blown over the first time I tasted the stuff on Titos's table. For years, I'd managed to survive with the profane belief that honey was honey, be it yellowish or brownish, viscous or runny, American or Greek. "She's as sweet as Tupelo honey," Van Morrison sings in a love song from my own corner of the world. And what is honey but sweetness, I'd thought—a rather expensive way for fructose and glucose to party?

But the honey from Kythira was unbelievably rich, with a mouthfeel I found almost creamy, the bright, lemony twang of thyme (the resinous essence of thyme, that is, without any of the grassiness I associate with the herb in my garden) keeping the honey from becoming cloying. It was complicated and, yes, beautifully sweet. It was also impossible not to love its tantalizing color: the shade new copper pennies would have if they could be melted into panes of stained glass.

My palate reacted to it strangely, as if confused, and within moments I caught what I refer to as my "honey buzz": a slow feeling of ascension, light sweat on my brow, some ringing in my ears, and just a tiny bit of tightness in my throat. I recognized this feeling, vaguely, and its origins were erogenous. Didn't the same thing come over me when I kissed Christine Wharton in the first grade at Crestwood Elementary in Madison, Wisconsin, in 1973? Whether brought on by anaphylaxis or angels, the sensation was undeniably pleasurable, and I wanted more of it. Immediately. Nothing I'd ever eaten had made me react like this, and the honey's kaleidoscopic flavor stayed with me for hours, then days. A week later I could still conjure the exact flavor of *that* honey on my palate without the slightest effort of my gustatory imagination.

Still, I had merely glimpsed the light. I hadn't yet been to the land of milk and honey where Yannis Protopsaltis lives.

In the meantime, I dreamt about Kythira, stumbling around blindly in search of information about the place and its bees. Actually going there just wasn't in the cards, and I quickly devoured the small supply of honey I purchased before flying home the previous trip. But there was almost nothing written about the island; all I could find was an occasional footnote about Kythira in old books (almost all referring to the island as Cerigo, its Venetian name). Online, there were the usual glossy websites designed by Greek travel agents, most of them clotted with half-translated text:

> The heavenly beauty of Cythera
> did the ancient Greeks to believe that
> this is the nicest protoperpatise
> gods and humans, the goddess of love.

Deliciously inscrutable stuff, but hardly helpful.

At last, I managed to track down an e-mail address for the Agricultural Cooperative of Honey Producers of Kythira and was astonished to receive a quick and courteous reply from Yannis Protopsaltis, not to mention an invitation to visit his bees in person. I'd soon come to understand that Yannis pretty much *is* the agricultural cooperative, and that his house (where I'd be staying when I found Kythira at last) is the center of all things apian on the island.

. . .

While standing on the ferry's upper deck (still twenty minutes out from port), I thought Kythira was only a mirage. Its mountains were soft and vague, cloaked in golden fog. But as the vessel drew closer to land and we passed the first solid outcroppings, the fog turned into flowers: billions of pale yellow blossoms bedecking a billion prickly bushes. A good place for bees, I thought. Greek islands in this region are usually arid stonescapes unfriendly to botany, but I'd soon see that Kythira is covered from top to bottom in plant life, most of it in the form of low-lying shrubs and wild herbs.

The Protopsaltis family lives in the village of Mitata, right in the heart of this profusion. It's a farming community with only a few working businesses and has nothing, really, to lure visitors. But it's easy to see why farmers and beekeepers would settle in this place: a corrugated plateau stretches around Mitata before rising to volcanic peaks on one horizon or dropping down to the sea on another. It feels like the top of the world. The village and the fields that surround it rest upon an ancient seabed, so the place is very fertile, vineyards and gardens as far as the eye can see. Here, the earth churns up a bounty of fossil-splattered rocks and enormous, petrified scallop shells (Botticelli's Venus tiptoes upon one of these in the famous painting), which farmers must haul from the fields during plowing. Beyond that inconvenience is a much more serious problem: when the big quakes come, this sandy and unstable substructure liquefies, and down goes the village every time. Forty houses and the village's largest church succumbed to the last one.

There are several honey producers in Mitata, and many signs along the road are decorated with cartoon bees, but the Protopsaltis's Aplynori House is the easiest to find. A tidy sign pointing down an alley promises in bold print that everything in that direction will be "milk and honey." Aplynori House is a three-level structure decked out with a handsome paint job and surrounded by a meticulous herb garden and a wall of flowers.

It turns out this well-kept pension is really just a front: behind the scenes they're doing serious agrarian business. Yannis is the honey in the equation and his wife, Eleni, the milk: I'm thrilled to discover that Mrs. Protopsaltis (née Petrocheilou) is as famous around the island for her cheese as Yannis is for his bees. Each morning in her ground-level workshop, she makes up to fifty wheels of Kythirian cheese. In winter, the Protopsaltis family lives upstairs, since the pension is in fact their house, which they vacate in summer and rent out to agriculturally minded visitors like me.

Yannis and Eleni are both slender and fastidious, and it's hard to keep up with their breakneck pace. They married when he was twenty-three and she

Figure 14. Yannis Protopsaltis and Eleni Petrocheilou in their land
of milk and honey, Kythira.

only seventeen, and I doubt they've stopped working since the moment they
met. Now in their forties, they move together as if part of the same body,
communicating with each other through gestures and eye contact and the
occasional perfunctory sentence, embodiments of marital efficiency. Yannis
wears the spectacles of a professor and keeps his curly black hair cropped
close, his lanky frame jittery with unspent energy. Eleni moves with an
equivalent amount of quick, feline grace, with a wide smile and flashing
brown eyes. Their two teenage daughters, Maria and Athanasia, look just like
her. They are shy to me at first, and like Eleni they are a little afraid to exercise their slightly halting, but perfectly good English. Yannis barely speaks
a word of it, on the other hand, and he makes no concessions for my own
insufficient Greek.

   When he guides me downstairs to show me around the honey shop
and cheese-making facilities, each question I pose to him elicits a flood of
erudition. I'd need a scribe and a team of pastoralists and translators to help
me navigate the facts, figures, and local history that burst the seams of his

being. He's not just a producer of Kythirian honey, but a true missionary of its virtues, one of the island's most knowledgeable agrarians, and a real scholar of its terroir.

Information comes at me fast and I must take notes in scribbled shorthand. Within ten minutes I know that the cliffs across the canyon have names, not to mention the caves hollowing their sides (which look to me like a pair of menacing owl eyes, but turn out to be called "dog" and "cat"); I'm shown how to shuck yellow split peas using an ancient mortar stone fitted with an olive-wood handle; I learn that the flowers I saw from the boat are actually two different shrubs, called *aspalathros* and *agathi* in the local dialect, and that the bees are indifferent to these yellow blossoms, which aren't for making honey; there's a short list of local shrines and churches any responsible visitor would seek out immediately, not to mention the hiking trails bisecting the island, which should be investigated soon; there are thirty-five hundred inhabitants of the island and sixty-four villages and Kythira is the thirteenth largest island in the Greek archipelago; wine can be made here from several local varieties including *petrolanos*, *alikaras*, and *doukomaki*; over there, he says, is a basket of antique farm implements, including some very old *chteni*, as in this region they call the little rakes used to harvest olives; though few farmers bother with official certification, perhaps as much as 80 percent of the agriculture on Kythira is organic, including most of the vineyards; the Greek honeybee is *Apis mellifera cecropia;* there are also dialect names for all the island's herbs, so wild sage is known either by the usual *faskomilo* or the local *atanaida*, and thyme is the usual *thymari* or the unusual *athribi*, though oregano is *rigani* both in ordinary Greek and in Kythirian dialect, for reasons he forgets to explain; on a shelf over here is the very first radio brought into the village of Mitata in 1945, just after the war; here on this other shelf you see a bottle of the beautiful red liquor we call *fatourada*, in which fiery *raki* is laced with cinnamon and other spices; and on Kythira there grows a wonderful variety

Kythirian Dissertation

of peach called "the breasts of Aphrodite," which are as sweet and delicate as the name suggests; on this island, they also make a kind of *trahanas* (or sour-milk porridge) called *xinochondro* that's often served with the unusual accompaniment of eggplant.

When he stops to sip his coffee, I seize the moment to get a self-serving word in: where, I ask, is the best place to eat in Mitata?

"Well, that's easy," Yannis says, "since we only have one restaurant here and it's all you shall require. But you should also drive down to Paleopolis, where my brother has a restaurant near an excellent beach. You know," he says without taking another breath, "Paleopolis is the site of ancient Skandia, originally a Minoan port that was maintained into the Hellenistic period until it was destroyed by a tidal wave in the fourth century, and . . ."

I want to listen to this bodhisattva of the hive forever, letting his knowledge pour over me. But when at last he stops to reload, as it were, giving me a moment to ask another question, it's only to let out a deep sigh and deliver this bit of bad news: I've got just twenty-four hours to learn everything Yannis has to teach me. He's leaving the day after tomorrow for Athens, he explains, wiping his brow with his forearm and looking down at his feet, suddenly bashful. The reason: his honey was just awarded top prize for all the thyme honey produced in Greece, and he and Eleni are being summoned to the capital to receive it in person. We'll have to go to the mountain tomorrow afternoon to visit the bees. I do my best to deflect his apologies with my own expressions of gratitude, very pleased with myself to have found the best honey in Greece—if not on the planet—by pretty much sticking my finger randomly into the telephone book of the Internet.

．　．　．

When Yannis excuses himself to attend to some business on the telephone, I seek out Mitata's one *taverna*. The village is spread out in a grid of more or less perpendicular alleyways, not the baffling labyrinth one typically finds in island villages. Having been demolished every hundred years or so, the village must have had its recent reconstructions guided by modern surveyors. Still, the place feels very Greek, each cottage along the road tidy and private, surrounded by prodigious gardens and immense terra-cotta pots. A friendly chorus of greetings follows in my wake: on nearly every porch someone is watering flowers, or shelling peas, or tinkering away the evening, and all my offerings of *kalispera* (good afternoon) are echoed back to me with corresponding cheer.

The main square is located on the edge of town, not at its center. It's a complete wreck, as if the last great quake happened only yesterday. First, there's a high-shouldered, brightly painted church at one end, garlanded with yellow "CAUTION" tape; jagged fissures are visible in the foundation and some snake up the walls and widen into chasms. The building looks like it might split in half at any moment. At one corner, walls have fallen away to reveal the skeleton of a concrete spiral staircase, its severed helix dropping off into thin air. The *plateia* itself, located right next to it, is little more than a raw dirt parking lot, though I see that it's been covered in a lattice of rebar—someone will be pouring cement there imminently. Though no work is currently going on, two men are standing with hands on their hips in the doorway of a handsome stone building, surveying the scene.

I'm surprised to hear them speaking English when I approach, and even more surprised to perceive the goofy lilt of Australian accents. One of them, whom I take to be a laborer, wears a sweat-stained ball cap and spattered overalls; the other man is ferociously tanned, with a slicked-back lid of white hair and a barrel chest. He introduces himself as Michalis and says he knows it will be his job to feed me; Yannis called ahead. Before I can enter the restaurant, however, I'm made to stand with them for a few awkward minutes pondering the mysteries of concrete, my own hands on my hips for no good reason. Michalis tells me that the quake that cracked open the church five years ago also knocked half the main square off the edge of the mountain. He points to a cliff at one end, where a new stone wall is being mortared into place.

When we've beheld the scene of tomorrow's labor with enough solemnity, Michalis grips my arm with an enormous calloused hand and guides me to a table inside, then begins speaking *in medias res* about his food.

"So tell me you like artichokes, mate, because they're perfectly in season right now. And you should be aware that I make my own olive oil here—my son Byron has a nice stand of trees just outside the village—and it is green and raw and will be good for your heart and blood. And we grow all our own vegetables, which know only sun and rainwater. And what about some *horta* and a morsel or two of tender goat?"

Music to my ears, of course. And the food is outstanding and expertly prepared by Michalis's wife, Katarina, who bops around the kitchen energetically. The artichokes' delicate hearts have been braised with fresh peas, lemon juice, dill, and a lot of beautiful olive oil. They are as light and fresh as spring itself, a perfect foil for the rich and fatty goat—whose slowly braised meat falls loose of the bone with just the lightest press of my fork. As for the wild greens, well, "those weeds were plucked from between the rows of my vineyard this morning," Michalis remarks. They've just been steamed and are still hot. I douse them with the juice of a fat lemon, dust them with coarse salt, and revel in their scratchy texture and dusky bitterness.

Michalis approves of my mission and doesn't seem surprised to learn that I've followed the honey trail here to Kythira. I'd have been a fool to go anywhere else, he tells me, "especially the Peloponnese. OK, on Crete they make some good honey too, but here on Kythira everything is much more concentrated and our honey is the most pure."

It occurs to me that even ancient Kythirians would have been bred to distrust both their northern and southern neighbors. After all, the kingdom of Sparta once held sway with an iron fist over Kythira and the whole region.

And everyone in Greece distrusts Cretans, while simultaneously viewing them with unconditional respect.

Michalis makes it clear that any honey producer on Kythira would have been a capable host—himself, for instance—but he gives a vigorous nod of the head when I bring up Yannis Protopsaltis, whom he refers to as a "very good boy."

"Yannis has done a lot for this village," Michalis tells me while opening my second beer and pouring another for himself, "and few people on the island know as much about its history as him. We're all people of the land here. Come and see my farm after lunch one day. All organic production and hard work, if you know what I mean."

"So why is the honey of Kythira so good?" I ask him.

"It's not easy to say. The island is covered in hardy wild herbs and flowering plants of all kinds. That's important. More than anything, the bees seem to love being here. And we protect the island from chemicals and . . . outside influences."

He utters the last bit gruffly, and I wonder what on earth he might mean by "outside influences." Turkish hornets? Italian wasps? Libyan horseflies? No, the abomination is closer to home.

"Watch out," Michalis mutters, narrowing his eyelids spitefully, "when buying honey from Kythira when you're not on Kythira. Bee farmers from the Peloponnese sometimes ship their hives over here by boat. The brigands let their bees raid our thyme for a week and then return to Corinth or Nafplion and try to pass the stuff off as Kythirian honey. Which it's not. Those bees are from the mainland! Some people are even more dishonest, merely slapping our name onto jars of inferior honey they buy from Bulgaria. Bah!"

As for this last point, I know he's right. Just days before, in the Athens agora, some friends pointed out a jar of unreasonably cheap thyme honey from Kythira. They thought they'd found a real bargain: only four euros? But when I studied the label's stylized Greek, I found that the honey was being sold under the brand name "KRYTHERA." That misspelling constituted an evil bit of false marketing. To the shop owner's consternation, and with not a little spite on my part, I took the time to loiter there awhile, warning my friends and also a few Norwegian tourists away from the stuff.

"Real thyme honey requires hard work and patience," Michalis continues, "since the season is short and the island is small. And the bee farmers here don't take any shortcuts by feeding their hives sugar water during the off-season. Over winter, you must leave a portion of the precious honey with the bees, since it's their food, after all. You can't be too greedy. We've also had many serious fires in the past ten years, robbing the bees of a lot of foliage. That's cut down on the supply. Then up goes the price. And so our honey is very expensive."

As for his Australian accent, he explains that there's a long history of connection between the two places; as many as forty thousand Kythirians emigrated down under after the Second World War. Only a very few, like him, ever came back. Michalis worked for twenty years in Sydney as a hotel chef, long enough to save up the money to build a small house outside Mitata and begin tending his family's land again.

"My dream was to trade the long hours of work in Australia for even longer hours here on Kythira," he jokes. "To be honest," he continues with a furrowing of the brow, "I work harder now than I ever have, but this is the kind of work that makes you live forever. There's no time card to punch and there's no boss to answer to. I take my dog out to the vineyard in the morning and boil myself a coffee under a wild olive tree and admire what I've accomplished with these old hands. I'm a very lucky man, finishing out my life this way."

. . .

Since I have only one morning to see Yannis and Eleni in action, I wake early enough to help them make the cheese. By the time I climb downstairs and step

Honey: The Thyme Honey of Aphrodite

inside Eleni's workshop a little after daybreak, a deep vat of milk is already steaming, a mechanical whisk stirring it in buttery circles. My hosts have been up for hours, and several empty milk cans are upside down and draining beneath a huge geranium outside, to the delight of the morning's first flies.

I'm still rubbing sleep from my eyes when the next delivery truck arrives, its shock absorbers squeaking beneath a load of full milk cans. Two very gamey shepherds—father and son—leap from the cab and begin slinging them off the pickup as if they are weightless, arranging them in a neat rows by the door of the workshop. The father soon stops to smoke and lets his son do most of the work. The boy is Apollonian: tall as a column, sunburnt, and absurdly handsome, his Afro of black hair tied back with a blue bandana. Though working diligently, so his father won't notice, I can tell he's flipping his mane about and flexing his biceps for the benefit of Yannis's daughters, who have just stepped from their basement apartment and are now pretending they don't see him. It's like a moment out of *Daphnis and Chloe*, this scene of pastoral flirtation, except Yannis's daughters study all day and night to get perfect grades and they'll probably finish their educations at good universities abroad. They are extremely sophisticated, self-confident, and worldly: no shepherd girls by a long shot. The poor boy hasn't got a chance.

Eleni makes four kinds of cheese. The one called Fratsia is made entirely from cow's milk. It's then aged a few months and sold as is, or transformed by Eleni in two other ways: either by lightly smoking it, as with a provolone, or by preserving it in olive oil to make a traditional *ladotyri*. Her most famous cheese, however, is named Mitato after the village itself. This is the real prize, and it's also the one we're making today. To a mixture of sheep's and goat's milk, Eleni adds about 15 percent cow's milk—which civilizes the other milks and contributes a bit of lushness to the finished product, aged three to six months. "Our village was named for a *mitato*," she explains. "These are natural limestone caves the shepherds once used as stables. Maria will show you some old ones when she takes you on a walk on Sunday afternoon. All of our milk comes from local shepherds, and so the name of my cheese remembers this history."

After the rennet is added and the curd sets, Eleni pulls the plug on the vat and suddenly we're standing in a fast-running stream of hot, milky water, which gurgles and whirlpools at the drain by the door. Yannis uses a kind of mesh shovel to transfer the curd onto a long steel table, where we wait with a pyramid of perforated plastic baskets. I help to press mounds of hot curd into these, where the cheese will drain and assume its shape. While I'm at work, it occurs to me that I have no idea where Eleni stores all her cheese. "Finish what you are doing and I'll show you," she tells me. Eleni packs three baskets for every one that I fill, but I'm too happy to feel embarrassed for my slowness. After all, I'm up to my elbows in cheese, in such a fog of dairy steam that I can barely see what I'm doing. The smell of hot milk is sacred to me. My maternal grandfather, Eugene Meier, owned a busy dairy farm in southern Wisconsin, and I remember standing beside him as a young boy while a massive vat of pasteurizing milk churned. The diesel engine of the shiny milk truck would be grumbling outside the barn, waiting to haul it away.

By the time Eleni wraps our twenty baskets in cheesecloth and transfers them to a kind of upright vise, where they will press and continue to drain for an hour, several more shepherds have dropped off their morning's milk. The cans are piling up quickly outside the workshop, and Eleni has a long morning ahead of her. Nevertheless, she declares it time for breakfast and walks me outside, where it is at least twenty degrees cooler, in the direction of a silver semitrailer. I'd seen the awkward thing from my balcony last night, and thought it had just broken down in Aplynori's backyard—an industrial eyesore blemishing the otherwise bucolic garden. But when Eleni flips open the heavy steel latch and the tall doors swing wide, I hear a compressor humming and realize that this is her refrigerator: five layers of wooden shelves line all the truck's interior walls, where hundreds of wheels of Fratsia and Mitato are sleeping in various stages of readiness.

She grabs a cheese from one of the lower shelves and hands it to me. "Let's eat," she says, and back we go into the house. By the time I've washed my hands and donned a clean shirt, Eleni has already mixed up a light batter and is dropping spoonfuls of it into hot oil. I'm too distracted to ask what she's cooking up, since on the counter that wheel of Mitato I carried in has been sliced open and cut into coarse wedges. Next to it, curiously, is a tall jar affixed with the kind of plastic pump you'd see on a soap dispenser.

"What's this?" I ask her, but she just smiles, bidding me to try it with a lift of her chin.

When I press down on the dispenser, a translucent ribbon streams from the nozzle onto the wedge of cheese I'm waving beneath it: it's thyme honey, of course, and an astonishingly rich accompaniment for the very ripe, very creamy cheese. I'm flabbergasted. Where else but in the promised land would Kythirian thyme honey be served in soap dispensers? It's like offering someone beluga caviar with a soupspoon. I could die of happiness. But no, not yet: there's a basket of good bread here, too. I tear off a hunk and smother it with honey, already feeling a little buzzed.

"Slow down, Christopher," Eleni jokes, "because Yannis is bringing different honey for you to try. That's the last you'll taste of thyme honey on this visit. Everyone on the island ran out over a month ago, since last summer's harvest was small and all of Greece was hungry for it. We put this jar aside for your visit."

At that, Yannis bursts in the back door with a huge jar of something the color of burnt caramel. He sets it before me with an authoritative nod of his head, waiting for me to identify this strange specimen. Sure, it must be honey, but it's so radically different from the stuff in the soap dispenser that I can only look back at him blankly. "Ereíki," he says, which means absolutely nothing to me.

I lift up the jar and tip it sideways. The honey is almost entirely opaque, though tiny champagne-like bubbles float in suspended animation throughout, reflecting light. It's also nearly solid—even when I sway it back and forth it doesn't budge. So I hand it back to Yannis with a shrug. He looks pleased to have stumped the pupil, then unscrews the lid and ladles three or four wedges of it into a small saucepan he's been heating, where the mounds begin to melt across the hot surface, glistening smears of tarnished gold appearing in their wakes.

Eleni has arranged the fry cakes in overlapping rows in a deep serving platter. Just when she extracts the very last one from the oil and piles it with the others, Yannis rushes over with his pan and douses the whole display with the warm honey—a fearlessly indulgent amount, I note, perhaps two cups worth—so that the fry cakes begin bobbing at first, then slowly sink, drowning a beautiful death. I scarf them down while they are still hot enough to blister the roof of my mouth, alternating with a cool wedge of cheese now and then. The fry cakes are much heartier than floppy American pancakes, especially given the accompaniment of the aged cheese. And the honey is fascinating and very mysterious: it's sweet, yes, but with a musky bitterness that is somehow reminiscent of both flowers and smoke. It's actually about as savory as any honey could be.

Yannis and I have a puzzling exchange about the secrets of this strange honey, and he might as well be talking alchemy. So Maria is summoned from downstairs to translate some of the technical vocabulary. When the thyme blossoms disappear by late summer, she explains, the honey is collected and the hives rest briefly before their next adventure. Soon, a different plant blankets the island with its blossoms: *ereíki*, a kind of island heather, which matures in autumn and blooms through much of the winter. Unlike thyme honey, which will remain fluid for years, heather honey is thixotropic, seizing up almost immediately after harvest (assuming the texture, I note, of something like miso paste). One shouldn't confuse this with crystallization, however, which is what will happen to most honey after a while (a brief application of heat will restore any honey to its previous state). Like thyme honey, it is extremely healthful, Maria says, and it's been used by healers since ancient times—*ereíki* honey is particularly good for dressing wounds and may have antibiotic properties.

I believe thyme honey is the essence of honey in its purest, most rarefied state, so for me *ereíki* honey is delightfully eccentric. I'd liken it to Laphroaig, which is about as far as you can take single malt Scotch in the direction of medicine while retaining some beauty and subtlety. *Ereíki* is an acquired taste, in other words, and very exquisite medicine.

. . .

All my wounds deliciously dressed, it's time to stand for my fitting. Yannis unearths a large cardboard box and begins unfolding bright white, space-age-looking, body-length bee suits, holding them up next to me to see which one might fit. When he finds one that is satisfactory, he refolds it and hands it over, telling me to be ready by noon. Then off he goes to join Eleni and the cheese.

I'm in danger of falling into a stupor, with such a belly full of sweetness, so I decide a digestive ramble is in order. But I don't get more than two hundred meters down the road before something big happens: I saw it and am here to bear witness.

A battered pickup truck and a gleaming Volvo meet at the narrow crossroads where one of the side alleys intersects the main artery running through town (itself not much wider than an alley). This is the first time I've seen more than one vehicle moving through Mitata at a time, and the drivers look surprised to encounter someone else on the road. The fact that a pedestrian happens to be there too, at this moment of convergence, is almost beyond comprehension. All three of us freeze, unsure what to do. Behind both windshields, the drivers' sunglassed faces remain impassive, if not a little hostile.

I'm tempted to beat a quick retreat, if only there were room to run, but I am pinned there with them. At last, the driver in the truck waves his hairy arm out the window and the Volvo inches through. I do my part in this bit of highway diplomacy, leaning back against a whitewashed wall to avoid being creamed by the exterior mirror on the Volvo's passenger side. Then the truck driver finds first gear and accelerates toward his business in the other direction.

Just like that: the most exciting thing to happen, traffic-wise, in Mitata in a long time. Then it's over, and the village falls back to sleep again. Within a few seconds it is so quiet that I can hear the murmuring song bees make while ravishing the white blossoms of a pear tree in a garden across the street.

.   .   .

"Smoke rolls and scarves in the grove," Sylvia Plath writes. "The mind of the hive thinks this is the end of everything." Yannis tells me that Stone Age human beings figured out that bees were calmed (or perhaps frightened into a catatonic state) by smoke. It would be hard to exaggerate the importance of this discovery. We've driven his red truck a few miles outside Mitata and have parked it in a flat area beneath the mountain known as Paleókastro—atop which the Byzantine shrine of Agios Giorgios shares space with the ruins of a four-thousand-year-old Minoan peak sanctuary. It feels like an appropriate location to review the history of human and bee interaction.

Yannis dissertates on this subject while lighting dried pine needles and stuffing them inside his bellowed smoker; when he pumps the device's wooden handle, it exhales a satisfying puff of bright white smoke. Bees are never truly domesticated, though we can learn to cooperate with their complicated system of matriarchal civilization. And smoke helps. Before our distant ancestors learned this fact, and also figured out how to fashion places for swarms to shelter, honey was only gathered opportunistically. Humming jackpots were located in the crooks of tall trees or in cliffside crevasses, and someone brave or stupid enough had to climb up and raid the comb with his bare hands, then somehow climb back down again.

That kind of hunting and gathering was abandoned long ago in favor of much more sophisticated commerce, and no doubt bees and humans have been cooperating beneath Paleókastro since very ancient times. This pseudohusbandry (or honey midwifery, if you will) is even legible in the region's mythology. The matriarchal Minoans, who worshipped here, brought with them from Crete their reverence for a bee goddess, as well as their tradition of embalming the dead with honey (indeed, the stuff is immortal, being the only food that will never spoil). According to scholars Anne Baring and Jules Cashford, this prehistoric Cretan bee deity gradually morphed into Aphrodite, who later Greeks sometimes called "Melissa," Queen Bee of Heaven and Earth, sweetest of them all.

Turn back the clock three thousand years and Yannis would be performing a sacred rite in service of the goddess's hives. Today, beneath Paleókastro, I'm struck with the feeling of *betweenness* that Kythira embodies: the mountains seem to be reaching down to embrace us, while at the same time we seem to be rising into them like the bees. The sky is utterly clear, and the noontime sun is working hard to vaporize every last bit of moisture from the flower-strewn ground. Here, the earth feels heavenly and the heavens seem, at least for a moment, earthly. Aeschylus has Aphrodite put it this way in a speech from the *Danaides:*

> The great and amorous sky curved over the earth,
> and lay upon her as a pure lover.
> The rain, the humid flux descending from heaven
> for both human and animal, for both thick and strong,
> germinated the wheat, swelled the furrows with fecund mud
> and brought forth the buds in the orchards.
> And it is I, who empowered these moist espousals,
> I, the great Aphrodite. . . .

No creature has as much power as the bee to bridge the liminal realms: raiding mountain blossoms to fill hexagonal combs, bringing nectar down to earth for mortals to enjoy.

I wriggle into my strangely sacerdotal white suit, being careful not to leave any skin exposed and tucking my pant legs into my socks. As far as I can see through the fine mesh of my bee burqa, there are yellow flowers in all directions. Within a few weeks, Yannis says, they'll wake up one day to find that the entire landscape has changed. The *agathi* here now will finish blossoming at about the exact moment that the thyme decides to put on its show. "Then even the air will seem to turn purple," he remarks dreamily. No wonder: there's an astonishing amount of thyme here. Every other bush is a clump of wild thyme the size of a large basket, and a pointillism of tiny purple specks is already asserting itself among the predominantly yellow canvas.

About fifty of Yannis's hives are scattered beneath Paleókastro, and he wants to check on these colonies before the thyme comes on. He has four hundred hives total, in several locations around the island. Normally, each hive will yield four to five kilos of thyme honey, which will sell for about twenty-three euros per kilo. The thyme honey is harvested in September, but there's no rest for the beekeeper after that, since the *ereíki* blooms next. The demand for heather honey is much smaller than for thyme honey—which means it's about half the price, only twelve euros per kilo. Without even crunching the actual numbers, it's easy to see that nobody will get rich on honey alone, though maximizing the precious thyme honey crop is obviously important.

I follow Yannis over to the first bee box and notice that he is careful to stand next to it, not in front of it—after all, this is an airport, and he wouldn't want to block traffic in and out of the half-inch landing pad at the hive's ground level. He unlatches the lid and lifts it without hesitation, puffing the bellows of the smoker a few times in a circular motion atop the frames, which calms everyone down immediately. Most of the bees retreat from the top crossbars down into the center of the hive. Then, propping the smoker

Figure 15. Yannis Protopsaltis inspects his bees beneath Paleókastro, Kythira.

between his knees, Yannis uses a little hooked tool to wedge a brood frame from the box and lift it to the light for inspection. It's a beautiful thing to behold, the uniform comb and the capped cells being tended by a mosh pit of workers. Other bees are dancing alone near the edge of the frame, their semaphore inscrutable, jagged, and fascinating.

Satisfied with what he sees, Yannis replaces the frame and selects another one, moving with expert dexterity and completely unperturbed by the bees that dive-bomb the mesh covering his face. Every once in a while, another puff of smoke is proffered, and the bees calm back down. Yannis spends more time with the third frame he removes, pressing his face close to the bees to study them. Then, with a very gentle hand and with great speed, he grabs one of the bees around the abdomen, pinning its wings down with his fingers, and lifts it in my direction. I can see a worried expression behind his mask. He points out a raised black speck behind the bee's head—it looks like a tiny wart, but it is actually a parasitic mite.

The great poet Virgil, who seemed a little obsessed with bees (dedicating the entire final book of his *Georgics* to them), cautioned Roman beekeepers about apian diseases and the hazards of entomological competition. Pity the hive subject to such infestation, and imagine the horror of the beekeeper who opens his hives to discover that

> the newt, out of sight,
> eats at the combs, the chambers swarm with light-shunning beetles,
> while the drone that does nothing sits down to food meant for others,
> or the cruel hornet closes in on the bees' weaker weapons,
> or moths, an ominous species, or the spider, hateful
> to Minerva, hangs its loosely spun webs in the doorway.

What Yannis has found is probably a varroa mite. The professor is impressed that I've actually heard of these little vampires, which suck the life out of young bees and can diminish production or even cause a hive to collapse. Full infestations are rarely a problem here, Yannis assures me, but one must always pay attention. He cherishes his job as the caretaker of the hives.

I've been afraid to ask Yannis about colony collapse disorder (what the experts call CCD), since it gives me nightmares. Across the world, whole bee colonies have been crashing suddenly and without easy explanation. If the bees go, all human agriculture goes with them—a terrifying prospect. Sure, bee colonies have always been subject to collapse now and then. Even Virgil makes note of this (he famously suggests that after such a collapse beekeepers can reboot their hives with an old Egyptian technique involving autogenesis and a rotting bull carcass). But I don't think Virgil could have foreseen a global apian catastrophe.

In 2006, there was nothing short of a "surge of CCD deaths," according to Rowan Jacobsen, who's written a compelling book on the subject.

In the United States alone, Jacobsen reported, "perhaps 800,000 of the 2.4 million colonies of honey bees . . . collapsed that winter. Thirty million bees dead, and no one knew why." Some tepid media attention followed (environmental portents rarely attract much interest in a country obsessed with the dating habits of celebrities), as did a lot of conspiracy theorizing: certain experts blamed newfangled viruses or pesticide use in addition to vampire mites; others said genetically modified crops were to blame; and some even held cell phones responsible (was global electromagnetic chaos the cause?). Though CCD was rampant throughout North America, Asia, and Europe (including some parts of Greece), Kythira saw none of it.

After he has replaced the last frame and refastened the latches on the hive, we make our way to the next cluster of bee boxes. I ask Yannis whether he thinks Kythira's organic farming methods might help protect the bees. He lets out a deep sigh before answering.

"Organic farming can't hurt, but I don't think pesticides are the main problem. It's more likely a result of climate changes, to which the bees are sensitive. And if diseases are to blame, then it's easy to see how they will spread when beekeepers move their hives from place to place too often," he explains.

I remember what Michalis said about thieving Peloponnesians, but I also find myself thinking about American apiarists who truck their bees all over the country, "renting out" their pollinators to orchards and farms, then moving them by interstate to the next place where the money is.

"Here on Kythira," Yannis continues, "there's rarely much need to move the hives, since there are so many aromatic plants available to them. We have the luxury of leaving the bees alone to do their work."

When we finish inspecting the hives and he is satisfied with the colonies' preparations for summer, we drive back to the house and Yannis bids me farewell with a vigorous handshake and a quick hug. He insists that I must find my way back to Kythira again soon. I'm inspired by this man's optimism, not to mention his humility, and I discover that there's a lump in my throat when he dismisses himself to pack for his trip to Athens. It's possible, I think morbidly, that Yannis is the last of the great beekeepers and that his bees might be some of the last to thrive on earth. What sad story might the hives be telling us about ourselves and our agriculture the next time I step foot on Kythira?

I don't see how the island can remain protected from CCD forever. As with all the traditional foodways I long to comprehend, there's the usual danger of the artisanal line dying out—knowledge of the old ways disappearing through human attrition. But in this case, my longing goes beyond culinary pleasure. The death of honey would be catastrophic. We can live without traditional bread and island cheese, and we can live without sweetness, too, but we'll never survive without bees.

.   .   .

A late afternoon meal with Michalis and Katarina goes a long way toward cheering me up. They are sitting at a corner table looking absentmindedly at the news when I arrive. But Michalis clicks off the television when I walk in. He says they've been waiting for me. I'm moved. I hadn't even confirmed that I was coming for lunch, in spite of Michalis's casual invitation yesterday.

"We're not having anything fancy, mind you," Michalis quips, "just some things from the garden I picked this morning."

Katarina arranges us each a generous plate: on mine alone, there are four baby zucchini with their yellow blossom ends still attached, two tender potatoes, and a mound of purplish-green *radiki*, the more or less generic name for weeds (one related linguistically to radicchio, a very fancy weed loved by the Italians). They've all been boiled lightly and flooded with Byron's delicious, scratchy olive oil. A half lemon has tagged along for the ride, bringing a little brightness to the proceedings. In the middle of the table, to be shared among us, is some bread and a plate of olives and cheese—Eleni's Mitato, of course, which all the restaurants on the island seem to serve.

When my friends taste Greek vegetables for the first time, they ask me why they are so good. I ask myself the same question all the time, and my usual answer is "because we're in Greece." That's certainly part of the reason: food is more beautiful when eaten slowly in a beautiful place. I get excellent produce in Pennsylvania and know that my friend David, an Amish farmer, works very hard to help it survive in our unforgiving local climate. But I swear that every Greek zucchini tastes like the Platonic idea of a zucchini—and that goes for peppers and tomatoes and eggplants and all the other vegetables, too.

"You must make the vegetables work hard," Michalis explains. "We get a little rain each spring just after planting and the soil stores up a bit of moisture. After that, I don't water them again. Most farmers irrigate too much. Not me."

That's hard to imagine, considering how much sun a Greek island gets, and how little rain between April and August.

"The plants are challenged and some don't make it, but those that do produce fruits of the greatest flavor and intensity. You can taste how hard they want to be," he says boldly, holding a gleaming wedge of potato up to the light.

This is the ultimate health food: a meal consisting almost entirely of plants dressed in olive oil, with just a garnish of dairy protein and some bread (delicately soured with some village baker's *prozymi*, I might add). Balancing one's diet in this way, Michal Pollan and so many others now preach, is the key to human longevity, not to mention environmental sustainability. If so, Michalis and Katarina embody its virtues perfectly—they look impossibly young for their ages.

Come to think of it, Kythira looks remarkably good too, considering how old it is. Against the odds, and in spite of Peloponnesians and earthquakes, human beings have found a recipe for sustainable life here, nurturing the island's bounty with diligence and respect.

While we're finishing our meal, Maria appears in the restaurant's doorway. She's been dispatched by her parents to find me, since Yannis has determined that I must see a few things before I leave his island. I say good-bye to Michalis and Katarina, promising to return again for my evening meal, and then set off with Maria on a tour of the Kythirian landscape. I feel sorry that she's been asked to give up a few precious hours of leisure to stroll around the village with the strange American—surely she has better things to do, including homework. But that feeling fades when I see how seriously she takes this task. Very much the honey professor's daughter, not to mention a viable scholar in her own right, Maria has come equipped with a clipboard full of detailed notes and pretranslated words she doesn't want to misrepresent in the rush of conversation.

"I've taken this walk many times with my father, over and over since I was very young, and though I know only a fraction of what my father knows, every detail is precious and I don't want to forget anything," Maria says with real zeal.

She points out where the village idiot lives (a madwoman who barks like a dog, occasionally speaks prophecy, and is generously taken care of by her neighbors) and shows me where the last big fire was extinguished (just on the verge of the main road). We visit a tiny church next, behind which Maria locates and opens a trapdoor so that I can climb down a creaky ladder to visit a cliffside ossuary. I emerge from that bit of spelunking with my hair full of spiderwebs, a little unnerved.

Then she guides me outside the village, into a valley where the *mitata* are found. For these, she reminds me, her mother named the family's most famous cheese. The remains of the old sheep and goat pens are still there, but mostly the old caves are now filled with weeds and sand. Along the road, she stops frequently to scrape away at the sandstone walls—we are walking through a kind of geology dump. Maria keeps handing me interesting fossils and petrified souvenirs, with which I fill my pockets obediently. At one point, she makes us backtrack a little, then has us scramble up a steep incline to enter another spooky cave sanctuary—this one an actual church carved into the hillside. It's cool and dank inside, and our voices echo. This is the shrine of John the Unbaptized, where mothers once brought their stillborns and dead infants. I ask Maria what they did with their babies after bringing them here, but she just shrugs.

"They left them here, I guess," she says sadly after a minute.

While we are walking back toward the village, swallows begin swooping across the rooftop of the valley, snapping up bugs in the violet light of dusk. Maria stops next to a rock wall and ponders it, running a hand over its striations.

"Weird," she says. "When we were here a few weeks ago this wall was riddled with fossils, but now there are none. The island seems to change every day. My father will find that interesting when I tell him."

Yes, Maria Protopsaltis is about to go off to university, probably far away from Kythira. But her father has made sure that she knows everything about the place she's leaving: its botany, its geology, its spiritual history, not to mention the habits of its famous bees. Someday, she'll inherit her family's cheese and honey business, if she wants it. To my surprise, she doesn't seem to resent this one bit, as so many teenagers might. The gift of real local knowledge is one she appreciates dearly, from what I can tell, and she's inheriting much more than just Greek culture from her parents. There are also ancient values at stake here, of the sort farmers have passed down to their children and grandchildren for as long as the island remembers.

In any case, alongside today's gloomy premonitions about the collapse of the bee-loving universe arises this counterweight: in Maria Protopsaltis I see the future of Kythira, and something hopeful in the uncertain future of Greece, and perhaps even (since by now I'm allowing myself to be swept up in the island's ever-optimistic salt breeze) the future of our otherwise hapless, uncooperative, and misguided species.

AFTER MIDNIGHT: WATERMELON, FETA, *TSIPOURO*

Greeks rarely eat their evening meal until well after dark. You'll often see Greek families—wide-awake toddlers in tow—being seated at a *taverna* after ten o'clock on a Saturday night. Diners not encumbered by their offspring will eat much later than that. And Greek meals are delightfully long: *mezedes* coming in waves, gradually, so that the appetite smolders, leaving room for a taste of fish or meat when it arrives at the end. Then there's the mandatory digestive stroll, or *volta*, leading almost always to a *zacharoplastío* ("sugar shop"), where it's possible to have a thimble of coffee and a wedge of something sweet.

Or, dessert and digestives are taken at home. My dear friend Kay Bash had a real knack for finding perfect watermelons at the open-air market in the suburb of Pylea, which she introduced me to soon after my arrival in Greece twenty years back. From behind every stall, farmers, fishermen, and butchers advertised their wares by screaming. Most adopted the kind of monotone, machine-gun staccato I associate with auctioneers, but others would fight through the cacophony by pitching their stylized caterwauling high into the air. That "fermenting mass of human-kind" (as Wordsworth puts it) turned me off at first, but the offerings at the market were so much fresher than at the grocery store. Soon I had my favorite hawkers, and I knew who sold the most interesting cheese and the freshest fish, and I came to love the wild, stinky, and exhilarating negotiations of my neighborhood *laiki*.

I also loved every wee hour spent on Kay's patio. A few candles would make light dance in the canopy of grape leaves overhead, and friends would drop by on their way home from dinner in the city. Music might happen, if someone had a guitar. And since it's unwise and frowned upon to drink *tsipouro* (or ouzo, for that matter) unaccompanied by food, Kay would offer us watermelon and feta.

There's no recipe, obviously. Thin wedges of very good sheep's-milk feta—of the crumbly, salty variety—are placed in between triangles of cold, very ripe watermelon. Nibble and sip. Chat and sing. It shouldn't work, but it does—that combination of salt and sweet, cream and melon—especially when brought together in the boozy licorice embrace of the *tsipouro*.

Epilogue

At the Still in the Hills

The rhythm of harvest on Thasos leaves little time for rest. About the same moment the *Evanthoula* is backed into its shed and the restaurant has been dismantled for winter, the grapes are ready. Some years this happens earlier than others, and it's not easy to predict what the weather will do. But just as soon as they are ripe, they must be picked and crushed and placed into vats for a month of fermentation: some for the wine and some for the *tsipouro*. Right on the heels of that, the olives will be ready and there'll be a thousand trees to strip. Meanwhile, the goats and sheep are pregnant and must be looked after. If there are moments of calm in between these responsibilities, they are given over to the orchards and to the garden, which have their own offerings to pick and put up for winter. The reward for all this hard work doesn't come until December, when it's time to make the *tsipouro*.

Since I'm not lucky enough to live on Thasos, I've been able to experience this stretch of island labor only in bits and pieces. I drop in to help for a week at a time, then fly home almost as soon as I've arrived, returning with some souvenir dirt under my nails. So I don't really know what it takes to make it through harvest season each year, but I know enough to appreciate the significance of that moment when the first drops of clear distillate run from the still in the hills. One December, I've promised both Tasos and Stamatis, as well as my *tsipouro*-loving self, I'll be here to savor that moment. At last, this is the year.

The family still—or *kazani*—is maintained by Stamatis and his cousin Nikos. It's tucked into an olive grove beneath Kleftoyanni Brachos, and Nikos says it's about 250 years old. I try to put that into perspective: while my own country was fighting its Revolutionary War, Tasos's Thasian ancestors were already up here making moonshine. The Kouzis clan is fortunate to have its own still. Almost everyone on the island makes some *tsipouro* for household use, but most have to bring their fermented grapes to the "legal" *kazani* in town, where for forty-eight expensive hours a rented distillery is at their disposal. They must work at a frenzied pace around the clock, in what I'm told are very tiring and debauched days and nights. By owning a *kazani* themselves, Nikos and Stamatis have the relative luxury of taking their time.

Not that the still sits idle, mind you. Uncle Nikos starts a fire beneath the kettle by early morning, and for almost two weeks he and Stamatis are here all day, filling and distilling and refilling and distilling, at a pace dictated by their own festivity. When darkness falls, they get to put out the fire and return home for the night. Sure, it's all technically illegal from the standpoint of the Department of Health, but as long as they don't sell their *tsipouro*, none of the authorities make any trouble.

Tsipouro begins as wine begins, with vats of grapes that have been fermenting for about a month. This proto-*tsipouro* is called *moustos* ("must") or *tsípoura* (annoyingly, since Greek is hard enough without near homonyms to contend with) and is often just made from the discarded skins and pulp left over after making wine. But it takes a huge quantity of skins and pulp to make just a little liquor. Stamatis prefers to use whole grapes, which he smashes and then pours into barrels, adding some fennel seed, quince, and orange to the purple mash. The mixture is stirred weekly and is ready when it stops gurgling, about a month later. Many people rely on sweet *sultanina* grapes, Stamatis explains to me, since they have the most juice and will yield huge volumes of *tsipouro*. But they are fickle, wimpy grapes and are almost impossible to grow without pesticides. He prefers to use *georgina* (it seems to be everyone's favorite grape here in the north of Greece), since it's friendly to organic cultivation. If you're going to drink a lot of *tsipouro* over the course of a year, it's easy to understand why you wouldn't want it to be laced with Monsanto's latest poison.

Stamatis told me a year ago that his *kazani* "was an elephant." Since I hadn't yet seen it, I had no idea what he meant by that, but I assumed he was referring to its size. So I was surprised to see how small the *kazani* was. The whole operation fits easily inside a ramshackle hut built out of old boards and some corrugated iron roofing panels. The still itself is just a big bronze kettle with a bulbous bronze cap. A long cylinder—that's the elephant's trunk—runs diagonally from the top of the cap through a deep vat of rainwater, where the vapor cools as it makes its way down toward the exit. Then it trickles through a layer of cheesecloth into a vessel at ground level. More sophisticated, nonelephantine stills accomplish this cooling with fancy coils and tubes and are certainly easier to control, but they're nowhere near as fun to look at. The Kouzis *kazani* is blackened from years of use, with oxidized patches of green here and there, and it's as dented and dimpled as the moon.

I get my first glimpse of the thing about ten o'clock one morning. To find it, I just follow the scent of wood smoke through the olive grove—the operation is only slightly clandestine. The second batch of the day has just begun running, and though I've not yet had breakfast, Nikos hands me a tiny shot glass, with which I interrupt the stream of steaming alcohol. Then, down the hatch. It's not quite *tsipouro* yet; in fact, it's called *souma* during this first distillation. OK, it's a pretty rugged beverage at this stage, especially given the time of day, but I'm not complaining. The fennel seed has just barely informed the flavor of the *souma*, and more than anything I taste grapes—the essence of the grape, really—transformed to clear spirit. And though I'd not

Figure 16. The still in the hills, Thasos.

usually accuse *tsipouro* of being subtle, this really is. It has a buttery, yeasty finish and very little fire. According to Stamatis's hydrometer, the *souma* only registers around sixty proof, which explains its mellowness. That will change in the second distillation, when more of the water is cooked away. The finished product will be up or over one hundred proof, and that's probably not the stuff you want to be drinking for breakfast. But for lunch, well, absolutely.

Every hour or so, a laborious process is repeated. The cap is removed, the cooked grapes from the last pass must be shoveled out quickly, and the vat must be rinsed with water. The fire is still raging beneath the kettle this whole time, so someone has to get down on his hands and knees in the smoke and steam and plunge his hand into the hot vat to scrub the insides with steel wool. A layer of sugar will have begun to cook on and must be removed, lest it burn and ruin the next batch. Then the vat is refilled with

Epilogue: At the Still in the Hills

moustos and stirred continuously until it comes to a simmer. The rickety old cap is set back into place and the connective seam is sealed with a paste made of ashes, water, and flour. After that, you wait for the spirit vapor to collect in the cap and begin dribbling down the trunk. To make this happen at the right rate, the fire must be managed with some care: too hot and the *moustos* will set on; too low and the distillation won't happen at a high enough temperature to cook off the hangover-making impurities.

For the first week, only *souma* is made, until every uncle has had a chance to run his grapes through the *kazani*. Then there's the more creative business of concocting *tsipouro* itself. The flavor of the final beverage really takes shape during its second distillation. In southern Greece, it is anathema to add fennel to one's distillate, which is drunk straight as kerosene and is usually called *tsikoudia* (in Attica) or *raki* (in Crete). If you want fennel in your fire, macho southerners will grumble, you should stick to ouzo. But in northern Greece, where I feel most at home, all the riches of the ancient spice trade are brought to bear upon their moonshine. Each family—and sometimes each man within each family—keeps a secret list of aromatics to be added during the second distillation. Everyone begins by adding a little salt, which helps clarify the liquor, but beyond that the options are myriad. Stamatis swears by his additions of Chian mastic, fennel seed, cinnamon, and clove, and because that's the *tsipouro* I drink most often and love the best, it's my favorite recipe in the world. But others on the island add things like basil, quince, lemon, orange, and even honey. No *tsipouro* is quite the same as another, so it's prudent to sample each one you encounter. This is what farmers do in the winter, after all. They visit friends, sample their liquor, compare notes, and then do what agriculturalists everywhere do: gripe about or celebrate the past growing season in vociferous tones.

It's hard work futzing with the *kazani* over and over, but in between there's a lot of downtime. By my third day at the still, I've come to recognize that making *tsipouro* involves hours of watching spirits trickle from the

Figure 17. Tasos emptying the still after dark.

elephant's trunk, breathing in alcoholic steam, sipping and tasting, and trying really hard not to fall into the fire. At some point, it's also a good idea to
eat something.

Tasos extracts a few two-by-fours from a pile of old lumber and gets
to work straightening out some rusty nails. Then he puts a pair of stumps
into place and fastens the boards on with a few whacks with the back of his
hatchet. Voilà! A Thasian picnic table is born. From a pile of trash behind
the shed he also excavates a kind of hibachi grill. He shovels in some hot
coals from the fire pit and almost immediately begins setting meat on fire:
thin ribbons of pancetta, some small pork chops, and piquant local sausages.

Stamatis hacks apart a tomato and some bread with his pocketknife, then plops a bag of still-curing *throumbes* on the table. And so we feast. An old Johnny Walker bottle is filled and refilled with last year's *tsipouro*, which can now be drunk in a hurry since more is on the way.

Tasos tells me that Stamatis and Nikos grew up together out here on the mountain, so they are like brothers. Their affection for each other is touching. Nikos is as sweet as Stamatis is salty. In fact, I can't help thinking of Nikos as a cartoon character, with his elfin countenance, darting eyes, raspy chuckle, and untrimmed salt-and-pepper mustache. When they plop down next to each other, physical differences evaporate—their distinctive profiles, dominated by long hooked noses, give them away as close relatives. Arm in arm, they sing verse after verse of every song they know, and they both know hundreds. In the pauses between songs, they talk, and I think that they could solve all the problems of the world with their moonshine colloquy. That said, they make no mention of the riots that have been rocking Athens all year, nor do they speak of the shame Greeks feel about their country's economic failure. Hours at the still are reserved for celebrating tradition and self-sufficiency.

And food. These *mesimeri* (midday) lunches never really end once they start, and such feasting goes on every day until all the barrels of *moustos* have been emptied. Only the menu changes. One day, Tasos grills the huge squid we caught from his rowboat and also boils a large octopus we snagged while braving the December waters. Another afternoon, I bring along a pot of garlicky lentils that I cooked up in the Archontissa kitchen. Friends "stop by" (that's not as easy as it sounds, since to get here one must navigate a half-washed-out, steep mountain road) and occasionally wives and sisters drop in to make sure they haven't been completely forgotten. Time itself might evaporate out here if it weren't for such subtle variations from day to day. This year, there's also a bit of family drama to help remind the men of their other lives.

For there's a new addition to the island: the lovely Karolin of Istanbul, Tasos's new wife. She comes to visit for a while each afternoon, arriving like a bolt of sunshine to the olive grove. In spite of her cosmopolitan upbringing, she seems perfectly at ease out here in the hills. She and Tasos are setting up house in the village of Potos and Karolin is learning to cope with the inefficiencies, torpor, and isolation of a Greek island in wintertime. On top of that, there are some negotiations ongoing with Eva, who hasn't made peace with the loss of her son yet, but will, I hope. The eventual arrival of grandchildren will help. Stamatis has already come around, since he sees, as we all do, that Tasos is completely out of his mind with happiness. When George Kaltsas comes across from Kavala to join us one afternoon, he sees the same thing, and he doesn't hesitate to tell Tasos as much. As for George, he's up to his usual tricks—eating raw olives right from the tree, talking poetry and theology, and looking robust, for which I am thankful.

The day before I leave, only four hours into lunch and after fourteen rounds of "S'agapo yiati eisai oraia" have left them weary, since they've been belting it out with such gusto, Stamatis and Nikos turn suddenly placid. They've been singing a famous old song from Asia Minor, whose declaration of love is so heartbreakingly simple that only the last verse translates into English with some of its pathos intact. "Open," the lover begs at last, "open just one shutter. Open just one shutter so I can see you there."

It's a beautiful song, but it can't be blamed for the seriousness we all read on Stamatis's face. No, he's got something to say to those gathered today. Karolin's Greek is coming along quickly, but since Stamatis seems to be addressing the newlyweds directly at times, Tasos whispers some portions of his speech in her ear.

"I used to run barefoot here," Stamatis says, his raised palm stirring the air, "and we had nothing. We were hungry sometimes, but we didn't need. Still, I set out with a plan for my life: to have my wife and my fishing boat and my home and to provide for my family and make life easier for my children. And I have achieved that and am here, at the end of my plan, at the end of what I hoped for."

Figure 18. Nikos and Stamatis Kouzis, in song.

Nikos nods his head in agreement. Their lives have not been easy, both men explain, but their ambitions have been fulfilled and happiness now comes down to working their family's land and waiting for the next generation to take the reins. It's hard for me to imagine an American giving such a speech, really, since most of the Americans I know seem determined to work themselves to death. There is no end to getting and striving. And to admit you've run out of ambition?

But Nikos and Stamatis take pride in this moment, even if they are suffering the sense of an ending that accompanies it. *Harmolypi*. That's the Greek term for what these men are expressing, their "joyful sadness." *Harmolypi* is the particular flavor of grief brought down from Parnassus by the Muse of History, who inspires Greeks to live, in spite of the reckonings of history. It's the grief Greeks expel through the sometimes playful, sometimes violent improvisations of the drunk man's dance. And the same grief inflects the creaky voice of the *rembetika* singer, whose ballads are sodden with the misery of diaspora, and the tang of hashish smoke, and the insistent erotic flush that keeps us tormented until sunrise. *Harmolypi* inflects Nikos and Stamatis's voices today, and it's not ordinary sadness, but an exhilarating and wise despair that brings us round, as if after long sleep, to ourselves—a beautiful sadness, then, which is immediate, ecstatic, and acutely felt.

Now that they've given voice to their *harmolypi*, Nikos and Stamatis return to singing, with Tasos joining in this time, so the family voice rings through the grove. But in midverse, Nikos nudges Tasos with his elbow. He's spied something through the trees up in the goat pen and evidently wants Tasos to go have a look. Nikos winks at me, too, so I follow Tasos up the hill. One of the goats has just given birth. There are two kids: one is jet black with a white diamond on his rump, and the other is the color of buttermilk. The doe looks dazed, with the little ones already prodding her udders. Both, I'm amazed to see, have been born with nubbins of horns. We watch for a minute to make sure she's all right, but when mama stomps her hoof at us, Tasos says we should clear out and let her recover from her ordeal in peace.

I walk just a few meters in the direction of the *kazani* when, from behind me, the doe emits a yodel that's so long and plaintive I have to turn back. Kleftoyanni Brachos looms atop the next ridge, its jagged peaks receiving the column of wood smoke from our *kazani's* chimney. Down at the rickety table, Stamatis and Nikos are knocking their glasses together and crooning so loudly that their voices are cracking on the high notes. Oblivious to that revelry, the goats are huddled in a neat cluster, safe for now beneath the canopy of a gnarled olive. With us out of her way, and having tossed her own complaint to the wind, the doe sets to work licking the afterbirth from her kids. When sunlight pours between the branches of the tree, I can see the wet fur of the black one glistening, as if slicked with oil.

Aeschylus. *Danaides*. In *The Myth of the Goddess: Evolution of an Image*, edited by Anne Baring and Jules Cashford. New York: Viking, 1991.

Amouretti, Marie-Claire. "Urban and Rural Diets in Greece." In *Food: A Culinary History*, edited by Jean-Louis Flandrin and Massimo Montanari. New York: Penguin Books, 2000.

Archilochus. "Political Fragments." In *Greek Lyric Poetry*, translated by M. L. West. New York: Oxford University Press, 1993.

Aristophanes. *Fragments*. Translated by Jeffrey Henderson. Cambridge, MA: Harvard University Press, 2007.

Baring, Anne, and Jules Cashford. *The Myth of the Goddess: Evolution of an Image*. New York: Viking, 1991.

Barnstone, Aliki. "Anemos." In *Blue Earth*. Oak Ridge, TN: Iris Press, 2004.

Bradford, Ernle, and Francis Pagan. *A Companion Guide to the Greek Islands*. London: William Collins and Sons, 1988.

Byron, Lord. *Don Juan*. Edited by T. J. Steffan, E. Steffan, and W. W. Pratt. New York: Penguin, 1983.

Callimachus. *Hellenistic Poetry*. Translated by Barbara Hughes Fowler. Madison, WI: University of Wisconsin Press, 1990.

Chesterton, G. K. *Alarms and Discursions*. London: Methuen, 1927.

Clampitt, Amy. *The Collected Poems of Amy Clampitt*. New York: Knopf, 1997.

Crane, Eva. *The World History of Beekeeping and Honey Hunting*. New York: Routledge, 1999.

Dalby, Andrew. *Siren Feasts: A History of Food and Gastronomy in Greece*. New York: Routledge, 1996.

Davidson, Alan. *Mediterranean Seafood*. New York: Penguin Books, 1976.

Dickinson, Emily. *The Complete Poems*. Edited by Thomas H. Johnson. Boston: Little, Brown, 1951.

Durrell, Lawrence. *The Greek Islands*. New York: Viking, 1978.

———. *Prospero's Cell and Reflections on a Marine Venus*. New York: E. P. Dutton, 1960.

Elytis, Odysseus. *The Axion Esti*. Translated by Edmund Keeley and George Savidis. Pittsburgh: University of Pittsburgh Press, 1974.

Emerson, Ralph Waldo. "From the Persian of Hafiz." In *Collected Poems and Translations*. New York: Library of America, 1994.

Fermor, Patrick Leigh. *Mani: Travels in the Southern Peloponnese*. New York: New York Review of Books Classics, 2006.

———. *Roumeli: Travels in Northern Greece*. New York: Harper and Row, 1962.

Gray, Patience. *Honey from a Weed*. New York: Lyons and Burford, 1986.

The Greek Pastoral Poets: Theocritus, Bion, and Moschus. Translated by M. J. Chapman. London: James Fraser, 1836.

Grout, James. "The Red Mullet in Rome." *Encyclopaedia Romana*, University of Chicago. Last modified February 11, 2012. http://penelope.uchicago.edu/~grout/encyclopaedia_romana/wine/mullus.html.

Hemingway, Ernest. *A Farewell to Arms*. 9th ed. New York: Simon and Schuster, 1995.

Herodotus. *The History*. Translated by David Green. Chicago: University of Chicago Press, 1987.

Hesiod. *Theogony, Works and Days, Shield*. Translated by Apostolos N. Athanassakis. Baltimore: Johns Hopkins University Press, 1983.

Hikmet, Nazim. "Occupation." In *Poems of Nazim Hikmet*, translated by Randy Blasing and Mutlu Konuk. New York: Persea Books, 1994.

Homer. *The Iliad*. Translated by Robert Fagles. New York: Viking, 1990.

Horace. *The Odes of Horace*. Translated by David Ferry. New York: Farrar, Straus and Giroux, 1997.

———. *Satires and Epistles of Horace*. Translated by Smith Palmer Bovie. Chicago: University of Chicago Press, 1959.

Jacobsen, Rowan. *Fruitless Fall: The Collapse of the Honey Bee and the Coming Agricultural Crisis*. New York: Bloomsbury, 2008.

Kalfopoulou, Adrianne. *Wild Greens*. Los Angeles: Red Hen Press, 2002.

Keats, John. *Complete Poems*. Edited by Jack Stillinger. Cambridge, MA: Harvard University Press, 1982.

Laurent, Peter Edmund. *Recollections of a Classical Tour through Various Parts of Greece, Turkey, and Italy Made in the Years 1818 and 1819*. London: G. and W. B. Whittaker, 1821.

Miller, Henry. *The Colossus of Maroussi*. New York: New Directions, 1941.

Naipaul, V. S. *In a Free State*. New York: Vintage Books, 1984.

Pausanias. *Guide to Greece*. Vol. 1, *Southern Greece*. Translated by Peter Levi. New York: Penguin Classics, 1984.

Plath, Sylvia. "The Bee Meeting." In *The Collected Poems*. New York: Harper Perennial/Modern Classics, 2008.

Seferis, George. *Collected Poems*. Translated by Edmund Keeley and Philip Sherrard. Princeton, NJ: Princeton University Press, 1995.

Seneca, Lucius Annaeus. "Natural Questions." In *Seneca*, translated by John W. Basore. Cambridge, MA: Harvard University Press, 1989.

Sikelianos, Angelos. "The Sacred Way." Translated by Edmund Keeley and Philip Sherrard. In *The Greek Poets*, edited by Peter Constantine, Rachel Hadas, Edmund Keeley, and Karen Van Dyck. New York: W. W. Norton, 2010.

Virgil's Georgics. Translated by Janet Lembke. New Haven, CT: Yale University Press, 2005.

Wordsworth, William. *The Prelude*. Edited by Wordsworth, M. H. Abrams, and Stephen Gill. New York: W. W. Norton, 1979.

Zanini De Vita, Oretta. *Encyclopedia of Pasta*. Berkeley: University of California Press, 2009.

INDEX

throumbes olives, 6, 19, 22–23, 25, 63, 118, 164, 227

tourism, 29, 104, 121–22, 146; agritourism, 32, 55

tsipouro, 1, 5, 14, 21–22, 63–64, 81–82, 118, 176, 180, 182, 183, 220, 221–25

tzatziki, 19, 29

village life, 29–30, 189–90

Virgil, 214

wood ovens, 29, 35–36, 48–49, 55, 63, 122, 134, 150, 156, 163–65

wine, 22, 46–47, 58, 148, 169–82, 184 ; Chian, 123; Cretan, 45–46, Domaine Skouras, 180–81; industry in Greece, 170–73, 189–90; Kythira, 199; Limnos, 187; Naoussa, 170–71, 173; Rapsani, 174–75, *retsina*, 46, 85, 172–73; Santorini, 171. *See also* grapes

Wisconsin, 8, 27, 31, 57, 66, 93, 189, 195, 206

xenoi: concept of, 120, 122

yigantes, 14, 92, 149, 159

Zanini De Vita, Oretta, 132–33

zucchini, 32, 40, 52, 63, 108, 140, 216–17